BAREFOOT HORSE KEEPING
—The Integrated Horse —

BAREFOOT HORSE KEEPING

—The Integrated Horse—

ANNI STONEBRIDGE AND JANE CUMBERLIDGE

THE CROWOOD PRESS

First published in 2016 by
The Crowood Press Ltd
Ramsbury, Marlborough
Wiltshire SN8 2HR

www.crowood.com

British Library Cataloguing-in-Publication Data
A catalogue record for this book is available from the British Library.

ISBN 978 1 78500 173 4

Acknowledgements
Deciding to become a hoof care professional has, quite literally, been life-changing. Choosing to do something that defies convention is never easy, but it has been both rewarding and at times extremely challenging. Numerous people have supported us and been influential in our barefoot journey. The authors would like to express their sincere thanks and respect to: our families and particularly Duncan Stonebridge for providing us with many wonderful photographs that so beautifully illustrate this book; the Barefootworks Co-operative team – Dawn Saunders, Liz Angus, Lesley Holehouse and Abi Hogg; the Dinnet Equine Herd Project – Wilma and John Doherty, and Cathy Todd; Bob Bowker; Lynda Davey; Brian Hampson; Dan Guerrera; Dorothy Marks; Kerry Ridgway; Mark Johnson; Paige Poss; Peter Laidley; Seaton Baxter; the Equine Sciences Academy; and HCP colleagues both in the UK and internationally, for the thousands of hours of discussions. Finally, we are grateful to our clients and their fascinating horses, without whom this book would not exist.

Typeset by Jean Cussons Typesetting, Diss, Norfolk

Printed and bound in Malaysia by Times Offset (M) Sdn Bhd

Contents

1 Introduction

The rationale behind this book comes from over twenty-five years' experience in delivering barefoot hoof care, saddle fitting, behavioural training and rider coaching. The authors have been horse owners, hoof care professionals (HCPs) and educators during this time, and have been intimately involved with the barefoot scene internationally. They apply their scientific education and transfer experience from prior careers to their work. Along with four other long-term HCPs (Dawn Saunders, Liz Angus, Lesley Holehouse and Abi Hogg),

they are members of Barefootworks Hoof Care Co-operative.

Barefootworks was established in 2006 as the first independent hoof care practice in the UK. The Co-operative is an industry group rather than attached to a training organization, but has links in training background and training provision to the Equine Sciences Academy, the American Hoofcare Association, the UK Natural Horse Care Practitioners Association, The School(s) of Barehoof Strategy and the American Association of Natural Hoof

The authors Anni Stonebridge and Jane Cumberlidge, and their dogs.

Barefootworks – the UKs first hoofcare co-operative.

Care Practitioners. A 'cross-training', evidence-based and critical thinking philosophy defines the integrated and holistic services the Co-operative provides, and sets Barefootworks hoof care apart from traditional farriery services and other hoof care providers.

This book is intended to provide a practical, accessible and objective guide to barefoot horse keeping. The content is informed as deeply as possible by empirical research and practice findings. The text is illustrated by photos from the authors' records, together with diagrams and graphics, and enhanced with case studies and commentary from other professionals.

Successful barefoot horse keeping requires education, planning and consideration, and can be complex and challenging. Whilst the authors appreciate that a number of readers will choose to perform their own hoof trimming, they strongly recommend that they secure the services of an experienced and educated HCP for regular checks. The authors define an HCP as a trimmer or a barefoot-educated farrier. If things take a turn for the worse, even the most open minded and optimistic owner-trimmer is unwise to take on and manage rehabilitation alone. The action of trimming itself is not difficult, but experience gained from hundreds of horses and thousands of feet allows HCPs to develop acute observational and evaluation skills. Extensive education and continuing professional development also gives HCPs the knowledge to analyse and provide solutions for the problems they encounter. In the authors' opinion it is not sufficient for the domesticated horse owner to 'leave it to Mother Nature', when the horse as a species has been fundamentally removed from its evolutionary origins. Feet respond to environmental pressures and do not 'know' what they need, even in barefoot horse keeping circumstances.

Trimming in practice.

It is recommended that anyone choosing to keep their horses barefoot should secure the services of a well recommended support team, including HCP, vet, dental technician, body worker, sympathetic saddler and trainer. The health of the equine foot is intimately related to the health of the rest of the horse. When troubleshooting is needed, in the authors' experience a co-operative team of professionals is the best way forward. Even if a horse never requires anything other than routine trimming, body work and dental care, interventions can impact on the entire body. For example, dental balance is vital to addressing movement asymmetry, and body work adjustments will not be maintained if the horse has imbalances in its feet.

THE RISE OF THE BAREFOOT INDUSTRY

There has been a sea change in the equestrian world in the last thirty years. In their book *The Revolution in Horsemanship*, Miller and Lamb wrote that 'the last fifteen years [have] seen the development of a whole new level of equine professional service industry'.[1] Expectations regarding the role and educational experience of the HCP have changed beyond all recognition. Barefoot horse keeping has generated a new industry category in parallel with farriery, distinctly removed from the traditional craft based specialism.

Many practising HCPs, including the

Equine dentistry. Image courtesy of Pete Markham from Loretto, USA (Equine Dentistry) [CC BY-SA 2.0 (http://creativecommons.org/licenses/by-sa/2.0)] via Wikimedia Commons.

Traditional farriery. Image courtesy of McLellan, David (Second Lieutenant) (Photographer) [Public domain], via Wikimedia Commons

Modern equipment for hoof trimming.

authors, began as horse owners looking for a more ethologically informed hoof care approach than was provided by traditional farriers. The discovery that such a service did not exist stimulated them to expand their knowledge horizons, just as the internet was beginning to change human communication and information exchange. Initially sharing knowledge through self-published books and websites, early barefooters started to amass information and to explore existing veterinary and farriery texts to find out more about the function of the integrated equine foot.

A few gurus emerged, who self-published some inspiring books, mainly based on personal practice observations.[2] Dissemination of this new information provoked a demand for clinics and hands-on trimming services. Occasionally overwhelmed, these individuals realized that a new market was emerging, and they diversified into training new HCPs to satisfy demand.

Trimming is physically demanding and inherently risky, as any job working with large animals can be. Establishing trimming schools was self-legitimizing, and allowed the early generators to imagine a futurity of trimmers ready, rasps in hand, to promote their ideas. The next line of HCPs emerged in the early 2000s, having attended training delivered by the gurus. The training they received

Students attend a
dissection clinic –
Shetland.

LANTRA

Equine Barefoot Care
National Occupational
Standards

May 2010

varied widely in quality, and often involved international travel to attend a self-certification course. On their return they compared the feet they saw locally with the ideology and technical advice they had learned. Some of it deviated significantly, but from trimming hundreds of horses and analysing effective approaches, they established 'what works' for the horses in their region under their care.

In 2010 the UK training organization LANTRA published the National Occupational Standards (NOS) for Equine Barefoot Care.[3] These standards were the result of a consultation process with representatives from the barefoot hoof care, farriery, veterinary and welfare professions, and cover all the basic aspects of providing barefoot hoof care services and running a barefoot trimming business.

Following the release of the NOS, the Department of the Environment, Food

National Occupational Standards for Equine Barefoot Care – LANTRA.

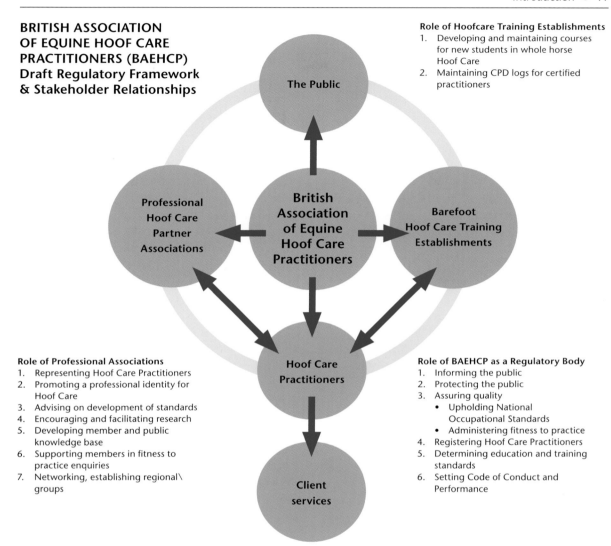

BRITISH ASSOCIATION OF EQUINE HOOF CARE PRACTITIONERS (BAEHCP) Draft Regulatory Framework & Stakeholder Relationships

The Public

Professional Hoof Care Partner Associations

British Association of Equine Hoof Care Practitioners

Barefoot Hoof Care Training Establishments

Hoof Care Practitioners

Client services

Role of Hoofcare Training Establishments
1. Developing and maintaining courses for new students in whole horse Hoof Care
2. Maintaining CPD logs for certified practitioners

Role of Professional Associations
1. Representing Hoof Care Practitioners
2. Promoting a professional identity for Hoof Care
3. Advising on development of standards
4. Encouraging and facilitating research
5. Developing member and public knowledge base
6. Supporting members in fitness to practice enquiries
7. Networking, establishing regional\ groups

Role of BAEHCP as a Regulatory Body
1. Informing the public
2. Protecting the public
3. Assuring quality
   • Upholding National Occupational Standards
   • Administering fitness to practice
4. Registering Hoof Care Practitioners
5. Determining education and training standards
6. Setting Code of Conduct and Performance

A draft regulatory framework for barefoot hoof care.

and Rural Affairs (DEFRA) has included barefoot trimming as a work package in the Review of Minor Procedures Regime project. At the time of writing, DEFRA has completed gathering evidence for the project, which will inform the development of options and the production of an impact assessment. DEFRA counted fewer than two hundred barefoot trimmers practising in the UK, including qualified commercial trimmers, owner-trimmers, unqualified and partially qualified trimmers. Regulation has substantial support within the commercial arm of the industry. The majority of practising trimmers recognize that regulation is an intelligent step to gain formal industry recognition and to develop industry standards. In 2014 the authors were involved in a voluntary professional group developing a draft regulatory framework. As the DEFRA Impact Assessment is completed, it is hoped that work towards a regulatory framework will be continued.

TRAINING FOR BAREFOOT HOOF CARE PROFESSIONALS

The demand for barefoot hoof care continues to grow. Thousands of barefoot horse keepers are joining social media groups, and there is on-going demand for specifically barefoot hoof care services.

HCP training is entirely self-funded, including the development of certification courses. Most UK certification providers recognized quality deficits in the original certification courses, and have designed their training programmes and assessment criteria to reflect or exceed the level of educational content and professionalism expected in other animal health care industries. The authors estimate that they have each spent more than double the amount on HCP training than it cost to achieve a bachelor degree, without affordable loans or grants. The cost for certification as an HCP in the UK is approximately £5,000, excluding travel and subsistence costs. In addition, each year HCPs are mandated to attend continuous professional development in order to maintain their certification, and membership fees to their certifying organization. A lot of training is modular, supported by self-study and online learning platforms. There are no formally recognized training criteria, so many courses range into other fields in order to replicate degree level programmes.

The authors are involved with UK industry efforts to achieve government recognition and training accreditation. At the time of writing in 2015, there are no government-recognized accreditation routes for professional barefoot hoof care training in the UK. The hoof trimmer, hoof care practitioner and equine podiatrist all provide a similar service, despite how they may promote themselves. The education most HCPs receive is extensive, crosses boundaries between equine disciplines, and allows HCPs to function as integrated equine health advisers with a hoof care specialism. A small number of farriers are educated in barefoot performance trimming, but despite early input from pioneering farriers there has been generally little movement from farriery towards attaining integrated barefoot knowledge. The rise of social media has perpetuated antagonism from both groups, despite the obvious benefits of knowledge sharing.

HCPs are educated to provide knowledge and support beyond working on feet. Almost all trimming training schools cover the four pillars of barefoot horse keeping: environment; trim; diet; and exercise. Training providers often run an educational business alongside a trimming or farriery practice, but are not yet linked to educational institutions. The main challenge in industry development is that HCPs are a small, nascent, vulnerable and factional industry group. Unlike other professionals, most HCPs are mandated to identify themselves with their original training provider after certification, rather than becoming an independent but certified practising professional.

Choosing a career as a hoof care professional may also be mediated by perception of risk. Effective professional insurance is difficult to purchase, and there have been several instances where HCPs have been prosecuted under farriery and welfare legislation. Farriery and trimming is a very physical job, and practitioners have a significant chance of work-related acute and repetitive strain injury.

Hoof trimming clinic – Aberdeenshire.

Why cross-training is essential in barefoot hoof care

As an integral part of equine anatomy, the hoof is a responsive and functional anatomical structure; however, the evidence base adopted for farriery training is insufficient to inform the 'whole horse' paradigm. With this 'whole horse' requirement also existing for barefoot hoof care, it has been essential that activists in the fledgling industry behaved as intellectual magpies. There are many areas of research that provide insights to explain and unravel complex functions and disease processes. The demand for barefoot trimmers has increased, and individuals with transferable skills, knowledge and experience have analysed the science of hoof function and care in order to evidence base their own practice.

The greater part of the barefoot community is not intentionally critical of traditional farriery, but their beliefs reflect a broader reaching and on-going educational journey than farriery training currently delivers. Academic research into hoof function is limited in real world application, therefore both industries need to translate, absorb, evaluate and distribute their research findings. Strong lines of communication can effectively manage the dissemination process more quickly than the 'jungle drums' approach. The authors would like to see the industries move closer and inform each other's practice to the ultimate benefit of the domestic horse.

In human psychology cross-training has

been highlighted as a significant way to speed up the acquisition of practical skills and intellectual knowledge. Integral theory applies this insight to the development of the individual, society, culture, and human thought and behaviour. As Ken Wilbur describes in the book *Integral Life Practice*, 'developmental models are in general agreement that humans beings, from birth, go through a series of stages or waves of growth and development. The lower, earlier stages are initial, partial and fragmented views of the world, whereas the upper stages are integrated, comprehensive, and genuinely holistic'.[4] *Barefoot Horse Keeping* provides a milestone in the evolution of barefoot

hoof care as it moves from its initial wave of development into an integrated future.

SOCIAL CAPITAL

Through the internet and social media, there has been a massive increase in instantly available information. Large numbers of people are joining online barefoot fora, and the choice to keep horses barefoot has been significantly democratized. It is clearly beneficial to establish social groups and social capital. Social capital is built on functional and reciprocal social relationships, including the opportunity to care for others. As humans have evolved alongside domesticated animals, other species have been folded into this social framework. An effect of domestication has been to confuse the requirements of other species with human requirements, which evidence shows is often to the detriment of the other species.

As humans continue to keep horses, professionals in supporting industries are often placed in the position of advocating for the horse as a different species through educating owners. HCPs from Barefootworks and other trimming organizations arrange educational seminars with specialists on a wide range of equine health and performance topics. By focusing owners on the endogenous requirements of the horse, it is possible to help owners maintain a productive and appropriate distance between themselves and their horses.

Writing this book has allowed the authors to illustrate the daily complexity of their work. Whilst on the one hand it is encouraging that so many people want to make the move into barefoot horse keeping, they are aware that demand for HCPs far outstrips supply. They hope that *Barefoot Horse Keeping* will provide an informative, intelligent and stimulating resource for horse owners, and inspire more people to consider a career as a hoof care professional.

Footprints in the sand.

Students at a Barefootworks Seminar with Dr Kerry Ridgway.

The author Jane Cumberlidge at work.

REFERENCES

[1] Miller, R.M. and Lamb, R. (2005). *The Revolution in Horsemanship and what it means to mankind.* Guilford, Connecticut: Lyons Press.

[2] Jackson, J. (1992). *The Natural Horse: Lessons from the wild for domestic horse care.* Flagstaff, Arizona: Northland Publishing; Ramey, P. (2003). Making Natural Hoof Care Work for You. Harrison, Arizona: Star Ridge Publishing; Jackson, J. (2002). Horse Owner's Guide to Natural Hoof Care. Harrison, Arizona: Star Ridge Publishing.

[3] LANTRA. (2010). *Equine Barefoot Care National Occupational Standards.* Coventry: LANTRA.

[4] Wilber, K., Patten, T., Leonard, A. and Morelli, M. (2008). *Integral Life Practice.* Boston, Massachusetts: Integral Books.

2 Trimming

WHY TRIM AT ALL?

The horse, in its original evolution in North America and repeated radiations and extinctions worldwide, developed the anatomical features to become the fastest distance-running quadruped on earth in arid regions of poorest forage. To assess the impact of the horse on human culture then, we must first turn, not to the well-watered heartlands of pristine civilization, but to the steppes and the deserts of our world.[1]

Horses and humans have interacted for six thousand years, an eyeblink in the history of the genus equus. For most of that time the horse has been used as a vehicle for cultural expansion and strategic military invasion and conquest. Characteristic of this relationship is the action of nomadic and transient human populations moving from remote, barren regions to invade or trade with 'sedentary centers of civilization... circumscribed alluvial states'.[2]

DOMESTICATION

Significant clues to the reasons why today's domesticated horses need hoof care are evident in the lifestyle of a historically domesticated horse.

Horse domestication probably first occurred in the fourth millennium BC on the Eurasian steppes, a great expanse of grasslands stretching eastward from Hungary for more than 6,400km to the borders of China... mobile horsemen... far-ranging routes across forbidding mountains and deserts... wide expanses of arid and semiarid lands... traversing barren regions... early nomadic movement across the Eurasian steppes... the extreme mobility of agro-pastoralism ranging over thousands of kilometers...[3]

The principal features of the lives of these horses were:

- Lots of movement
- Geographical distance
- Arid landscape
- Native grasslands

Distance and deprivation were drivers of horse domestication. Horse physiology is adapted to living in an arid environment where food is scarce and movement is a survival requirement. Nomadic populations in the fourth millennium lived at a distance from trading centres, and utilized horses to travel and transport goods to make a living. Trade centres developed in geographically suitable locations, which is why many cities are sited on major rivers and coasts. Around human habitation there sprang up an agricultural community to provide food. Nomadic horse keepers also traded horses, and passed on their horse keeping beliefs and their tools into developing urban communities. Early nomadic travel was done completely without recourse to horse shoeing, because the horses were adapted to their living environment. As modern barefoot horse keepers are often aware, the horse does not adapt well to living in constrained urban environments, therefore as they were forced to co-exist close to human habitation, the well known problems of domestication developed. The wiry, lean Steppe horses became fat pasture dobbins with sore feet.

The modern Steppe

According to information from the China International Horse Fair 2014,[4] Mongolia is still a horse breeding centre for China, producing half of all Chinese racehorses.

Mongolian Naadam race rider. Image courtesy of InvictaHOG (Own work) [Public domain], via Wikimedia Commons

Modern Steppe horses are significantly more functional than most domestic horses, and the differences in body shape, condition and fitness are clear. What is less obvious are the differences between their feet. In 2011 a group of researchers and vets visited the Mongolian Derby to evaluate the hoof morphology of the horses competing. None of the horses received hoof care, and they lived permanently on the Steppe. The team reported that 'few conformation abnormalities were observed, and hoof shape and size was within the normal expected range for horses of this size. The hoof conformation in this population of Mongolian horses represented the natural interaction of the hoof with the environment'.[5]

BAREFOOT BELIEFS

Two common barefoot horse keeping beliefs are that:

- A natural environment and lifestyle will optimally maintain the feet of both wild and domesticated horses; and
- Horses themselves are best placed to judge how their hooves should be shaped and will self trim appropriately given sufficient movement on hard surfaces.

Both of these beliefs have attractive logic, but both contain a number of assumptions that warrant a detailed examination of their origin and validity.

One of the driving texts behind the natural environment and lifestyle movement is a book entitled *Paddock Paradise* by American farrier Jaime Jackson. Paradoxically, the Paddock Paradise approach is about providing less paradise and more healthy deprivation, in order to improve the lives of domestic horses in the twenty-first century. His theory is that feral horses self-manage and are successful in the wild, therefore their lifestyle and hoof form are the ideal model for healthy hooves. So if horse owners can provide a 'wilder' life for domestic horses, why should they need trimming?

Paddock Paradise puts horses in a simulated natural environment. Its core intent is to stimulate natural movement and socialization patterns that are essential to a biodynamically sound horse. As an example, Paddock Paradise is inherently the perfect place for the healing or prevention of navicular syndrome and laminitis, today's greatest killers of domestic horses. It readily enables natural feeding patterns that are consistent and integral with the horse's digestive system. And it facilitates the implementation of a safe (i.e. founder free) diet in a controllable feeding environment.[6]

Self-trimming

Paddock Paradise presents a series of adaptation models for horse keeping, but can it be sufficiently 'wild' to manage a horse's feet? The authors' experiences of 'wilder' systems over the last fifteen years suggest that this belief is not valid, and there is considerable individual variation between horses and systems.

Many adapted systems include trackways; some track designs have been found to stimulate movement more than others.[7] The structure of the track needs to motivate movement. If plentiful grazing opportunities exist in the track area, horses will remain stationary. Without adequate abrasion from natural wear on hard substrates, or human intervention in terms of hoof trimming, their feet will get longer. This is evidenced by the feet of feral horses from very soft environments. Longer feet are adaptive for softer going; the longer-toed hoof does not sink into soft ground and acts like a snow shoe, spreading the horse's weight over a wide area. Wild and feral populations in softer regions can maintain good posture while moving on softer ground and the balance of the body is maintained. Horses that live in harder and more abrasive terrain develop feet with thick, densely calloused soles and thick short hoof walls to protect them from their environment and allow them to move about comfortably.

The authors provide hoof care for a herd of feral Konik ponies for the RSPB at Loch of Strathbeg in north-east Scotland, introduced for conservation grazing purposes. The herd lives on 250 acres of marshland.

Feral Konik horse on RSPB Reserve, Loch of Strathbeg.

Domestic ridden horses routinely live on soft ground but are ridden on hard surfaces. Their feet are adapted to soft ground, as the duration of riding time is too brief for hoof morphology to adapt. The best solution is to design a permanently harder living environment. Here they can abrade their feet and build up sole density to create a foot that functions on hard substrates.

Body asymmetry in horse and rider is common. Without trimming, most horses in a relatively short period of time start to develop imbalances in their feet that affect their biomechanical function and comfort.

Domestic foot newly adapting to an enriched living situation. Despite the extent of the abrasion the horse remained sound throughout.

Biomechanics will be discussed in detail in Chapter Six, but this is the main reason why even in Paddock Paradise systems detailed attention must be given to foot balance.

ASSESSING THE HORSE FOR A TRIM

In simple terms, trimming can be described as removing areas of hoof overgrowth which the horse has not abraded, in order to optimize their skeletal alignment and biomechanics.

A number of elements have a fundamental effect on the way the hoof looks, feels and functions. These elements are both intrinsic to the horse, for example its conformation, or extrinsic, relating to how it is trained, used and kept. They form a series of very complex interactions, making the hoof far more than simply the sum of its parts.

Hoof care professionals, or owners practising hoof trimming, need to develop an in-depth appreciation for the subtlety of these relationships. Once this is attained, the limitations of considering the hoof in isolation, or 'leaving it to Mother Nature', become obvious. It may already seem complex, but the surface has barely been scratched. Horse owners are being encouraged to take charge of their own horses' hoof care, but without expert knowledge it is easy to get out of one's depth, feel overwhelmed, or be tempted not to trim at all and 'see what happens'. Owners need the support of an experienced hoof care professional. Don't go it alone: trimming is a necessary part of most Western domestic horses' management.

HOOF BALANCE

Hoof balance is widely acknowledged as being critical for optimal hoof care and lameness prevention, but it seems that there is less professional agreement regarding just what constitutes 'balance':

> Hoof balance has been the term used by veterinarians and farriers to describe the theoretical ideal shape or conformation of a given foot, the position of the hoof relative to the limb above and the way the foot should be trimmed; however, hoof balance lacks an intrinsic definition.[8]

The scientific explanation for why hoof balance is critical is as follows:

> A straight alignment of the bones through their axis is considered optimal for physiological function. Misalignment of the bones of the digit… has an incidence of 72.8% in the forelimb of lame horses.[9]

In an ideal situation, particularly when imbalance is suspected, a hoof care professional should have access to radiographs. In practice, however, this is uncommon, but it is possible to reliably identify the location of the pedal bone without radiographs, which is an important skill. Through many dissections, hoof care professionals have identified external markers which determine where the pedal bone is located.

External markers

The white line is produced by the terminal papillae, located around the distal border of the pedal bone. The shape of the pedal bone can be identified by referencing the junction made by the outside edge of the sole and the inside edge of the white line. The bone sits higher in the hoof capsule slightly behind this junction. Denser areas of sole are often visible under the periphery of the bone, or in pathological feet bruising can sometimes be observed.

The 'straight alignment' of the digit bones, the pedal bone, and long and short pasterns is referenced by observing the hoof pastern axis, or HPA. The HPA has been used as the gold standard for evaluating balance, and is considered to be correct 'when the horse is standing still and the metacarpus/metatarsus is perpendicular to the ground and viewed from the lateral side, the HPA… forms a straight line'.[10]

Having the hoof pastern axis correctly aligned places the orientation of the pedal bone in the optimal position to have a 3 to 5 degree palmar or heel angle. This angle allows the sinking of the rear of the pedal bone within the hoof capsule during the landing and loading phase of the stride.

If the hoof pastern axis does not form a straight line, it is described as either broken back (associated with long toes and low heels), or broken forward (common with heels that are long and high). In the normal foot, HCPs should achieve the correct HPA by appropriately trimming the height of the

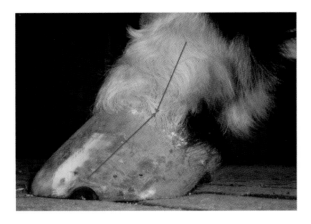

Broken back hoof pastern axis.

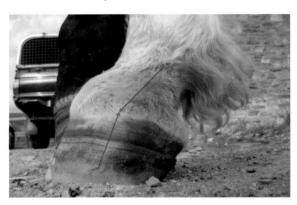

Broken forward hoof pastern axis.

heels and occasionally the toe. If significant adjustment is required, this needs to take place gradually and be supported by body work and postural re-training.

Whilst the hoof pastern axis can provide us with a mechanism for evaluating anterio-posterior balance, it is not useful for evaluation of medio-lateral (side to side) balance, which can cause lameness and performance deficits.[11]

The T-square approach

One traditional method for achieving medio-lateral balance is the T-square approach. This

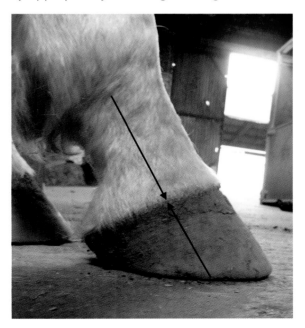

Correct hoof pastern axis HPA.

places an actual or virtual inverted T shape with the long stem along the back of the cannon and pastern, and the cross-piece across the heels. The heels are trimmed to be level with the cross-piece. The rationale behind the T-square approach is to make the height of the hoof equal on each side to orientate the solar surface of the pedal bone to be parallel to the ground, when looked at from the toe or heel as the horse is standing square.

Whilst the T-square approach may be theoretically correct for a perfect limb, it makes no allowances for the effect of loading during movement, for any rotations going on within the limb, or for the fact that body mass and therefore the effects of gravity are not placed symmetrically above the foot. The hoof capsule is also highly deformable, and quickly adjusts to the substrate the horse is moving on, so whatever balance was achieved at stance on a level surface can quickly disappear.

Supporting the observations of HCPs, 'it is fairly certain that the horse's hoof is another example of a smart structure'.[12] Smart structures are capable of sensing and reacting to their environment. In addition to carrying mechanical loads, smart structures may alleviate vibration, monitor their own condition and environment, automatically perform precision alignments, or change their shape or mechanical properties.[13] The mechanical behaviour of the hoof is modified by the external shape and material properties of the hoof itself; the gait, speed and direction of the horse; the substrate it is moving over, whether it is ridden or not; how it is trained to carry a rider; its saddle; and what hoof care and protection it receives. The hoof will respond in the immediate instance by deforming and wearing, and over time both the external and internal hoof structures may remodel.

When evaluating medio-lateral balance, HCPs use a variety of landmarks. Many evaluate the 'live' sole, the waxy surface located underneath the exfoliating sole.[14]

Dissections of healthy domestic and wild horse feet found that the depth of the sole is relatively even across the hoof, and can be up to 18mm thick in hard desert populations.[15] In most domestic feet, or in wild feet that do not live in hard environments, this depth of sole is not common. With care and skill, the live sole can be exposed without removing essential material, and can be used as a more reliable guide for trimming to balance the pedal bone than the T-square can achieve. Medio-lateral balance can also be assessed by referencing the widest part of the foot and the P2/P3 pivot axis in the coffin joint.[16]

The above methods for assessing foot balance are described as '*static balancing*'. The development of sophisticated equipment such as motion capture, strain gauges and force plates has enabled researchers to gain insight into how horses move and load their limbs, and it is now possible to assess balance dynamically. However, these methods are still not without controversy. For many years HCPs and vets believed that 'ideally, the horse's foot should strike the ground as a unit, with the entire weight-bearing surface hitting the ground together'.[17] Challenging this belief, a study by the appropriately named Van Heel *et al.* in 2004 suggested that this often was not the case. They found that:

> Lateral asymmetrical landing was the preferred way of landing in front feet and especially in hind feet of trotting horses... Trimming aimed at complete symmetry under static conditions did not change this preference. In the front feet, 63.3% of all measured untrimmed landings were located on the lateral side of the foot. After trimming, 57.8% of all landings were lateral asymmetrical.[18]

In-shoe force measurements have given insight into hoof balance. Reilly[19] showed that neither static nor dynamically balanced hooves have equal force distribution across the foot at mid stance at rest, walk and trot, and statically balanced hooves have equal force at trot alone. A higher medial load at rest is to be expected as proportionately more of the horse's body weight is located centrally, however, once the horse moves, in order for it to be able to protract the leg out from under the body, the body weight needs to be shifted away from the leg about to move forward. Interestingly, the statically balanced hoof almost exactly shifts the percentage of force measurable in the medial side, or inside half of the foot, to the lateral side from rest to walk, whereas no such symmetry of load exchange was found in the dynamically balanced foot.

THE BIOMECHANICS OF MOVEMENT

Biomechanical research into equine movement deals with the stance phase, i.e. when the foot is in contact with the ground, and the flight phase, when the foot is moving through the air.[20] In the real world, however, both parts are inseparable because stance and flight are interdependent elements of equine movement. The conformation of the horse links the biomechanics of both the stance and flight phases, more specifically the set of the joints in the limb from the shoulder down in the foreleg and from the hip down in the hind leg. As David Gill explains, 'it is from the ball and socket joints of the shoulder and hips that the vast majority of all medial and lateral motion originates'.[21]

Ball and socket joints enable movement in any direction, but the ligaments surrounding the joints limit that range of motion, so 'the flight arc of the hoof represents the summation of all the joint movements in the limb'.[22] In the perfectly conformed horse, the arc of flight of the foot forms a straight line, but in the real world HCPs see all sorts of deviations.

So what do HCPs need to look at in limb

The stifle moves outwards

The hock moves inwards

The fetlock moves outwards and rotates laterally

Biomechanics of the action of the hind limb.

joints? Limb movement is controlled by a complex sequence of joint flexions and extensions from the hip and shoulder down, which are directed by the various muscle contractions and the shape of the joints themselves. In the hind leg, as the hip joint flexes this causes a series of rotations: the femur rotates, which in turn causes the stifle to move outwards, the hock to move inwards,[23] and finally the fetlock to rotate outwards.

In order for the arc of flight to be straight, the degree of inward rotation of the hip and hock has to be counterbalanced by the outward rotation of the stifle and the fetlock. This is further compounded by the fact that the fetlock, as a ginglymus joint, has three-dimensional range of motion.[24] Ginglymus joints produce a small lateral rotation, which in the case of the fetlock can be felt by lifting and manually manipulating the joint. Understanding what goes on biomechanically explains why horses prefer lateral landing in the hind legs – in order to land symmetrically, the stifle, hock and fetlock would not only have to perfectly counterbalance the various rotations through the leg initiated by the hip joint, but also compensate for the additional rotation caused by the ginglymus fetlock joint itself. Most horses, unless they are successfully trained to shift more of their weight onto their hind limbs and tone their core muscles, do not have this range of rotation control.

The fore leg has another complex series of ginglymus joints, which again control the arc of flight. Due to the lack of bony connection to the rest of the skeleton, the conformation and posture of the foreleg can change with time as the young horse develops. The position of the elbow is a key factor controlling whether or not the limb will be straight, or have a toe in, or toe out conformation.

When the hoof is loaded with the horse's body mass, measured as peaking at 1.2 times the animal's body weight at trot and more than twice that at gallop,[25] it is important that the skeleton is correctly aligned to optimally distribute that load and avoid injury.

An intelligent trimming approach, which minimizes stress to joints and connective tissue, is to optimize the hoof shape of each digit based upon the horse's anatomy to evenly distribute the biomechanical forces encountered by the foot. Critically important to this is the shape and location of the pedal bone relative to the hoof capsule, and the alignment of the rest of the digit and the skeleton above. Evaluating and responding to individual biomechanics with a long-term trimming plan is more effective than shooting for a predetermined landing pattern or geometric symmetry.

EVALUATION OF THE FOOT

There are a number of criteria which compose the 'ideal' foot for a working barefoot horse, although not all are required for functional feet.

The 'ideal' foot

Viewed from in front, the slope of the walls should be either symmetrical or the medial wall slightly more upright. Walls should form

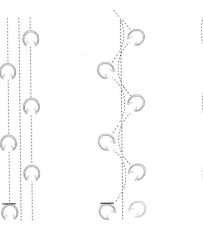

The influence of conformation on the flight pattern of the hoof.

| *Front* Ideal | Toed-out | Toed-in | Base-wide | Base-narrow |
| *Hind* Ideal | Cow-hocked | Bow-legged | Base-wide | Base-narrow |

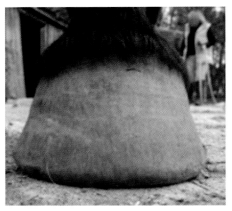

A good example of a self trimming domestic hoof – dorsal view.

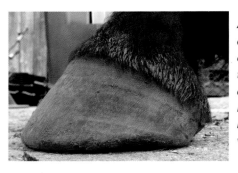

A good example of a self trimming domestic hoof – lateral view.

a straight line from the coronary band to the ground without any change in the angle of growth. The coronary band should be level with no dips or bulges. There should be no sign of bruising, and ideally no event lines (concentric ridges in the hoof wall). There should be no cracks or splits in the wall other than minor surface defects. The bottom of the hoof wall should be beveled or abraded to form a smooth curve.

Viewed from the side (lateral view), the slope of the toe and heel should form a straight line from the coronary band to the ground without changing angle. The hoof pastern axis should be straight. The slope of the toe and the heels should be a similar angle, although the heels may be slightly more acute. The coronary band should slope from the toe down to the heels without any dips or bulges. The angle formed by the hairline and the heels should be slightly less than a right angle. There should be no evidence of bruising or event lines. There

should be no cracks or splits in the wall other than minor surface defects.

Viewed from the bottom (solar view), the widest part of the foot should bisect the hoof so that at least 50 per cent of the hoof makes up the heel area – this may increase to approximately two-thirds. The sole should be a solid colour, either pale or grey, and free of dark or red areas. The frog should be located centrally within the hoof capsule. The heels should line up with the back of the frog. The depth of the co-lateral grooves should be even on both sides. The width of the white line around the circumference of the sole should be even and should fill up the space between the sole and the wall. The wall should be generally of uniform thickness, possibly with slight thickening at the toe and thinning at the quarters. The bars should be clean and well angled, and not show a distinct crack at the end of the laminar bar. The distance from the apex of the frog to the toe should be roughly half the length of the frog, so that the frog forms two-thirds of the length of the foot. The central sulcus of the frog should be open and shallow. The surface area of the lateral side of the foot should be the same as, or very slightly larger than, the medial side.

A good example of a domestic hoof receiving regular maintenance trimming– solar view.

THE NEUROSENSORY ROLE OF THE BARS AND DIGITAL CUSHION

As hoof care professionals, we often discuss the biomechanics of locomotion and proprioception, but beyond that we rarely consider the neurosensory role of the equine foot. Large mammals produce characteristic footfalls, which in some species have been found to be utilized in seismic communication.[26]

Although a multi-toed species, elephants have dense fatty foot pads interlaced with cartilage, like the horse's digital cushion, and they also walk on their toes supported by their foot pads. In other mammals, such as dolphins and some whales, fat is used for acoustic purposes. The fat in a sperm whale's head, for instance, serves to transmit acoustic vibrations, which are focused in its bowl-like skull. Researchers have found that elephants press down on their foot pads to facilitate the detection of seismic vibrations.[27] Having a fatty pad between the ground and the bony column allows seismic waves to be transmitted into the body without impedance from the air. When horses are

African Bush Elephant. Image courtesy of Muhammad Mahdi Karim Facebook. The making of this document was supported by Wikimedia CH. (http://www.gnu.org/licenses/old-licenses/fdl-1.2.html)], via Wikimedia Commons.

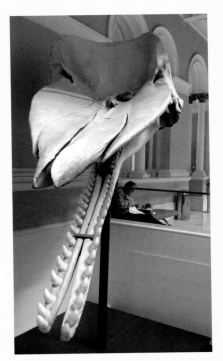

The bowl like skull of a sperm whale.

listening intently, they lift their heads and angle their front legs slightly underneath them. This action will compress the digital cushion. The authors hypothesize that the digital cushion, and the 'dirt plug' that horses gather in the collateral grooves of the frog, will also reduce impedance and improve detection of the seismic vibrations produced by the footfalls of dispersed herd members. The bowl shape of the solar surface of a healthy pedal bone and the bars themselves may also focus vibrations to the area of the foot most densely provided with nerve corpuscles.

REAL WORLD EXAMPLES

The following examples constitute a selection of some common challenges faced by HCPs. Discussing them is useful because it introduces and highlights where and when things frequently go wrong and how this may affect the horse.

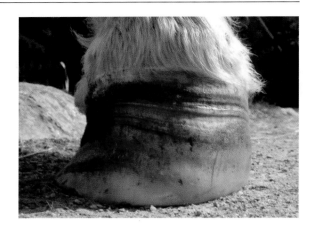

Self trimming left hind foot of a three-year-old hunter gelding.

	Real world example	Effect on the horse	Summary
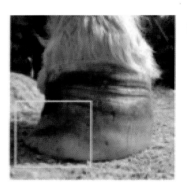 *Medial flare.*	Medial flare	Uneven loading through the limb and uneven joint spaces. On a hind limb this causes lateral rotation of the distal limb, cow hocks, toes out. The joint spacing on a limb such as this will be narrower medially and wider laterally. Without corrective hoof care and body work this will potentially lead to damage to all the joints in the hind limb. Ridden, the horse will have difficulty going forward and difficulty engaging the hind quarters.	Uneven joint wear Cow hocked Toe out Training resistance
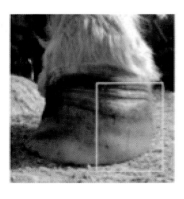 *Overloaded lateral wall.*	Overloaded lateral wall	Overloading of lateral heel and quarter lateral wall in the long term can lead to sheared heels. Lack of natural wear on the medial wall maintains excessive lateral wear resulting in misalignment of the limb as if the horse had a medial wedge. This interferes with the flight arc causing the horse to excessively adduct the hind limb. Excessively asymmetrical loading of the limb causes muscle tension throughout the body.	Excessive lateral heel wear Uneven heel height Medio-lateral imbalance Plaiting Altered flight arc Muscle pain Back tension resistance Training resistance

	Real world example	Effect on the horse	Summary
 *Wall bruising.*	Wall bruising	Leverage from the medial flare causing tearing and pressure necrosis of the laminae. Ongoing discomfort and potential for abscess formation in damaged laminae tissue.	Abscess Leverage
 *Distorted growth rings.*	Distorted growth rings	Excessive medial wall length and leverage is causing new growth to be compressed and the coronary band to be proximally distorted.	Leverage Coronary band pressure Uneven wall length
 *Pressure deformation.*	Pressure deformation	The medial toe pillar is creating a focus of pressure causing the hoof wall to bend, preventing the horn receiving sufficient hydration. This is evidenced by the surface tubules drying out. The result of this excess pressure also causes a bruise which will be maintained each time the foot is loaded.	Pressure Wall bending Bruising Poor hydration

REAL WORLD EXAMPLES

The following examples constitute a selection of some common challenges faced by HCPs. Discussing them is useful because it introduces and highlights where and when things frequently go wrong and how this may affect the horse.

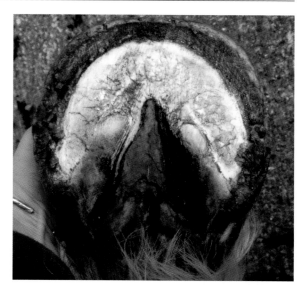

Overgrown foot of a sixteen-year-old cob gelding.

Damage to hoof wall.

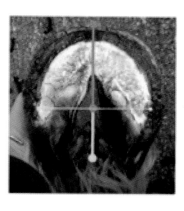

Long toe.

Real world example	Effect on the horse	Summary
Damage to hoof wall	Proximally to the toe pillar, the combined effect of all the imbalance problems has caused the hoof wall to materially degrade, leading to complete loss of structural integrity. The hoof capsule has distorted inwardly to such an extent that the vascular structures beneath have serious potential for damage.	Wall collapse Abscess Disrupted blood supply
Long toe	Toe length becomes excessive when the foot in front of the widest part of the sole is longer than the foot behind it. A long toe delays breakover, which will cause interference in the stride by delaying lift off in the front feet with the potential for causing overreaching. Tripping and stumbling are also common with toe first landing. The weight bearing and shock absorption functions have been brought forward in the foot, directly under the DIP joint. This can lead to excessive forces being transmitted to the joint and the impar ligament, which is implicated in navicular pain.	Overreaching Tripping Stumbling DIP joint problems Soft tissue damage Navicular pain

	Real world example	Effect on the horse	Summary
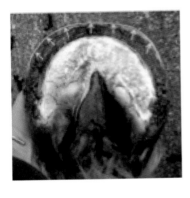 *High heel.*	High heel	High heel tips the landing zone closer to the DIP joint, and provides compression at the back of the foot. Excessive heel height prevents ground contact and frog pressure. The frog will therefore atrophy and be unable to dissipate shock and pressure effectively. Excessive heel height will also provide internal pressure leading to bruising and potential abscess. The horse will shift its body weight onto the front of the foot, making it more difficult for the horse to lift off its forehand and maintain a balanced stance. Training resistance problems are common in horses with long heels.	Frog atrophy Poor shock absorption Bruising Training resistance On the forehand
Excessive wall length around toe providing leverage.	Excessive wall length around toe providing leverage	Leverage can cause painful tearing in the white line and distal laminae, leading to the horse having problems breaking over and turning comfortably. Leverage will also distort tubule alignment. Referred pressure from long toes and flares can cause pressure anaemia higher up the hoof wall, leading to cell damage and pain.	Toe zone pain Damage to white line Damage to laminae Breakover problems Uncomfortable turning
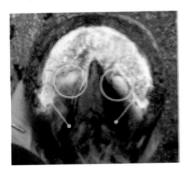 *Folded bars, with pooling in non laminar bar and fracture.*	Folded bars, with pooling in non-laminar bar and fracture	Underneath the folded bar horn, the horse can experience painful pressure leading to corns and abscesses. Management of bar length and fold is a critical part of optimizing comfort at the back of the foot to encourage heel first landing.	Corns Abscess Weak caudal foot

REAL WORLD EXAMPLES

The following examples constitute a selection of some common challenges faced by HCPs. Discussing them is useful because it introduces and highlights where and when things frequently go wrong and how this may affect the horse.

Long toe and collapsed heel of an aged cob x gelding.

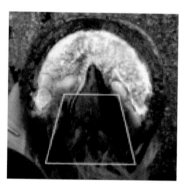

No structure to the back of the frog.

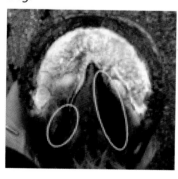

Thrush in collateral grooves.

Real world example	Effect on the horse	Summary
No structure to the back of the frog	A well developed and healthy caudal foot provides shock absorption whilst controlling heel expansion on landing. Where the back of the foot is weak, the horse can feel pain and be reluctant to utilize the caudal foot effectively.	Excess concussion Caudal pain
Thrush in collateral grooves	Persistent thrush weakens the frog tissue and can be indicative of metabolic challenges. Where thrush is not eliminated by appropriate treatment and good hygiene, further diagnosis or investigation is required.	Frog damage Metabolic problems Hoof hygiene

	Real world example	Effect on the horse	Summary
	Excessive heel length but no vertical height	The heels are pulled forward by the length of the toe, causing the heels to grow almost horizontally. Because the toe is long and weak, the horse has no choice but to overload the heel buttress as the most robust part of this foot. Negative palmar angles and broken back hoof pastern axis are common with this kind of foot, as there is no support for the bony column in the caudal foot.	Weak heels Caudal pain Negative palmar angle Broken back hoof pastern axis

Excessive heel length but no vertical height.

	Heel buttress migrated over seat of corns	Heel buttresses are overloaded, causing the tubules to bend, leading to hoof wall being overlaid over both seat of corns areas. This is likely to cause bruising due to pressure necrosis in the sole at the seat of corns. Abscesses are common under the overlaid heel, and under the distorted bars.	Seat of corns Bruising Abscesses

Heel buttress migrated over seat of corns.

	Under-developed frog and digital cushion	This frog is approximately a third of its potential width, extremely thin and weak. It is incapable of providing any shock absorption, or resistance. The digital cushion is underdeveloped, leading to a loss of vertical height in the foot. Had the caudal foot had sufficient stimulation in earlier life the frog and digital cushion would have developed to meet their potential, supported the caudal foot and allowed the heel buttresses to attain vertical height. At this age potential for improvement is significantly limited and this horse will require support in terms of boots and pads if ridden.	Weak frog Thin frog Need for protection Inability to shock absorb

Under developed frog and digital cushion.

	Real world example	Effect on the horse	Summary

Contracted heels.

| | Contracted heels (Although this presentation is commonly contracted heels, it may also be as frequently caused by under-development) | The heels are well inside the toe bends, and the potential for heel expansion is very small. Poor shock absorption and painful pinching of heel bulbs. Heel expansion is limited, which will have a significant impact on the ability of the horse to employ the hoof mechanism to assist the movement of blood through the foot. | Heel pain Poor blood flow |

Heel bulbs displaced caudally.

| | Heel bulbs displaced caudally | Due to lack of material strength in the frog, digital cushion and lateral cartilages, the body weight of the horse has displaced the heel bulbs. This contributes further to the poor shock dissipation potential of the foot. Horses with this type of foot presentation often walk as if they are wearing flippers. | Tenderfooted Excessive heel first landing |

Thin flat soles.

| | Thin flat soles | The collateral grooves are shallow with no depth whatsoever around the apex of the frog. This indicates the foot has extremely thin soles. This means the horse will find walking on hard uneven surfaces painful, and lacks solar protection of the pedal bone. The foot is prone to sole bruising and excessive flexion of the sole, particularly if wet. The completely flat sole indicates that the pedal bone could be sitting too low within the hoof capsule. This may cause peripheral loading of the pedal bone and eventual pedal osteitis. | Sole pain Bruising Excessive sole flexion Pedal osteitis |

	Real world example	Effect on the horse	Summary
	White line infection	Peripheral loading of the pedal bone has the potential to damage the circumflex artery. This results in disruption of blood supply to the peripheral hoof wall and white line. The tissues in this area are insufficiently robust to withstand natural attrition and bacterial/fungal infection.	White line infection Loss of structural integrity

White line infection.

	Thin, weak hoof walls (Hoof wall is made up of intertubular horn and tubules. The number of tubules does not vary from horse to horse, being approximately 600. The material strength of the wall is imparted by the quality of the intertubular horn)	Excessive wear to walls, prone to chipping, splitting and cracking. The hoof wall is lacking intertubular horn, which provides material strength. Excessive flexion in the quarters of a hoof with poor intertubular horn leads to separation and cracking	Excessive wear Chipping Cracking Separation

Thin, weak hoof walls.

EVALUATION OF THE HORSE PRIOR TO TRIMMING

Assessing the horse's biomechanics is often conducted by asking the owner to walk and trot the horse up in hand. Close observation should be able to address a range of questions:

- Is the horse sound? Are there any unusual rhythms, heaviness or lightness in its footfalls that could indicate lameness or imbalance?
- Does it have a distinct asymmetrical arc of flight? This could cause excessive wear or compression on the landing heel.
- Where does each foot breakover? An off-centre breakover causes more wear to one side or other of the toe.
- Does the horse land toe or heel first? This could cause excessive wear, or no wear, either of which could disrupt the HPA as a result.
- Is the horse level in the body or croup/wither high?
- Is it moving with more weight over the front or hind legs?
- Does it lightly swing through the stride with a lifted back or drag its feet along with a dropped back?
- Are there any obvious conformational issues, for example, rotated joints or base narrow/wide?
- Is there any asymmetry in the knees, shoulders, hocks or pelvis, looking at the horse from the front or back?
- Does the horse have a preferred stance?

Movement, conformation and observable deviations give a huge amount of information about the balance of the feet. For example, if the slope of the heels is much flatter than that of the toe, the distance from the apex of the frog to the toe is significantly more than half the length of the frog, the heels are located forward of the most caudal aspect of the frog, the anterio-posterior (AP) balance of the foot is incorrect. Where these features are found, it is also highly likely that less than 50 per cent of the foot will be located behind the widest part, there may be a dish in the wall at the toe, and the HPA will be broken back. This means that excessive force is being directed through the navicular bone as the skeletal alignment has shifted, the heels will have become crushed as the normal energy dissipation mechanisms cannot function optimally due to the misalignment of the skeleton, the soft tissues of the foot and the hoof capsule. In terms of movement, the horse is likely to be prone to be short strided, trip and stumble frequently, be on its forehand or land very flat.

Problems with AP balance and a broken back HPA do not suddenly occur overnight but develop over time, steadily getting worse if not addressed. By understanding the relationship between each of these observable features, it is far easier to catch changes in AP balance at an early stage. Correcting an early imbalance may be as simple as increasing the frequency of trims.

It is important to be aware that foot balance is dynamic and constantly adjusting to the forces exerted on the digit. This being so, evaluating balance should also be dynamic – i.e. one cannot expect to balance the foot and it to stay the same, but must monitor the changes in the foot shape and movement of the horse over time. By adopting an integrated dynamic approach, it is possible to stimulate changes which bring the horse closer to ideal as far as its individual conformation will allow. Progressively less rebalancing should be required at each trim to maintain the medio-lateral and anterio-posterior balance of the hoof capsule in relation to the pedal bone.

This kind of work is often a team effort, especially where a long-standing imbalance is evident in the foot. In this situation there are likely to be imbalances higher up in the body, which may require a specialist body worker, therapeutic exercises, adjustment to tack, and correcting any imbalances in the rider.

With this number of factors to consider, combined with different 'expert' opinions as to what constitutes balance, it is easy to see where the complexity lies. However, one factor remains constant throughout: no two horses are the same. By respecting the horse's anatomy and learning to read the various landmarks on the outside of the foot, matters do become clearer.

THE OWNER'S ROLE

Under normal circumstances horses should be seen by an HCP every five or six weeks. On a day-to-day basis the owner has a vital role to play in monitoring their horse's hooves, overall health and well-being, and knowing when to alert the professionals in between. After all, no one is in a better position to observe the horse than its main carer.

The hoof is a dynamic anatomical structure, which undergoes constant change. Often hooves can change quickly, especially in spring and autumn, the times of the year when horses' hormonal balance is undergoing seasonal changes. It is not unusual for problems to occur between trim dates. Routine health monitoring by keeping journals or notes can be very helpful in early intervention and in retrospectively analysing the etiology of disease processes.

Other useful items to record include:

- weight
- condition score
- digestive health
- wormers or other chemicals used
- heart rate
- temperature
- eating and drinking behaviour
- unusual behaviour
- foot comfort
- digital pulse

DIGITAL PULSE

It is good practice to learn how to feel for a digital pulse, both at the pastern and at the fetlock. For the majority of horses, the digital pulse should be undetectable or very faint. Where it is clearly present, it typically indicates some degree of inflammation and constriction within the hoof capsule. As the hoof capsule cannot expand, the inflammation compresses the dense network of blood vessels, restricting the blood flow, resulting in a noticeable pulse. The stronger the pulse, the greater the degree of inflammation.

Many horses who show signs of 'footiness', particularly in the spring and summer months, also have a digital pulse. Very commonly this coincides with a rise in the levels of non-structural carbohydrates in the grass. By regularly checking for a digital pulse, it is possible to obtain an early warning of potential issues, enabling steps to be taken to reduce the levels of sugars and starches in the diet before more serious problems, such as laminitis, take hold.

KEY POINTS

- Early nomadic domestication maximized the horse's opportunities for movement far beyond what is generally available today.
- Hoof balance is unique to each individual horse, and is critical for long-term soundness.
- Evaluating what constitutes balance is complex and multi-factorial.
- Modern domesticated horses are rarely able to maintain appropriate hoof balance and self-trim without significant modifications to typical horse keeping practices.

- Owner vigilance regarding health and fitness is the most critical part of successful horse management.
- A professional partnership team working well is essential for both health maintenance and troubleshooting.

REFERENCES

1. Kelekna, P. (2009). *The Horse in Human History*. New York: Cambridge University Press.
2. *Ibid.*
3. *Ibid.*
4. www.horsefair.cn/eabout.php# www.mongolianexperiment.com/mongolia/culture/a-little-about-mongolian-horses/attachment/3315789031_cf5c57e96f_b/.
5. Gordon, S., Rogers, C., Weston, J., Bolwell, C. and Dooloonjin, O. (2013). The Forelimb and Hoof Conformation in a Population of Mongolian Horses. *Journal of Equine Veterinary Science*, 33(2).
6. Jackson, J. (2006). *Paddock Paradise: A guide to natural horse boarding*. Harrison, Arizona: Star Ridge Publishing.
7. Hampson, B. (2010). *Australian Brumby Research Unit*. Personal lecture notes. Barefootworks Seminar, Aberdeenshire, Scotland.
8. O'Grady, S.E. (2009). *Guidelines for trimming the equine foot: A review*. 55th Annual Convention of the American Association of Equine Practitioners. Las Vegas www.ivis.org/proceedings/aaep/2009/z9100109000218.pdf (accessed 12.03.2010).
9. Page, B.T. and Hagen, T.L. (2002). Breakover of the hoof and its effects on structures and forces within the foot. *Journal of Equine Veterinary Science*, 22(6):258-63.
10. O'Grady, *Guidelines for trimming the equine foot*.
11. Singer, E. (2003). 'Understanding hoof balance', *Horse & Hound*. www.horseandhound.co.uk/horsecare/392/47715.html (accessed 12.07.2010).
12. Thomason, J.J. (2007). Biomechanics of the Equine Foot, in A.E. Floyd and R.A. Mansmann (eds), *Equine Podiatry*. St Louis: Saunders Elsevier, 49.
13. www.structuralwiki.org/en/Smart_structures (accessed 03.09.2010).
14. Ovnicek, G. *Hoof balance made easy*. www.hopeforsoundness.com/education/articles/handouts/hoof-balance-made-easy.html (accessed 11.08.2010).
15. Hampson, *Australian Brumby Research Unit*. Personal lecture notes. Barefootworks Seminar.
16. Laidley, P. (2004). *Hoofworks: Barefoot Basics*, CD Rom, Ferny Hills.
17. Rooney, J.R. (1998). *The lame horse – revised, updated and expanded*. Neenah: Russell Meerdink Company Ltd, 117.
18. Van Heel, M.C.V., Barneveld, A., Van Weeren, P.R. and Back, W. (2004). Dynamic pressure measurements for the detailed study of hoof balance: the effect of trimming. *Equine Veterinary Journal*, 36(8):778–82.
19. Reilly, P.T. (2010). In-shoe force measurements and hoof balance. Journal of Equine Veterinary Science, 30(9):475–8.
20. Merritt, J.S., and Davies, H.M.S. (2007), 'Biomechanics of the Equine Foot', in A.E. Floyd and R.A. Mansmann (eds), *Equine Podiatry*. St Louis: Saunders Elsevier, 49.
21. Gill, D.W. (2007). *Farriery: The whole horse concept*. Nottingham: Nottingham University Press, 31.
22. Back, W. (2001). The role of the hoof and shoeing, in H. Clayton and W. Back (eds), *Equine Locomotion*. London: W.B. Saunders, 147.
23. Gill, *Farriery*.
24. *Ibid.*
25. Thomason, J.J., 'Biomechanics of the Equine Foot', 49.
26. O'Connell, C. (2007). The Elephant's Secret Sense: the hidden life of the wild herds of Africa. Oxford: Simon & Schuster.
27. *Ibid.*

3 Environment, Herd and Human Interface

This chapter will discuss considerations for an ethologically sound lifestyle for barefoot horses, how the lifestyle of the domestic horse has a critical impact on integrated hoof health and barefoot success, and how to understand and manage herd dynamics. The authors will apply research findings from wild and feral herd studies to domestic practice. Human activity, culture and historical beliefs significantly impact on the life of the modern domestic horse, and the chapter concludes by making suggestions for integrating human and horse needs and requirements in a way that positively supports whole horse health. The authors also introduce an Equine Barefoot Welfare Manifesto, which underpins a twenty-first-century model for domestic horse keeping.

WHAT SORT OF LIFESTYLE IS BEST FOR THE HORSE?

The headline message for this section is simple: horses are horses, not humans.

Horses of the Camargue. Image courtesy of Jeremy Atkinson (originally posted to Flickr as Camargue horses) [CC BY 2.0 (http://creativecommons.org/licenses/by/2.0)], via Wikimedia Commons.

Wild horses in the Bolkar Mountains, Turkey. Image courtesy of By Zeynel Cebeci (Own work) [CC BY-SA 4.0 (http://creativecommons.org/licenses/by-sa/4.0)], via Wikimedia Commons.

Australian Brumbies, Northern Queensland. Image courtesy of n.hewson at http://flickr.com/ photos/43207063@N06/6112166362 via Wikimedia Commons.

Horses are a large prey species that in the wild inhabit an expansive geographical space, and require the company of a family of other horses to stay properly healthy. This lifestyle is much more than most owners of domestic horses can provide, so what kind of space and herd structure is good enough?

Researchers of wild, feral and domestic horse herds throughout the world agree that horses choose space over restriction, and company over isolation. These strategies have kept the species equine caballus alive over millions of years and will probably continue to do so. Space and company are two protective lifestyle factors for all horses, and are significant mitigating factors against ill-health throughout a horse's lifetime. Horse owners also need to acknowledge and keep in mind that human species requirements are distinctly different from equine requirements.

How can horse keepers make the space their horses live in be the right kind of space? Horses are a geographically diverse species, and can adapt to many different habitats. It is possible to successfully keep quite large domestic herds healthily in quite small spaces, when ethologically appropriate adaptations have been made. In traditional situations, keeping horses in habitats where there is little environmental stimulation beyond grass to graze, can cause a horse's lifestyle to become impoverished and detrimental to their well-being. Examining the approach taken by zoologists in designing captive environments and strategies that encourage species-appropriate behaviour highlights how different the life of a domestic horse has become. Making this comparison is useful as it highlights tried and tested approaches to inform horse keepers about ways they can adapt their horses' lifestyle.

ENVIRONMENTAL ENRICHMENT

Environmental enrichment refers to how knowledge about the behaviour of wild animals informs how they are kept in captivity. Often enrichment concerns the modification of enclosures to encourage the 'natural' behaviour of captive species. Evaluation has shown that this approach, done intelligently, is successful in improving the health and well-being of many captive animals, with some exceptions. For instance, it is very difficult and costly to set up a sufficiently large and varied 'sea-like' area for cetaceans, bringing into question the ethics of keeping cetaceans in captivity at all.

In zoology the development of enrichment approaches has been driven forward by the challenges presented in keeping environmentally sensitive species in captivity. Ruth Newberry writes:

> ...environmental enrichment is defined as an improvement in the biological functioning of captive animals resulting from modifications to their environment. Evidence of improved biological functioning could include increased lifetime reproductive success, increased inclusive fitness or a correlate of these such as improved health.[1]

Modifications such as including trees and climbing frames in chimp enclosures, or pools of water in penguin enclosures, are intended to stimulate species-appropriate behaviours. Newberry explains how to increase the biological relevance of environmental enrichment, and goes on to suggest an important point, which is relevant to modification efforts in domestic horse keeping. She argues that careful evaluation is required to determine whether assumptions about enrichment actually work. Early attempts to make captive environments more stimulating included providing things like human toys and piped music, which beyond an initial

Environmental enrichment is standard in zoos. Image courtesy of Spawn Man (Own work) [GFDL (http://www.gnu.org/copyleft/fdl.html) or CC BY-SA 4.0-3.0-2.5-2.0-1.0 (http://creativecommons.org/licenses/by-sa/4.0-3.0-2.5-2.0-1.0)], via Wikimedia Commons.

novelty impact had little intrinsic value, nor did they improve the lives of the captive animals exposed to them.

COMPARING STANDARDS FOR CAPTIVE AND DOMESTIC ANIMALS

In modern zoo keeping environmental enrichment is centre stage, and has evolved into a daily practice in animal husbandry supporting the extensive conservation aims of many of today's zoological operations. Advised by behaviour scientists, organizations such as the Association of Zoos and Aquariums (www.aza.org) have a specific and detailed approach to environmental enrichment, which covers captive species' behavioural, physical, social, cognitive and psychological needs.

In the UK the Department of the Environment, Food and Rural Affairs (DEFRA) publishes the Secretary of State's Standards for Modern Zoo Practice (SMZP). The standards cover animal welfare, public safety, and practice and governance for zoological facility managers. The most recent standards set out relevant instructions for environmental enrichment. Zoological establishments must

Captive herd animals in an enriched environment. Image courtesy of Kevin1086 (Own work) [CC BY-SA 3.0 (http://creativecommons.org/licenses/by-sa/3.0)], via Wikimedia Commons.

found their care plans for captive species on up-to-date information on species biology and husbandry. Zoos must also 'seek to meet the physiological and psychological needs of the animal'[2] in arranging their accommodation.

Whilst evidence-based environmental enrichment standards and strategies for captive animals have been formally compiled and adopted by the zoological community, paradoxically the same attention has not been given to domestic equines, despite the much larger global impact such standards could achieve.

DEFRA also produces a *Code of Practice for the Welfare of Horses, Ponies, Donkeys and their Hybrids*.[3] The content of this publication varies substantially from the SMZP. Unlike the SMZP, the document on equids does not place responsibility on horse keepers to base their practices on species-appropriate evidence. For example, the document accepts that it is an appropriate ethological management decision to keep horses in buildings for extended periods of time, although the species is known to have territorial ranges spanning between 152 and 826km^2.[4] The Equine Welfare Code of Practice document excludes any mention of ethology, and fails to consider the psychological or cognitive requirements of the species. The tone suggests that horses simply have considerable resource demands, and are an inconvenient species that the land has to be protected from, rather like small unruly tractors.

In the Equine Code of Practice 2009, guidance on environmental standards is limited to provision of shelter; pasture at 1.25–2.5 acres of 'suitable quality' grazing per horse, less if housed or only occasionally turned out; adequate pasture management, with removal of horses from the land if the ground is being damaged; and provision of an 'adequately sized and well-drained' area for feeding and lying down in wet conditions. The document includes long sections on the construction of buildings and fences. A large and practical section on diet emphasizes condition scoring and ways to prevent obesity. Other sections mention tethering, neither supporting nor precluding; rugging; and supervision. There are four small sub-sections on behaviour, suggesting that not all horses will actually benefit from 'turnout' (an accepted term for

time horses spend away from buildings), and that 'no-turnout' situations are acceptable. Two of the sub-sections on behaviour indicate that it is acceptable to discipline and restrain horses for treatment as long as it is appropriate, timely, reasonable and proportionate. The document excludes any mention of behaviour training, or habituation of equines for handling or treatment. There is a brief section on company, which emphasizes that herd life is preferable but social isolation is acceptable, and advises on managing fighting, stress, bullying and aggression, and supports the social isolation of stallions. As would be expected, there is a long section on health and welfare problems, old age, managing end of life care and euthanasia.

A wide range of 'accepted norms' and beliefs originated in the extensive history of equine domestication and human use. The horse is highly adaptable in domesticity, and

The Hope For Horses Campaign is spearheading legislative change for equine welfare in the UK. Image courtesy of Mark Johnson.

can survive in a wide range of less-than-ideal living situations. However, more professionals and horse owners are arguing for changes to animal welfare rights in this area. Numerous examples of neglect and cruelty are sustained by the lack of government action to maintain even adequate welfare standards for domestic animals.

ENFORCE UK LAW – PROTECT HORSES NOW! UK horses are protected by Animal Welfare law – but this is infrequently enforced, leading to suffering and death for thousands of horses. THIS MUST STOP!! We demand that Government prevent suffering by properly overseeing local enforcement of the law, ensuring that neglect is investigated and offenders prosecuted.[5]

Whole horse health equals hoof health; the horse is an integrated dynamic living system, and a horse-healthy lifestyle will support and protect their feet. It is essential that horse keepers consider the integrated needs of the horse in the same way that zoo keepers care for captive zoological species.

MOVING ON FROM 'NATURAL' HOOF CARE

Barefoot horse keeping practice has formulated the following four pillars of barefoot success:

- Diet
- Environment
- Trimming
- Exercise

Feral horses mutually grooming.

Finding the right balance for each individual horse requires planning and consideration of all four pillars. The adoption of the ethology of wild and feral horses in order to look for a 'correct' model for natural hoof care might seem a route to pursue this, but it was based on limited observations of feral mustangs living in only one habitat.[6] In very arid environments the hoof adapts its form in several ways to allow the horse to move more comfortably over hard substrates. The sole thickens and dries out, and the hoof wall thickens

Mustang feet displaying the short, strongly bevelled wall created by a dry, arid environment.

Mustang feet.

and develops a significant bevel around its peripheral rim. In addition, the nutritional paucity of the forage means that feral desert herds do not experience the same levels of laminar abruption from internal gut changes as horses in more lush environments.

The authors and other professionals have observed and monitored the feet of thousands of domestic and feral horses in the UK, and have noted that in a more temperate climate the desert-adapted foot is not common to feral horses. More recent evidence questions whether the lifestyle and feet of the domestic equine can ever be considered 'natural', and what evidence exists to support the assertion that wild and feral feet adapted in one geographical location can ever constitute 'correct' foot morphology.[7]

The authors of this book propose, based on empirical and practice findings, that the horse and its feet are in a situation of constant dynamic change in response to environmental demands. There is therefore

Konik horses on an RSPB reserve in North East Scotland.

no single correct morphological or 'natural' hoof, but a number of dynamic hoof morphology vectors depending on the range, substrate and climatic conditions. Barefoot horse keepers need to adopt a methodical philosophy, which connects environmental modification and intelligent ethical horse keeping practices with functional improvements in the feet of domestic horses. Any such philosophy also needs to acknowledge the artificial demands that humans place upon the species, and integrate evidence-based ways to develop sufficient strength and resistance to support those demands.

ENVIRONMENT

Environment can be defined as:

- the circumstances, objects, or conditions by which one is surrounded;
- the complex of physical, chemical and biological factors (including climate, soil and living things) that act upon an organism or an ecological community and ultimately determine its form and survival; and
- the aggregate of social and cultural conditions that influence the life of an individual or community.

Environment is paramount in getting barefoot horse keeping to work. In environmental enrichment terms, 'environment' encompasses diet, trimming and exercise, and adds more species specifics. The 'right' environment for horses is one where the species can survive in good health and reproduce successfully, which is somewhat more detailed than the four pillars. The limits on what barefoot horse keepers can do to construct a good environment for their horses

are simply limited by human knowledge, resources, commitment, imagination and creativity.

FREEDOM OF CHOICE?

When humans interact with horses, despite romantic notions of 'liberty', there are very few occasions when the horse has a genuine right to choose whether or not to engage. This is not to say interaction is always negative for the horse, but trainers and riders need to acknowledge that humans removed choice from the domestic horse the first time they herded them into an enclosure. But basic daily interaction can be positive, low stress and rewarding, which can build confidence and emotional resilience in the horse, and is essential for human safety. Under normal circumstances domestic horses will choose the comfort of their herd over the company of humans. With progressive positive experiences teaching them that humans offer safety, security, comfort and food, horses and humans can develop a base for effective communication and healthful relationships. This statement may seem self-evident in light of the history of horse and human relations, but archaeological evidence shows that most interaction was coercive. It is important to maintain continual awareness of the distinction between species requirements, to be responsible and ethical, and to acknowledge that a horse will have its own perspective on human interactions.

Perspectives on environmental 'control'

There is a common belief amongst horse keepers that domestic horses are unsafe and 'accident prone', and are likely to get hurt in any but the most spartan of enclosures.

The author's son and Max enjoying a beach drive.

Recently gelded feral stallion and family showing good condition – North East Scotland.

A group of young feral horses deftly traversing steep slopes.

Herding a family group of feral horses – youngsters, mares and recently gelded stallions.

However, evidence shows that domestic horses are most often injured by fencing when they are prevented from moving to get to other horses or to food. Observation of horses living in complex environments where there are many potential hazards suggests that, given an intimate knowledge of the terrain, they are very capable of avoiding damage. The horse has a sensitive proprioceptive system that is well designed for survival in an all-terrain environment. Many domestic horses are not exposed to complex environments from birth nor do they learn how to cope with them by living in an established herd, and therefore they may not learn how to stay safe. The following narrative describes a visit to an unusual UK feral herd, where the horses had what could be described as unintentional freedom of choice.

There are several important features that made this observation visit interesting in comparison with the horses the authors see from domestic herds:

- the low levels of illness and physical damage in comparison to domestic horses. From our experience of years of delivering hoof care, witnessing only one lameness in almost a hundred horses would be extremely unlikely;
- the good physical condition of the majority of the herd despite limited winter supplementary feed. There was no obvious need to disband the herd for reasons of poor condition;
- hoof balance was being maintained even when the majority of the living environment was grass and moorland with less abrasive substrate;
- the physical ability of even the youngest of the herd to move competently in a complex, varied environment, as evidenced by how they moved around the terrain and the lack of physical damage from discarded human 'junk';

Feral horse footprint showing typical hoof morphology for North East Scotand.

Recently gelded feral stallion.

PRO COMMENT

In 2011 one of the authors visited a farm in north-east Scotland where the equine charity World Horse Welfare (WHW) had been alerted to the existence of a large feral herd of cross-bred Highland ponies. The owner of the herd of over ninety animals, which had lived on the farm in naturalized family groups for over ten years, was increasingly unable to manage feeding the herd in the winter. There were concerns for their welfare and uncontrolled breeding (at which they were clearly successful). The plan for WHW was to assist the owner in cataloguing the whole group, neutering the colts and stallions, and disbanding the mainly unhandled herd to domestic homes. A manageable number of horses would be left on the property.

Spread over the property in small harem groups and colt bands, the horses averaged around 14.3hh and were of stocky build, with some slightly finer horses within the herd. The owner had limited breeding records, but anecdotal evidence suggested that a number of stallions, including a thoroughbred, had contributed over time to the genetic mix of the herd. By observation, the majority of horses in the herd had characteristics of Highland ponies, and the youngstock could be matched to the relevant stallion by proximity and resemblance.

It was originally a hill sheep and cattle farm, with the farm buildings situated away from the road halfway up a very beautiful river valley. The horses had free range of approximately 1,000 acres of mixed terrain, consisting of large areas of open heather moorland with rocky tracks and gullies, grassland fields around the farm buildings which they shared with sheep and store cattle, the grassy river valley and bottom, with some deciduous woodland on the slopes, and coniferous woodland areas higher up into the moorland.

On arrival at the farm, it was clear that the place had been in decline for some time. Much of the fencing was damaged and the farm buildings were surrounded by rusting car wrecks and other farm junk. Domestic horses often have scars resulting from accidents with fences and other objects, and therefore one would expect, given the amount of junk and the number of animals free grazing the property, that the feral herd would have many limb scars. In fact, there was only one mare who exhibited any scars, and they were on her shoulders, probably the result of an over-aggressive stallion. There were large numbers of youngstock grazing in and around the farm junk, but when any group moved off it was clear from the pattern of pathways and hoof prints over and around the old fences that they had a clear understanding of how to move around the property in the safest way.

A group of young colts were playing a high-speed game, racing around one of the farm fields then diving down a steep slope through the trees to gallop flat out through the river. One did slip over briefly, but not on the slope: it was when he turned at speed and lost traction on the flat bottom field. Only one horse out of the entire herd had any obvious lameness. One yearling showed the acute pain symptoms of a hoof abscess in a front foot. He was made to gallop when his harem band was chased by WHW staff in an all-terrain vehicle in order to 'round him up' for treatment – a practical demonstration of adrenalin in action, presumably. Generally their feet showed little evidence of laminitis, and the reasonably good anterior-posterior, medio-lateral balance and slightly longer toe length found in feral horses living in naturalized areas in mild and wet European climates.

- the frequency of movement between the herd groups for social interaction or 'visiting';
- the low numbers of obvious casualties. There was no evidence or reports of any horse deaths, although cattle carcasses had been removed from the farm;
- the existence of approximately six mature stallions (recently gelded) in breeding condition showing no serious physical damage from sparring or fighting;
- a clear monarchic structure. There was an obvious overlord, a senior stallion whose progeny were band stallions in harem sub-groups; and
- the clear psychological difficulties the mature band breeding stallions were experiencing two weeks after gelding.

Unfortunately for such a healthy group of horses living in an unusually diverse UK environment, the Dallas Herd was disbanded by WHW in 2011, although recent reports suggest there may be some breeding stock left.

PERMANENT INTERACTION WITH AN ENRICHED LIVING SPACE

Space and herd movement

In her book *The Horse in Human History*, Pita Kelekna writes:

> ...the horse, in its original evolution in North America and repeated radiations and extinctions worldwide, developed the anatomical features to become the fastest distance-running quadruped on earth in arid regions of poorest forage.[8]

Just like humans, if horses do not have to move around they frequently choose to be sedentary. Studies comparing the movement of feral horses with domestic horses find that mean daily distance moved in domestic herds increases with the size of their living space.[9] Basic daily movement is a substantial protective factor in horse health. Movement levels in wild and feral herds vary dependent on the food and water resources available.

A herd of Mongolian wild horses in their natural state. Image courtesy of A. Omer Karamollaoglu from Ankara, Turkey (Herd of Mongolian Wild Horse) [CC BY 2.0 (http://creativecommons.org/licenses/by/2.0)], via Wikimedia Commons.

Desert-living horses, such as Brumbies (Australian feral horses), are forced by environmental exigencies to adapt to very arid conditions by increasing their movement between watering holes and grazing areas. There is evidence that the ability to travel up to 65km from water for up to four days is a physiological adaptation of desert living equids.[10]. These distances sound impressive but may be related to hoof pathology and are viewed as excessive for the species. Further research which combined findings on wild and feral movement suggests that 'natural' daily movement for equids ranges from 5 to 10km (3.1–6.2 miles) per day. This level of movement can be seen in domestic horse herds living in enclosures greater than 10 acres.

Maximizing the size of a horse's living area is a priority, as horses that are very closely contained can become agoraphobic. Horses can be healthy if they are kept on small but environmentally enriched areas, but this is likely to take investment in the form of ground preparations, structures, fencing and things that encourage the horse to indulge in natural behaviour, such as moving, foraging, rolling and rubbing. Horses living in small spaces additionally benefit from having the mental map of their surroundings artificially extended by riding and/or walking horses out in hand around the area where they live.

In observations of modern domestic herds with large ranges, an important factor in horse health is the movement engendered by herd interaction.

If the terrain is very arid and plant density is sparse, each horse is going to require a larger area to find sufficient forage than horses in a more fertile area. In the UK a rule of thumb has been 1–1.5 acres of permanent grassland per horse.[11] The UK is an excellent environment for growing grass, and there are few areas in the UK where grass is not

The forty acre enclosure of Dinnet Equine Herd Project, Aberdeenshire.

Domestic Paddock Paradise system.

present all year round. However, in a more arid environment, like Namibia, a much larger area is needed to equal the plant yield.

The most sensible approach to managing grazing in the UK is to ensure that at any one time only 30 per cent of the available turnout is in use. Any property also needs

DINNET EQUINE HERD PROJECT

The Dinnet Equine Herd Project introduced a mixed herd of seven domestic horses to 40 acres of silver birch forest in 2012. During the first two weeks we observed many interesting changes. The most obvious one was in how much the horses were moving around the area and around each other. Predictably for those horses at lower fitness levels and the more obese horses, it was quite simply boot camp. It also became clear that social skills varied within the new herd, which led to some horses not coping well with the increased interaction and behaving aggressively. Over time the herd settled, gained fitness and lost weight, but during the grazing season they continued with the high level of movement. Most of the DEHP horses are ridden, and their riders found that their basic level of fitness was greater than it had been prior to their entry into the project.

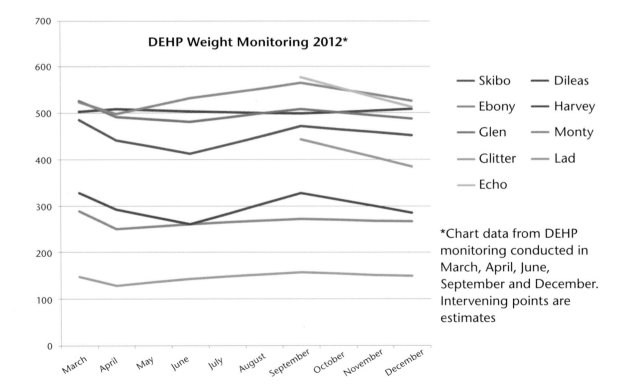

*Chart data from DEHP monitoring conducted in March, April, June, September and December. Intervening points are estimates

Weight monitoring chart - Dinnet Equine Herd Project.

Feral horses in the Namib Desert. Image courtesy of Stuart Orford [CC BY-SA 2.0 (http://creativecommons.org/licenses/by-sa/2.0)], via Wikimedia Commons.

Conventional horse keeping in the UK.

to ensure that changes can be made quickly if the weather changes drastically; the use of yarding systems with run-in shelters is an excellent way to manage periods of bad weather or illness.

Alternative shelter and yarding systems allow horses to be permanently kept in social groups.

Rotational grazing provides a practical way to manage grazing without using trackways. There are three important stages in grass growth that need to be taken into consideration in order to effectively manage grazing and protect land.[12] Grass is in what is known as the vegetative stage when it is less than 5cm long. There will be more about grass in Chapter 4, but suffice it to say here that in this stage the grass is 'stressed' – i.e., it is trying to prepare itself for regrowth after a reduction in grazing pressure by storing sugar in the leaf. On short grass horses will always be eating more sugar per mouthful than on longer grass.

Track systems and dispersal areas

Horses in the wild walk between water sources and foraging areas, where the herd disperses to eat. Many barefoot horse keepers have installed track systems with slow feeders to encourage their horses to move as much as possible. There is no formal evidence that track systems increase the rate of herd movement more than turning horses out in larger areas, but they are very useful in some parts of the world for reducing access to high calorie grasses. One notable concern with some track systems is stress. Dominant herd members may move others around a track system and may monopolize feeders. The challenge for track systems is how to include unpressurized foraging opportunities into a system to properly stimulate species-appropriate grazing behaviour. Track systems with additional cellular grazing areas allow barefoot horse keepers to integrate research findings about

PRO COMMENT

Even on track systems, if the track route stays the same or feeders and other objects are not moved regularly, boredom can be a common source of aggression. Get to know what plants are good for horses and what grows locally. Adding scattered edible stimuli, such as green bark branches, dried nettles, rosebay willow herb and meadowsweet stems, raspberry canes, fresh or dried rosehips, tiny pieces of dried apple and carrot, and even scattered grass nuts, encourages movement and foraging behaviour and avoids feeder pressure and bullying. Home dehydrators are readily available at good prices and are a very useful tool for making best use of seasonal gluts in fruit and vegetables that can be stored and used through the winter to add variation and interest. Adding narrow places into the track, with jumps and scattered objects where food can be hidden, also changes movement patterns and introduces varied use of balance and proprioception.

growing healthier and less calorific grasses[13] with enrichment strategies to maximize herd health.

Habitat enrichment

This category is of specific interest to hoof health. Providing a range of different ground surfaces or substrates can dramatically improve hoof condition, and can prepare horses for riding on different surfaces outside their living enclosure. Spending some time on virtually any kind of stone ground surface, possibly excepting lava rock which is exceptionally abrasive, has been found to be useful in conditioning feet, from the cobbles promoted by Xenophon[14] to the pea gravel and quarry waste put down in the tracks and loafing areas of many Paddock Paradise-style enriched systems.[15] Rocky areas do not need to be tidy

Pea gravel is often used in enriched systems in tracks and loafing areas

or flat, but to avoid injuries from penetrating rock fragments choose materials that are rounded in profile. River rock is ideal, but successful surfaces can be constructed out of virtually any rock, including crushed slate.

Developing resilient feet is not the only reason for modifying the herd area with stone. When horses actively move over rough stone areas, with each footstep they will abrade a small quantity of horn from the surfaces of their feet in contact with the ground. Even when they live in and around fairly sizeable rocks, as they pass over and between them they will brush them with their feet. This is an effective way to allow them to maintain their hoof wall length and bevel between trims, and can extend the period between trimming.

Horses in enriched systems develop their own paths. Moving over granite boulders encourages peripheral hoof abrasion.

Loafing areas

Loafing areas, where horses choose to rest and sleep, are useful focal points to provide a deeper layer of conformable material like pea gravel, sand or bark chippings which can improve hoof circulation and health.[16] Horses naturally choose softer areas for loafing, but they will choose visibility over comfort every time. A loafing area needs to have good visibility, and be big enough for several horses to comfortably lie and roll in. Removing a layer of topsoil and lining the area with membrane before adding an 8cm minimum depth of surface will protect the land underneath and prevent mud from building up, as well as giving a supportive surface that horses can pack under their feet when resting. Over time stone surfaces do need to be topped up, but it is worth planning properly and making a substantial foundation the first time they are laid so they do not need to be completely re-done. Horses also enjoy climbing on stone and gravel piles so it is not essential that a loafing area is flattened mechanically.

Added objects

Environmental enrichment standards highlight that animals interact with certain objects. DEFRA's Standards of Modern Zoo Practice describe this as a category of materials or objects designed to aid and encourage an animal's normal behaviour patterns in an enclosure and minimize any abnormal behaviour.[17] For equines, these could be loafing areas, trees and bushes (edible or otherwise), pools or water sources, substrates and browsing vegetation.

Horses are motivated by eating, moving, visual space and socialization. Enrichment objects could include:

- food items to forage for;
- space to graze and browse;
- loafing areas and sand pits to rest, roll and sleep;
- rubbing posts to rub and scratch;
- pools, muddy wallows and water sources for drinking and rolling;
- places to feel safe to play, relax and sleep in comfort in social groups; and
- places that are higher to watch for approaching danger.

Depending on the existing topography of an enclosure intended for horses,

PRO COMMENT

For rock crunching feet, dry them out. Barefoot horse keepers often install pea gravel surfaces in their track systems. Whilst pea gravel can be a helpful habitat addition in loafing areas, experience suggests that in some parts of the UK pea gravel tracks can cause problems for horses. In a wet northern UK climate horses often have very soft soles. The authors have been called to horses who have suddenly developed 'footiness' without inflammation or pulses, which turned out to be caused by them grazing in boggy areas for long periods and softening their feet. Long grass will also hold rain and dew for longer than open areas, keeping the feet damp. When sole horn is soft and the horse moves onto stones, the sole will easily deform and the foot will become sensitive. Wet sole horn is also very easily abraded, and can be excessively removed as the horse moves across stones. In drier climates sole horn builds up thickness, and being dry it is more resilient to abrasion so growth will keep up with wear, and the solar margin can 'callous' under pressure. A dry enough climate to achieve this is not common in the northern UK, therefore the authors advise installing pea gravel in some loafing areas, but in addition install in covered areas a deep layer of highly absorbent bedding material to help dry out soft, soggy soles. Even when all the other barefoot ducks are in a row, horses in northern UK climates are often more comfortable in boots and pads for riding, which is likely a result of sole softness.

Feral horse rolling in the sea. Image courtesy of T353&4 (originally posted to Flickr as IMG_1732) [CC BY-SA 2.0 (http://creativecommons.org/licenses/by-sa/2.0)], via Wikimedia Commons.

simple additions or modifications may be required. As horses interact with objects and opportunities in their enclosure, it can increase the time they spend in movement and being occupied rather than just eating, thus supporting all-round health and hoof health in particular.

Some horses are particularly attracted to water features and will choose to wade or roll in shallow water. They may also dig shallow pits in the ground and roll on, lick and ingest soils. Other objects may be specific to the individual, and there are certainly horses that enjoy picking up objects and nosing or tossing them around. Colts and male donkeys in particular are inclined to play with objects in their enclosures.

PRO COMMENT: DINNET EQUINE HERD PROJECT

One rainy evening in spring I was watching the herd in the Dinnet Equine Herd Project as they foraged at the edge of a clearing in the birch forest. Usually at that time of day they range over a relatively small area, there is plenty of movement and they are all grazing within sight and sound of each other. One of the geldings found a particularly interesting smell at the base of a tree and started to dig up the soil there. Despite the rain it was still very dry under the tree and as he dug sprays of dry soil flew up under his belly. Sniffing loudly and bridging his body with excitement, he dropped and rolled on the spread soil several times in quick succession. The other geldings came over, attracted by his excitement, and moved him off the spot, taking turns to roll themselves. The mares moved in too, ranging at the periphery of the excited group of rolling geldings. After a minute or so the senior gelding leapt up after four or five rolls, and galloped off through the trees. The others did the same a second or two later, and the whole herd had a wild fling through the forest. Intrigued, I hurried over to the tree to see if I could identify what it was that had excited them. Even though I got down on all fours to have a really good sniff, I couldn't identify anything in the soil. A few months later I met a lady who was a specialist in fungi. She told me about red squirrels who collect certain types of fungus and use them as a stimulant!

Mammals and fungi

In 1995 Scottish Natural Heritage carried out a study into the food choices of red squirrels and analysed their stomach contents for evidence of fungal spores. To their surprise they found that red squirrels may be little furry gourmets – they had been eating both true and false truffles (elaphomyces muricatus; hydnotrya tulasnei and melanogaster ambiguus), pea truffles and ceps.[18] Many other animals, including deer, have been found to consume fungi, some of which are psychoactive. Horses co-evolved with a wide range of fungi and may also find them attractive and edible.

Interactive horse 'toys'

These objects include treat-dispensing balls or multisided shapes with slots or holes that the horse can nuzzle and roll around to gain food. Be aware that interacting with these objects can be extremely frustrating for horses. The horse is not cognitively adapted to delayed gratification; when they see food, they eat it. Sorting through mixed low calorie forage materials with lips and tongue, smelling, tugging, lipping, peeling and tearing with teeth are all alternative normal horse eating behaviours.

AN END TO STABLING AND SOCIAL DEPRIVATION

Equine welfare is dependent on not only physical comfort but mental comfort as well. Confining a thinking animal in a dark, dusty stable with little or no social interaction and no mental stimulation is as harmful as providing inadequate nutrition or using abusive training methods.[19]

Social deprivation is the most prevalent form of sensory deprivation in domestic horses. In many parts of the world horses are kept in individual management systems, and,

Healthy horses should not be prevented from rubbing on solid objects.

with the increase in one owner–one horse situations, individual housing, including for turnout, is on the increase. Many horse owners agree that isolating horses leads to problems, but without peer-reviewed evidence government welfare organizations will be reluctant to move towards a more ethological model.

Evidence comes from a recent study by a team of British researchers. They examined stress levels in horses in several different housing conditions. In this study 'housing'

In the Dinnet Equine Herd Project nine horses now live in a 40 acre enclosure of mixed birch forest, grassland and marsh. Having this range of habitat allows them to move around and engage in many different behaviours, but they are mainly interested in foraging. Throughout the year they have become specialists at finding tasty plants. Around the base of each tree is a protected area or microclimate, which is slightly warmer than the surroundings, within the drip line of the canopy and protected enough to allow early plant growth. Early in the spring the horses are often found foraging for blades of grass around the base of the trees and around stone piles where other little protected shoots emerge. This involves a lot of energy and stimulation for very little in terms of calories, helping to manage their weight. As well as eating behaviours, the herd chooses particular trees for rubbing sessions. They are trees that grow at a 50–60 degree angle so each horse can get different parts of its body underneath the trunk and push in several different directions, including upwards. This kind of angle also allows a rubbing tree to be used by different sized individuals: the smaller the pony, the more acute the trunk angle. Even horses with evidence of sweet itch use these rubbing trees, which for anyone used to dealing with sweet itch seems impossible to allow. Living in a consistent herd with a diurnal movement pattern mitigates intense and prolonged rubbing. Tree rubbing tends to be a social activity where the horses take turns. Serious rubbers are often moved off the selected tree by other herd members wanting a turn, and learn to keep up once left behind as the herd moves on to a new area.

relates to the level of social contact between individuals. The team used four conditions:

- single stables with solid walls;
- single stables with interconnecting bars;
- pairs of horses housed in a barn system; and
- group housing in a paddock.

The study used non-invasive measuring methods, so that the experimental situation did not increase the horses' stress levels. The researchers measured adrenal activity via fecal cortisol, and stress levels by thermal eye imaging, both of which have been found to be reliable but non-invasive measures.

Unsurprisingly, the study found that horses housed singly had significantly higher levels of adrenal activity, and were more difficult to handle than horses housed in any other way. Horses housed in groups with full contact in turnout paddocks were easiest to handle and least stressed.[20]

In another study on social restrictions on behaviour in young horses, significant effects of social deprivation were found, even at the level of separate but adjacent stabling. Two groups of two-year-old stallions in Denmark were housed either singly or in groups of three for nine months.[21] Housing young horses in groups in buildings without turnout through

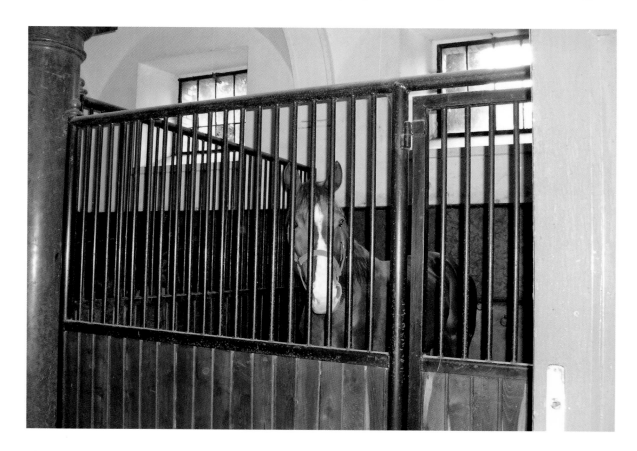

The typical lone stabling arrangement of the modern domestic horse allows for no socialisation. Image courtesy of Magellan (Own work) [GFDL (http://www.gnu.org/copyleft/fdl.html) or CC-BY-SA-3.0 (http://creativecommons.org/licenses/by-sa/3.0/)], via Wikimedia Commons.

In healthy herds rolling is a group activity.

the winter months is a conventional European management situation to minimize pressure on the land. In Dutch Friesian studs the authors have observed barn-housed groups of colts being kept in much the same way as young cattle. The Danish study found several interesting findings relevant to modern-day practice. On subsequent turnout those that had been grouped together remained near each other in the herd, but singly stabled horses did not remain in contact with their box neighbours. Singly stabled horses would be found on average closer to the nearest horse during turnout than the grouped horses were, and showed more overt aggressive behaviour and increased levels of mutual grooming and play. The grouped stallions were observed to use submission and subtle displacement behaviour more frequently in their interactions.

The authors suggest that the concept of 'turnout' is a misleading and restrictive term to use in the care of equids, who should be given permanent access to large enough living enclosures to encourage natural levels of daily activity.

Buildings

Horses can be habituated to containment inside buildings, but it is not a 'natural' experience for them. If it is essential that a horse is brought into a building for treatment or care, bring a sensible calm companion with it, and ensure it has enough time to settle down with some food before trimming or other intervention is planned. A horse is reinforced by learning to associate buildings with food for which it will not have to forage or compete, rather than wanting to come in 'to get out of the rain'.

The rise in popularity of 'duvet' days and extremely limited turnout for horses spells bad news for their hoof and general health. Footfall studies have shown that horses kept in stables even for only part of the day do not choose to move as much as those who free range.[22] Lack of movement has significant consequences for a horse, from slowing peristaltic action to changing the blood flow to the foot.

There are some horses who appear to enjoy staying indoors. In these cases there is likely to be an aversive reason why they do not prefer to be outside. Common causes include competition for food, bullying or discomfort caused by weather or insects. Choosing to stay in buildings is not a normal behaviour for a horse, will impact on hoof and general health, and should be resisted.

Domestic horse from Dinnet Equine Herd Project listening for the herd approaching.

PRO COMMENT

One summer I was asked to do a hoof assessment on a young Arab stallion who had recently been adopted as a rescue by one of my clients. This horse was six years old, and had never been out of a loose box or shared his personal space with any other animal since weaning. Whilst his basic needs for food and water had been taken care of, he was under-developed in every other way. His legs were spindly and weak, his feet were almost tubular and his movement was mechanically compromised in almost every dimension. About the only thing he had going for him was his testosterone, which had given him reasonable body condition. His new owners, long-term horse keepers with a sympathetic approach, were keen to get him introduced to the outdoors but their early experiences with him left them confused and disappointed. He was extremely agoraphobic, to the extent that in the paddock he did not graze but paced a loose box-sized shape next to the fence line, calling and sweating. Bringing him back into the barn was the only thing that would reassure him. Over time, and by very slowly increasing his time outside, initially by walks in hand, he learned to accept being outside. The following year I saw him again, and he had by then learned to accept an older broodmare as a companion. His behaviour outside had settled a lot, and he was not that different from any other young, conventionally kept stallion. His attitude to the mare, however, varied between foal behaviour and stallion behaviour.

THE SENSORY LIFE OF THE HORSE

The Association of Zoos and Aquariums explains:

> Animal sensory systems are typically specialized by species and play crucial roles in their survival. Sensory enrichment is designed to address the animal's sense of smell, touch, hearing, vision, and taste and elicit species-specific response, territorial, reproductive or hunting behaviors.[23]

Smell

Horses are an olfactory, or smell-orientated, species. Research by Dr Bob Bowker has defined scent glands around the frog,[24] which allow horses to gather information on the other horses sharing their habitat. When a lone horse is returned to its herd, it will sometimes drop its head and appear to cast about or check out the ground in front of it before deciding which way to go. The horse is looking for a hoof scent trail to locate the rest of the herd. A strong sense of smell accounts for those times when horses take lost people home in the fog or at night. It has also been suggested by other researchers that the chestnuts (vestigial toes) above the knee on the medial side of the legs contain scent glands. An unusual traditional use for shed or trimmed chestnuts is as a proprietary calmer. If there is or was any basis to the claim, it is probably because of the scent gland association.

Sniffing other herd members or objects, dung piles or urination spots keeps horses up to date with herd activity, health and breeding state. Horses may prefer that not all the dung piles are removed from their habitat. If there is enough space some herds will develop and use latrine areas, and these can be managed to allow them to express this behaviour and control parasites.

PRO COMMENT

Smell is a frequent discussion topic during hoof trimming appointments. We can tell a lot about the state of the horse's health by its smells. The strongest and most obvious smells often indicate a disease state, such as thrush or an internal infection emerging through an abscess. Occasionally, when an abscess is about to breach the soft skin above the coronet, flies are attracted to the olfactory messages emerging before we can register them. I have occasionally used the behaviour of flies to help locate an emerging abscess! Horses with Cushing's disease also seem to have a particular and recognizable smell about them. When coming into contact with strong disease smells, horses are very unlikely to react. There are, though, other smells that are interesting to them. It is on occasion necessary to trim chestnuts and ergots as if they become very long they can interfere with the horse's skin and movement. A horse will often take pieces of chestnut or frog into their mouths and mumble them, or will take several deep sniffs of the fragments if they find them on the floor. Young horses and mares will lick hoof trimmings and the top of the hoof stand, and my gloves often need a very long sniff for information on who was trimmed last!

Many horses necessarily share their enclosures with wildlife.

In the wild horses also encounter smells from other species, including predators. Many domestic enclosures get visits from wildlife, and some horses find other animals' smells and sounds fascinating.

Touch

Tactile stimuli are also important elements of a horse's habitat. Horses enjoy rubbing against solid things. Moving through bushes and undergrowth can also help to dislodge shedding hair and biting insects from the belly and legs.

The Bog Myrtle plant is known for its insect repellent properties.

HERD COMMENT

Scotland is well known for its midges, and during the summer the horses at the Dinnet Equine Herd Project are no stranger to these tiny biting pests. In the herd enclosure there are plantations of low bushes containing juvenile birch trees, bog myrtle and other plants. When the midges are particularly bad the herd can be found in the bushes, which grow in the low marshy areas where the midges actually breed. Bog myrtle (latin name *myrica gale*) is a well-known plant traditionally used for its insecticidal properties and the herd has apparently discovered its usefulness.

Vision

As a prey species, horses need good visuals, can be claustrophobic and prefer open spaces. During training, graded exposure is sometimes used to help a horse become comfortable in contained spaces such as stables and trailers. If a horse usually inhabits a very open space, riding them in indoor arenas, enclosed lanes or forestry could be overwhelming due to the reduction in visual depth, and the increased proximity of objects that the horse may find threatening. Including varying visuals in an enclosure can be as simple as establishing trees and bushes that break up the horizon or the openness of the enclosure, give a greater sense of space, and can serve a dual purpose of providing additional browsing or foraging interest at different times during the year.

If horses are regularly isolated, for instance for rehabilitation after injury, owners often add mirrors to their boxes with the intention of providing a social substitute or visual stimulus. In practice, horses quickly habituate to anything that remains in the same place for long, so the use of mirrors may be of very limited value in comparison to a box companion, touchable neighbour or a busy yard to watch.

Behaviour such as jumping or barging out of stables, going over or through fences and gateways, pulling away and bolting is often caused by an overwhelming fear of something that seems inconsequential or invisible to humans. Particularly when caring for young horses, think twice about choosing to bring them in during very wild weather conditions as they may show increased fear or be overwhelmed by their surroundings.

HERD COMMENT

With the evolution of the horse associated with mainly grassland, we expected the herd to prefer the open spaces provided by the glades and grassland of the Dinnet Equine Herd Project. After an initial couple of weeks while the herd members were clearly finding their feet in the enclosure and working out their social gremlins, we found that they were happy to inhabit all areas of their enclosure at different times. The topography of the landscape in the enclosure means that they are rarely if ever exposed to bad weather unless they choose to be. When locating the main herd after an absence for riding or other activities, the horses appear to use seismic vibrational transmission and listen for evidence of their location.

Taste

Current horse-keeping advice suggests that maintaining a consistent diet is very important to equine health. However, without making an enormous change in the main food sources, a wide range of different tastes can be safely introduced into their diet. Hedgerow browsing

Horses enjoy eating Rosebay Willowherb.

whilst walking in hand provides the horse with interesting access to new flavours across the year and benefits their feet. Wild foraged fruits and herbs can be easily preserved from fresh when in season, or are available from specialist feed suppliers.

EQUINE SOCIAL LIFE

Animals of social species should normally be maintained in compatible social groups. They should only be kept isolated for the benefit of the conservation and welfare needs of the group, and where this is not detrimental to the individual specimen.[25]

Wild and feral equine harem groups average between six and twelve individuals and typically include the dominant stallion, a head mare and lead mare, one or two other subordinate mares and some related youngsters. Unless there is a large range area or the horses are very busy, larger numbers than this can increase interpersonal pressure to a stressful level. If resources are plentiful, a number of harem groups containing distantly related individuals can co-occupy an area.[26] Harem groups co-occupying habitat may share resources such as drinking sites and access trails, on a rotational basis.

Establishing a herd is an essential part of an environmental enrichment strategy, and there are several factors to consider to encourage normal behaviour, particularly movement. Prior to doing so, though, address enclosure safety. It is important to ensure that the space is large enough and contains sufficient edible resources for the number of horses in the herd, and that enclosure fences and other permanent fixtures do not provide places where horses can become trapped. A less obvious consideration is the size differential between herd members. Smaller animals are at more risk if larger horses decide to engage in vigorous behaviour. An

Recently gelded feral stallion and his two sons.

Horses of different sizes can rub along well together. The small coloured mare demands respect in Dinnet Equine Herd Project.

interesting way to provide depressurized zones in mixed-size herds is to use 'pop-holes' through fences into specially designed small horse dispersal areas.

Mixed gender herd structures

The horse is a harem group species. Harem groups are defined as animals that live in small groups of often unrelated individuals. This factor is an advantage for modern horse keeping as horses do adapt relatively well to living outside their immediate family. In harem groups with a breeding structure, juvenile members are discouraged from remaining in the group once they reach breeding age. Interestingly, there is some evidence that in the wild some family members, particularly colts, are allowed to remain with the dominant stallion as a subordinate or 'apprentice' male. These individuals are often related to the dominant male and can support him in his defensive role, and may even be allowed to serve some harem mares. Observations in Brumby herds suggest that this relationship may encourage the physical development of the subordinate horse. Colts who have not been 'apprenticed' in this way may not reach breeding condition and remain more juvenile in appearance.[27]

In wild or feral herds young horses are mainly moved on from the herd by the dominant male, and sometimes by the senior females, when they reach breeding age. Young males may band together on the periphery of the herd when there is lower pressure on resources, or may move away completely. Older non-patriarchal stallions may also be members of these all-male groups. Mares may be selected by the dominant stallion, or may choose to leave or join a herd of their own accord.

When there is significant competition for resources and larger population densities, the tenure of a dominant stallion may last as little as a season before a stronger competitor takes over the herd. However, when resources are plentiful and where population densities are lower, there is correspondingly less frequent turnover of the patriarchal stallion.

Experiences with established domestic herds suggest that where there is no movement of individuals in and out of the herd, and sufficient food resources are available, activity levels will be low. Traditional single gender herds do not encourage social interaction at the same level as a mixed gender herd. Mares are all about making friendships, and can become very comfortable and quiet with each other's companionship: 'There is a bond of mutual interest, which unites mares within a harem band, and, as individuals, each benefits from the protection of the herd.'[28]

A strong head mare is the backbone of the herd. There have been many observed instances where losing the head mare has initiated a grieving and chaotic period for the herd. Head mares provide the decision-making capacity. Herds work well where the head mare is a confident and well adjusted individual, but if a herd contains a number of mares who do not have these qualities, moving them around as a group can be challenging. In studies of feral herds, darting or otherwise capturing the head mare has been used successfully to 'ground' a wild herd so they stay in one area for study. The male members of the herd are likely to protect the herd rather than decide to move it, and will actively prevent younger and less assertive mares from taking a lead and making a decision. A strong head mare will also interact with and help 'train' younger members of the herd, which can be a considerable advantage with curious and ebullient growing youngsters.

Young horses

Young horses have lengthy physical and psychological development stages. Standards for Modern Zoo Practice[29] makes specific mention of developmental stages, although this is excluded from their guidance on equines.

Young horses are most appropriately developed within their maternal herd until they reach breeding age, from which time a change in social group to one that includes horses of a variety of ages and genders will be most appropriate and least stressful to their development. Traditionally young horses are weaned at six to ten months of age, when they are separated from their maternal herd. They or their dam may be removed by forcible

separation and transported to a completely new property and herd, where they may then be kept indoors to stop them injuring themselves by trying to escape and find their mother. When their behaviour is seen to have 'settled', they are put into a herd consisting mainly of other young horses until they are old enough to start training or to be sold on. Many young horses are sold straight from weaning either privately or through sales and markets. Weaning experiences like these are often extremely stressful. As well as the risk of physical damage to horses, humans and equipment through panicking behaviour, weaning has been linked to the development of gastric ulcers.

Weaning and separation from the maternal herd at a very young age carries a serious risk

A group of young horses relaxing.

of placing the horse under a level of stress that is going to damage its physical and psychological well-being. With young horses that have been weaned at months rather than years old, particularly if the horse is experiencing physical or behavioural problems, including being unusually calm for its age, investigation for gastric ulcers is a sensible choice. In studies, over 50 per cent of foals with no obvious gastric disease were found to have gastric ulcers, which the researchers related to stress.[30] A Danish study in 2009 cited fasting as a risk factor for the development of gastric ulcers.[31] Observation of foals weaned in an abrupt traditional fashion indicates that disturbances in eating and drinking behaviour are common, and anecdotal evidence suggests that gastric ulcer problems which began in foalhood can extend into adult life, through lack of identification and the long-term maintenance of stress responses. The chapter on troubleshooting contains further information on gastric ulcers, but ulcers in any part of the intestinal tract can have a significant effect on hoof health and sensitivity.

In recent years some breeders have begun integrating a more ethological model into their breeding practices in order to eliminate the destructive and unnecessary effects of abrupt weaning.

Out of doors our stallions live with mares and youngstock, or as a bachelor herd in sight, sound and smell of the mares, separated from them by a wall topped by normal electric fencing. Indoors they all feed ad lib from shared bales and can mutually groom over the partitions. We have found that some of our own horses are happier sharing a large loosebox than occupying one on their own, so that is what they do . . . Some people are quite alarmed to be told that some of the double-occupiers are stallions. The fact that they have to be told before they realise it says a great deal. . . .[32]

The older mare at centre provides a confident model for her younger companions.

Gastric ulcers, persistent parasites, developmental problems, attachment problems and anxiety can all be linked to abrupt weaning and may cause lifelong complications for a horse. Young horses who have had a stressful weaning experience require a consistent and well-balanced herd as a priority. These youngsters may have problems adjusting to change, and may benefit from ulcer treatment and additional digestive support to help them cope with any changes.

Mixed age herds

Mixed age herds keep old horses mobile and young horses safer. Separating herds by age is common in domestic horse keeping, where many establishments have 'the oldies' and 'the youngsters'. Life in the wild is harder, but domestic horses can reach far greater ages due to nutritional advantages, and with geriatric domestic horses reaching their late twenties and thirties, horse owners often find themselves caring for a horse through many twilight years. Old horses can be very sedentary, and with old age can come a range of health and mobility problems. Owners often wish to protect older equine companions, perhaps by excluding them from the busy and curious life of young horses. It can be mutually beneficial, however, to establish a mixed age herd if the older members of the group are healthy enough and the young members are not over-enthusiastic.

Young horses spend a lot of time playing, growing and sleeping, but their lack of life experience can lead them into trouble. When healthy older horses move and play with youngsters, they keep themselves physically and psychologically active, and maintain their basic fitness and mobility. For the young horse, having the guidance of older herd members is an essential part of healthy development.

Youngsters learn by observing the behaviour of older horses. With the right mix of personalities, the young horse is in a place where it can build social skills and confidence, and learn how to react and stay safe in different situations and complex environments. In a mixed age domestic herd, it is prudent to monitor older horses' stress levels, and ensure there is sufficient forage and space for herd members to spend time apart. Any sign of depression or weight loss could indicate a stressful situation.

How big is a big enough herd?

Getting the herd size right has traditionally been governed by how much grass grazing is required to keep a horse in good condition, but in reality there are several more factors involved. It may seem appropriate that horses would be happier in larger groups as the burden for threat vigilance could be shared between greater numbers of horses, but it turns out that horses prefer a small but consistent group of between six and twelve individuals. In many domestic settings the protective effect of a larger group is mitigated by the pressure more horses put on less space and fewer resources. Even in large open fields a horse may feel pressure on its personal space if it cannot choose to leave the visual presence of a horse it feels threatened by. A common sight on many yards is a group of twenty horses sharing several acres with feeders in the winter. Access to the feeders will be restricted by the dominant horses in the herd. Others approaching may have to 'run the gauntlet' to get access to forage.

Environmental overcrowding can lead to high levels of aggression, passivity and non-reactiveness as herd members adapt their behaviour to a pressurized living area. Horses in artificial domestic environments may also have poorly developed social skills, which

Ring feeders are convenient for humans but can provide a source of tension in a herd.

will lead to unusual or excessively expressed behaviours.

This is a particular problem for domestic stallions. A colt raising service[33] allows young males to experience an ethologically appropriate developmental period. Colts are taken into the nursery herd as foals, and subsequently into a herd of youngsters and mares. When individually appropriate, they move into the bachelor herd to complete their development prior to a decision being taken regarding gelding.

Circadian rhythms and behaviour

Andy Beck, in his book *Horsonality*, discusses the night-time behaviour of the herd:

As dusk comes on, groups of horses tend to close up, facilitating an increase in communica-

tion between them and improving the defensive alert, and this is what we might expect since dusk is a favourite hunting time. During the night the herd continues to graze while remaining in tighter formation than during the day; the level of alertness, even during periods of rest and stillness, is also higher, and the group can easily be spooked into high-speed flight. More movement takes place during the hours of darkness and for this reason the Japanese researcher Hayakawa... recommended that yearlings be grazed during this time to improve muscle development, rather than during the day which has been the traditional turn-out time for housed horses.[34]

Clearly, if we want to maximize movement potential, if there are any restrictions on the size of the herd range for practical reasons for instance, giving the herd access to the maximum range at night will serve this purpose better than day-time turnout and night-time restriction.

Attachment problems

Horses kept for extensive periods of time in small, stagnant herds are likely to develop a deep and strong attachment to the other herd members. This can make separating any individual stressful for them and their herd mates, and problematic for their humans. If this situation has persisted from birth, they are also much less likely to develop appropriate social skills with other horses.

Inter-species social groups

Whilst horses are able to socialize with other species, permanent isolation from other horses should be avoided. Several welfare documents refer to the acceptability of keeping isolated equines with other animals. Be aware, though, that in other species of mammals (humans, dogs) which have been observed growing up in situations of social deprivation, the lack of early socialization has been seen to affect their cognitive development and the effects may be extremely persistent or even irreversible.[35]

AT THE HORSE–HUMAN INTERFACE

The horse as a species has no evolutionary mechanism that protects it from human intervention or prepares it for interaction with humans. Human choices in horse breeding have selected for some behavioural characteristics including trainability, but at the end of the day a horse will always choose to behave like a horse. In order to establish

healthy attitudes and predictable behaviour, owners need to take responsibility for expanding their horse's cognitive capabilities and choose training approaches that help the horse become physically and mentally resilient to the artificial demands humans place on them.

Walking horses in hand is a useful way to expand their mental territory.

Trail riding is excellent for helping horses develop fitness and confidence.

Driving is a fun and useful way to keep smaller ponies fit and healthy.

Travelling horses regularly can be a source of stress.

Ground work including lunging and agility can help horses develop cognitive skills.

Horses and cognition

The term 'cognition' refers to conscious mental activities, such as thinking, learning and remembering. Varied groundwork and riding training in low stress environments can enhance a horse's cognitive abilities. Recent research has defined that horses are capable of many different cognitive tasks, and are not simply reacting on 'instinct' or responding to conditioning as was previously believed. Evelyn Hanggi explains in a paper reviewing equine cognition research:

> In the wild, [horses] must cope with food and water of inconsistent quality or unpredictable distribution, predators that change locations and habits, and a social system in which identities and roles of individuals must be discovered and remembered. Domesticated horses may face even more potentially bewildering conditions. In addition to dealing with similar situations encountered in nature, many domesticated horses must live in largely unsuitable environments, must suppress instincts while learning tasks that are not natural behaviors, and must co-exist with humans who sometimes behave bizarrely, at least likely from an equine standpoint.[36]

Habituation

All domestic horses learn from habituation to objects and situations. Habituation describes the way in which young horses learn to discriminate between objects and experiences that are important, and those that are not. Habituating a youngster is common sense and accepted practice in horse training. It may be simple, but it is a very important experience and needs to be managed effectively.

Discrimination learning is happening the first time a young horse experiences anything new. Initially anything and everything may

PRO COMMENT

When introducing young horses to trimming, it is critical that the handler or hoof trimmer does not become affected by the horse's emotional state, but concentrates on having a calm and positive attitude, regardless of how the youngster behaves. Managing unintentional signals is especially important for safety in horse–human interaction. Experienced professionals learn to keep their heart rate low in order to maintain focus in the horses they work with.

Trainers need to be calm, positive and reinforcing.

be exciting and interesting, and the young horse can be emotional and reactive. If the young horse is guided through the experience without being allowed to become overwhelmed, it will habituate to the multitude of new stimuli.

Equine learning theory – making choices about learning

Incorporating a wide range of different learning experiences into a horse's training can significantly improve its performance in specific activities. Cross-training has been found in humans to enhance cognitive development across the board, and research in equines is moving in the same direction:

> Many horses could benefit from opportunities for generalization . . . horses in specific riding disciplines are frequently not allowed to participate in activities other than what interests their riders. As a result, they go through mechanical motions that rarely enhance any cognitive skill. Evidence of this can be seen in a recent study that showed that, compared with horses involved in other disciplines, high-level dressage horses displayed the lowest level of learning performance in simple tests. It was hypothesized that because these horses are trained to perform highly sophisticated, precise behaviors, riders give them minimal freedom; therefore, they are inhibited from learning to learn or generalizing.[37]

Desensitization

Desensitization is a common approach used in horse training, and is useful with individuals that are reactive to stimuli like touch and moving objects. With the increasing popularity of natural horsemanship and 'spook-busting' clinics, many horses have been exposed to desensitization procedures. These clinics tend to consist of graded exposure to a range of potentially fear-inducing stimuli, and the horse is encouraged to engage with the object repeatedly until it stops showing fearful behaviour. When done for specific purposes, such as learning to carry objects on the body such as equipment and humans, and when changes in attitude from fearful to engaged and calm are positively reinforced, desensitization is a very effective process.

Positive reinforcement or negative reinforcement?

There is debate in training circles on the distinction, effectiveness and ethics of different types of behavioural training. In studies, both negative reinforcement (removal of an aversive stimulus after the correct behavioural response) and positive reinforcement (application of a reinforcer, usually food, after the correct behavioural

DESENSITIZATION AND LEARNED HELPLESSNESS

In horse training systematic desensitization has a place, but extreme desensitization experiences such as 'sacking out', where the horse is exposed to a flapping tarpaulin until it stops reacting, can cause a problem called learned helplessness. When an animal or human is exposed to very frightening stimuli from which they cannot escape, a well known stress response is to psychologically retreat or 'shut down'. After an initial period of flight, the horse may outwardly appear to become calm and even relaxed, but not necessarily engaged with the human. If the horse has tried to flee from the aversive stimulus but has not been able to (if tied or contained in a small enclosure), they do not learn to associate their behaviour with a reduction in the aversive stimulus. Learned helplessness may be associated with lack of engagement in future learning situations, and panic attacks. Some researchers have associated certain kinds of round pen training with learned helplessness in horses.

response) have both been found to be effective training approaches. Close observation of horse trainers at work reveals that a combination approach with the stress on the positive is an effective approach to equine learning. Proponents of 'single approach to reinforcement' training, whether positive or negative, have their justifications, but research findings suggest that 'ideally trainers and handlers should incorporate intelligent use of both positive and negative reinforcement into a well-balanced program'.[38]

Troubleshooting training

It is critical to assess the horse's basic emotional state in every training situation and if it is displaying generalized anxiety (basic signs are elevated heart rate, rapid breathing and body tension), to thoroughly relax it through touch, breathing, carefully removing and reintroducing frightening stimuli, and controlled movement. If horses are continuously exposed to certain objects when feeling fear, some individuals may learn to permanently fear these objects,

PRO COMMENT

We love our clients to develop good riding relationships with their horses so they can keep them fit and healthy, and help their feet stay strong and conditioned. I recall two stories that show how observation is important when deciding whether desensitization is appropriate for some horses but not others.

In order to be able to hack out his horse safely and condition her feet, one of our clients decided to go to a 'spook-busting' clinic as the mare was scared by white lines on the road and poles in the school. The horse was relatively calm at home, but had learned to be worried about schooling sessions in other arenas. This had happened because her rider believed her anxiety was 'silliness' and thus tended to keep the pressure high to 'ride her through it', and did not reinforce her with breaks or food during sessions. After coming home from the clinic, the rider reported that the horse was having on-going trouble with lines and poles. It was clear what had happened. At the clinic, neither the trainer nor the rider acknowledged that the horse already had a high level of anxiety and fear about being in arenas, which was much more long-standing than the pole problem. At every arena visit the horse felt fearful, and exposing her to scary new objects had sadly escalated her general fear in arenas.

By comparison, one summer one of our young horses was ready to start his ridden training. He was a young Arabian gelding who was born and raised at home. As a foal he had a precocious and confident personality, and therefore he quickly occupied himself in various 'helpful' ways around the fields and yard, including watching other horses being ridden on and around the property. At that time I used a join-up method in the round pen for starting, but this boy taught me something useful about flexible thinking. He would not be driven away from me for anything, and calmly turned back towards me each time I tried. Eventually I decided to listen, and tacked him up (he was prepped for this), and climbed on. After five minutes happily trundling round the pen stopping and turning, we went out for a ride with his older herd mate (on a route he knew well from walks in hand), and went for a canter up the bridleway!

HEART RATE AND HANDLING

Swedish researchers have identified that an increase in a human's heart rate affects the heart rate of the horse they are leading or riding

The heart rates of horses, ground handlers and riders were monitored to see if humans inadvertently communicate fear and anxiety to horses. Using heart rate as a fear indicator, the researchers asked a sample of people with varying levels of horse experience to walk and ride horses between two marked points in an indoor school. Participants were informed just before the fourth pass, that an umbrella would open as they rode or led the horse past. The umbrella was never opened but heart rates in both horses and humans increased (and average rein length of riders decreased) on the fourth pass.

Increase in heart rate is part of the 'startle' response, and in a social situation prepares the herd to react to potential danger. This study confirms the experience of many riders that when human heart rates increase, it is possible to inadvertently trigger the horse's startle response.[39]

An innovative project trying to solve problems with night-time aggression at taxi ranks associated non-nutritive sucking with lowered heart rate, and hence distributed lollipops to taxi queues and reported lower levels of aggression. Japanese researchers have also found that chewing gum can increase available brain serotonin, and lead to mood elevation.[40]

which can escalate flight behaviour patterns.

Horse training skills and human personality

Good trainers understand how learning theory can be applied in horses, but not only that, they have certain personal characteristics, which they may have taken time to develop. Horses prefer humans who are positive, assertive (not aggressive), calm and have excellent timing. Emphasizing and developing these characteristics helps hoof care professionals manage a physical job with energy efficiency. There are times when emotional management is also essential for human and equine safety.

A good trainer sees each horse as an individual, and identifies their strengths and weaknesses, both physical (biomechanical) and psychological. Emotional control can be learned but is a challenging and long-term process. Despite the fact that many horse owners wish to train their own young horse, it may often be more appropriate, and safer in the long run, to find a good trainer who can confidently guide the horse through its initial riding experiences, help it start to develop good balance and biomechanics, and establish a positive attitude about learning.

Physiologically, we can think of a single stressful facet of the horse's world as lowering the threshold at which other events become frustrating. Therefore, a horse that is in an inappropriate social group may be less responsive during training and, equally, a horse that has encountered inconsistent training may be more likely to be distressed by marginally frustrating aspects of its world when not ridden.[41]

Coping with separation and absence

In domestic situations horses are removed and returned to the herd for human purposes, which can be destabilizing to other herd members, particularly for those left behind. Horses should never routinely be left on their own in this way, as there is a much greater chance they will panic and try to escape to find other horses, hurting themselves in the process. Occasionally the authors meet horses and ponies which are kept individually. Whilst outwardly they can appear calm, they are actually emotionally shutting down. Escape has not been possible, so these horses to varying extents are also displaying a degree of learned helplessness. Horses can be helped to deal with staying on their own by gradual exposure. For example, a horse can learn to associate a pen or stable with positive food rewards and rest. If they need to be regularly left on their own, it is essential that the enclosure is safe and that they are taught to associate it with a positive emotional state.

Early resilience training

The movement of individuals in and out of the herd is an expected part of domestic horse life, and a structured approach is most effective for preparing young horses for this experience. This process needs to include opportunities to leave the herd with a safe and relaxed older horse and confident, calm handlers. If a mare with foal at foot is confident to leave the herd, coming out for a feed and a fuss, progressing to going for short walks in safe areas is an ideal place to start. As the young horse grows, continuing to leave the herd regularly for short periods with a friend can establish a comfortable behaviour pattern. It is very important to monitor the emotional state of the horse as it goes through this process. Make each trip a calm and enjoyable

experience by including tasty things to eat, grooming sessions, hedge browsing and visits to interesting objects. If the horse begins to feel distressed at all, then go back a step. Turning for home earlier than planned is not a failure. Remember that training is often 'two steps forward, one step back', and allow the youngster to develop confidence and bravery at its own pace.

There is some evidence that an optimal amount of early handling can help horses learn how to function in a human context. Hand-reared foals have been found to be less emotional when placed in a novel environment,[42] but horses that have been extensively handled do not perform as fast in maze tests as minimally handled horses, but are faster than completely unhandled horses.[43] In the authors' experience, hand-reared horses are often more difficult to train and handle, can be aggressive, and can have social problems with other horses. They are often most responsive to their main human early care giver. Experience in training older horses who have received minimal or no handling also supports an optimal level of early handling. Older horses can be more established in their behaviours, and less curious about novel situations. In contrast, too much early handling by horse owners can teach a youngster to over-habituate to humans and their communication can lose salience. Young horses do not generally need to be extensively handled daily, but should receive regular planned learning experiences with an emphasis on attitude rather than behavioural repertoire.

Hear these three: TTT; Hear their chime; Things Take Time!

Horse training and development does not fit into a time-pressured human agenda. 'Fundamental differences between horses lie in the time needed to train a specific quality.'[44]

Feral foals growing up in family groups.

Taking time with early training can result in a low-stress animal with an optimistic attitude, who voluntarily participates in training sessions and actively enjoys learning. A horse with a good attitude will co-operate with general handling and care, will enable you to exercise them enough to help them stay healthy, and will very likely be great fun for the whole of their active life. Sharing life with another species is a privilege, and allows humans to gain much-needed perspective on what it means to be human, as those 'chinks of light shine through half-blinded windows into another's world'.[45]

Choosing land for horse keeping

Finding an appropriate place to keep horses can be a considerable challenge. The UK is a small island group and land is at a premium. Most grassland now used for grazing horses has been at some time managed to maximize plant density for growing farm animals or crops. Often this has been achieved by merging fields to improve machinery access, removing hedgerows, woods and competitive plant species, and ploughing and re-seeding with high yield grass strains. When looking for horse property, consider the topography of the land as well as the acreage. Marginal land, woodland, slopes and rough-looking areas may be less accessible to farm machinery, but can provide varied and healthy environments for horses.

Finding a rough and unimproved environment, including woodland, can be a significant gain for horses' health and the owner's pocket. High-density plant growth on ex-agricultural land, together with high

Dinnet Equine Herd Area.

grazing pressure, means that many horses in the UK do not need to move much at all and consume high calorie, low fibre food. Without daily exercise and grass management, many owners struggle with the challenges of cumulative weight gain and metabolic problems.

In mid-summer in the Dinnet Equine Herd Project the horses have been observed to take approximately eight steps per mouthful of grass or 'pause to forage'. The grass is sparse, and in most of the 40 acres of herd area it competes for sunlight with the forest tree canopy above, meaning that it delivers less energy per mouthful than the grass in the adjacent field. During the winter months the horses are given supplementary hay made on a local farm. There is still forage in the herd area, but it is so low in energy that it would be equivalent to plant density in a much more arid zone.

How can livery yards be encouraged to change?

Enrichment standards for wild animals in captivity are becoming globally accepted, so how can horse owners start to persuade yard owners and managers to integrate enrichment standards for domestic equines?

Encouragingly, more yards are introducing enriched horse keeping systems. These are designed either by the owners, or by owners assisted by specialist consultants, and include track systems with gravel, sand, stone and chipping surfaces, slow feeder systems, imaginative shelter designs, cared-for grazing dispersal areas and well nourished soils. Many people have never seen these approaches in situ, nor observed the health of the horses living in them. They may also have concerns about herd safety and need

PRO COMMENT

It is very hard, almost impossible, for some of our clients to change their horse's living accommodation. A lot of the time livery yard owners are very reluctant to change anything, or make what they see as compromises for individual horses. Sometimes horses with conditions such as laminitis are forced to live for many years in the same circumstances that triggered the disease in the first place.

reassurance about this aspect, plus – if the property is a business – there needs to be a market. An association between enrichment systems and 'natural' horsemanship may have excluded people who do not share this training modality. Encouraging yard owners to identify with enrichment is a horse-centric approach.

The internet offers a wealth of images and information about successful, tidy and inclusive enriched systems. Emphasizing the equine health and ethology evidence base, rather than the 'natural' perspective, may increase demand and encourage people to believe that it can be successfully done with any herd.

Track system with extensive new pea gravel surface.

Comfort for humans

Horse owners spend significant amounts of time interacting with their horses. Attractive systems need to acknowledge, accommodate and effectively manage (often fee-paying) human needs. A schooling arena with a good surface within view of the herd can be a massive advantage to any facility, and when ethical training approaches are encouraged, training is a very beneficial lifestyle enhancement for humans and horses.

These modifications come at a cost, which can be offset by a change in property infrastructure. In traditional horse keeping systems, buildings are usually seen as a priority. In enrichment systems, buildings are mainly used for storage of fodder and

Horses make their own pathways within their environment.

Track systems fence horses out of the centre of a field, which can then be used as a dispersal area or grown on for forage.

It is important that livery yards consider human and horse needs.

equipment, with run-in sheds and yard systems being the main approach taken for horse accommodation.

Livery yard owners are not always resistant to change, however. Moderate and achievable trials of a simple electric-fenced summer track system, or rotational paddock grazing and topping rather than strip grazing, are not massive departures from the norm. Measure change using accepted methods such as weight tapes and condition scoring, and take weekly photos. Keep a visible change chart in the feed or tack room. Having a supportive, rational and friendly attitude, backed up by good information and an inclination to compromise, will be more successful than being critical, demanding or basing requests on feelings or emotions. Change must feel good to be held, so share, mark and celebrate positive outcomes, but be realistic and ready to go back to the drawing board.

As more thought is put in to properties designed to allow enrichment modifications to take place, and horse owners choose these properties over traditional livery systems, they will become generally more acceptable. Social media has a large part to play in mediating the development of new belief systems and helping people co-operate by sharing experiences and information. Barefoot trimming services have emerged in response to demand from the horse-owning community. Many trimmers were

PRO COMMENT

When I started my hoof trimming business, I had no idea of the amount of time I would spend trying to change other people's beliefs to help them change their horses. Many, if not all, of the people I work for pursue their happiness to a greater or lesser degree through relationships with their animals. This is generally horses and dogs, but other animals can be involved too. Relationships with animals can often transcend or replace their human family relationships, and my clients believe that living with or alongside animals increases and enhances the physical and emotional rewards of life.

Each working day I meet five to ten horses, a few dogs, probably a cat or two and an assortment of ducks, hens, deer, rabbits, guinea pigs, etc. Then there are those animals who live alongside us: mice, rats, insects and birds of various kinds – particularly jackdaws, robins and small garden birds. I usually meet many fewer people than animals, birds and insects. Some days are much more rewarding than others, though. None of the animals I meet tries to be anything more than themselves, and the people accept them for who they are, and they accept, enjoy and nurture all the other animals around, sharing their space and the resources. I never feel that a horse, unlike a human, is openly critical of its owner, or that the chickens clearing up the hoof trimmings are going through an emotional rollercoaster about the swallow excrement on the ride-on mower. If humans could try to be a little more like that, it would be great!

By our choice to work with horses and other animals, with the intention of helping them cope with us as a species, we are entering into a caring profession. How can we foster these human and animal relationships and genuinely respect the nature of the animals we wish to relate to? It leads to some uncomfortable realizations, particularly when entire societies have intentionally subjugated the lives of animals to our own ends for thousands of years.

Imagine a windy wet night when you decide to further your horsemanship experience by 'going native' with your horse for a night. You are really interested in how your horse copes with the weather, partially because he seems to be fine, and a little bit of you wants to justify to your husband why you are not using that stable block you insisted he build. So you bundle up in lots of coats and, without switching on your head torch (for authenticity), you stumble up to the top of the field where your horse and its herd are standing under a tree. It is very dark, and even with layers and waterproofs on, the cold starts to seep in quite soon. You huddle in the tree roots to keep out of the wind. You may be a little scared, and will quickly find that staying alert in the dark is tiring and you are now quite cold. Your horse and its herd, however, are clearly napping, with one or other horse taking turn to keep watch. They lower their heads in the rain, and occasionally shake their necks, showering water droplets. A branch crashes down from the tree behind you and the horses take off. One minute they are there, the next they have vanished, flat out into the dark. It is so windy that you feel more than hear the rhythm of their hoof beats as they leave. You wait for a little while, initially uncertain what the crash was, and then wonder whether the herd will see you in the dark and run into you if you try to find your way down the hill right now. Snuggling down under the tree you wait for a bit and perhaps doze off, but you are woken up a little later by a soft snuffle as the herd slowly grazes its way back towards the hill top and spot you. You didn't hear them walk back up the hill. Slowly you unfurl your legs, and rub the warmth back into your hands before switching on your torch to light your way home.

Take a minute to think about the differences between the experiences of the horses that night, and your own imagined (or real, if you have done this) experience. How successful were the horses at adapting to the situation? How successful were you? If the falling branch had been a predator, who would have survived?

prior members of that community who have sought out information to help them provide an alternative to traditional farriery. As time goes on, could new-style livery yards set up by owners interested in enrichment advertise their enrichment plans to attract new clients? Could we see the emergence of national enrichment standards to improve domestic horse welfare?

Taking the equine perspective

Changing the cultural concepts of horse keeping towards environmental enrichment provides a range of convincing and rational arguments. Promoting the welfare of domestic horses is an incontrovertible human ethical responsibility. In a truly integrated approach, considering spiritual and/or empathic beliefs that underpin human behaviour towards horses can be an important motivator towards maintaining good welfare standards over the long term. The following exercise may make entering the life of a horse more comprehensible:

Evidence has been presented in this chapter in order to illustrate why and how barefoot horse keeping is expanding the range of domestic practices into integrated whole horse health. In their daily trimming practice the authors consider all of this information, to carefully select and determine how it needs to be emphasized and applied to the horses they support.

The benefits of establishing a herd life for domestic horses are obvious.

AN EQUINE BAREFOOT WELFARE MANIFESTO

Hoof care professionals, barefoot horse keepers and many other associated equestrian professionals are spearheading an ethological and ethical movement, which will, it is hoped, impact on the welfare of every domestic equine, whether barefoot or shod. There is considerable support for a flip in perspective from horse keeping practices based on tradition and assumed knowledge, which have advantages for humans, to equine-centric systems responsive to up-to-date research and practice findings.

In 2005 Tomas Teskey wrote:

As more and more horse owners demonstrate success in working their horses without steel shoes, unheeding farriers and veterinarians alike will become increasingly uneasy at remaining entrenched in the metallic end of the hoof care spectrum. Utilizing the knowledge of natural hoof form and function as the basis for bare-foot hoof care advances our success with horses, whereas holding fast to an untenable paradigm leaves hoof care mired in the past.[46]

The Equine Barefoot Welfare Manifesto is proposed by the authors in conclusion to this chapter, as an ethical and evidence-based ideology for twenty-first-century horse keeping.

The authors:

- support the development of evidence-based ethological standards for domestic equines;
- promote a global awareness of the specific requirements of equine species;
- accept that domestic equines cannot live a 'natural' life, nor have freedom in all areas of behavioural expression;
- propose that horse owners are responsible for protecting their horses from the impact of a domestic life; and
- choose not to support the deployment of metal horse shoes for the purposes of allowing humans to benefit to the detriment of a companion animal species.

Five aims for domestic horse keeping:

- Permanent interaction with a herd within an enriched living space.
- An end to individual stabling and permanent housing in buildings.
- Global acknowledgement of the impact of social isolation and abrupt weaning.
- Global acknowledgement of the multidimensional sensory life of the equine,

and an end to practices that negatively impact upon it.
- Global acknowledgement that riding or otherwise training the horse to perform for human benefit is an artificial extension to species specific behaviour, and places the horse's physical and psychological health at risk.

REFERENCES

[1] Newberry, R.C. (1995). Environmental enrichment: Increasing the biological relevance of captive environments. Elsevier: *Applied Animal Behaviour* Science, 44.

[2] Association of Zoos and Aquariums. (2014, January 14). *Enrichment.* Retrieved 16 March 2015 from www.aza.org: www.aza.org/enrichment.

[3] Department of the Environment, Food and Rural Affairs (DEFRA). (2009). *Code of Practice for the Welfare of Horses, Ponies, Donkeys and their Hybrids.* www.defra.gov.uk.

[4] Kaczensky, P., Ganaatar, O., von Wehrden, H. and Walzer, C. (2008). Resource selection by sympatric wild equids in the Mongolian Gobi. *Journal of Applied Ecology*, 45:1762–9.

[5] Hope for Horses UK. (2014). www.hopeforhorses.co.uk/our-petition. Producer: M. Johnson. Retrieved 20 March 2015 from Hope for Horses: www.hopeforhorses.co.uk.

[6] Jackson, J. (1992). *The Natural Horse: Lessons from the wild for domestic horse care.* Flagstaff, Arizona: Northland Publishing.

[7] Hampson, B. (2011). The Feral Horse Foot – The Australian Brumby Studies. In P. Ramey (ed.), *Care and Rehabilitation of the Equine Foot*, Dexter, Missouri: Hoof Rehabilitation Publishing LLC, 36–57.

[8] Kelekna, P. (2009). *The Horse in Human History.* New York: Cambridge University Press.

[9] Hampson, 'The Feral Horse Foot'.

10. Berman, D. (1991). *The ecology of feral horses in central Australia*. Armidale: University of New England; Hampson, B., de Laat, M., Mills, M. and Pollitt, C. (2010). Distances travelled by feral horses in 'outback' Australia. *Equine Veterinary Journal*.

11. British Horse Society. (2005). *Guidelines for the keeping of horses, stable sizes, acreages and fencing*. British Horse Society Welfare Department.

12. Myers, J. and M. (2012). *Horse properties – a management guide. Australia*: Equiculture.

13. Watts, K. (2011). Safer Grass. Producer: K. Watts. Retrieved 22 July 2015 from Safergrass. org: http://www.safergrass.org.

14. Xenophon. (2006). *The Art of Horsemanship*, ed. M.H. Morgan. Mineola, New York: Dover Publications Inc.

15. Jackson, J. (2006). *Paddock Paradise: A guide to natural horse boarding*. Harrison, Arizona: Star Ridge Publishing.

16. Bowker, R.M. (2011). The concept of a good foot: its evolution and significance in a clinical setting. In P. Ramey (ed.), *Care and Rehabilitation of the Equine Foot*, Dexter, Missouri: Hoof Rehabilitation Publishing LLC, 2–34.

17. DEFRA. (2012). *Secretary of State's Standards of Modern Zoo Practice*. www.defra.gov.uk/ wildlife-pets/zoos/.

18. Turnbull, E. (1995). Not only nuts in May… Mycologist, 9:82–3.

19. Hanggi, E.B. (2005). *The Thinking Horse: Cognition and Perception Reviewed*. Retrieved 15 March 2015 from Equine Research: www. equineresearch.org/supportf-iles/hanggi-thinkinghorse.pdf.

20. Yarnell, K., Hall, C., Royle, C. and Walker, S.L. (2015). Domesticated horses differ in their behavioural and physiological responses to isolated and group housing. *Physiology and Behaviour*, 143.

21. Christensen, J.W. and L.J. (2002). Effects of individual versus group stabling on social behaviour in domestic stallions. *Applied Animal Behaviour Science*, 75.

22. Hampson, 'The Feral Horse Foot'.

23. Association of Zoos and Aquariums, *Enrichment*.

24. Bowker, R.M. (2008). *Contrasting Structures of Good and Bad Feet*. Author's personal lecture notes. Barefootworks Seminar, Aberdeenshire, Scotland.

25. DEFRA, *Secretary of State's Standards of Modern Zoo Practice*.

26. Beck, A. (2007). *Horsonality – An insight into equine behaviour*. www. equine-behaviour.com. New Zealand: Self-published.

27. Hampson, B. and P. (2011). *Improving the foot health of the domestic horse: the relevance of the feral foot model*. Rural Industries Research and Development Corporation.

28. Beck, *Horsonality*.

29. DEFRA, *Secretary of State's Standards of Modern Zoo Practice*.

30. Murray, M.J, Murray, C.M. and Sweeney, H.J. *et al.* (1990). Prevalence of gastric lesions in foals without gastric disease: An endoscopic survey. *Equine Veterinary Journal*, 2(1):6–8.

31. Luthersson, N., Hou Neilseen, K., Harris, P. and Parkin, T.D.H. (2009). Risk factors associated with equine gastric ulceration syndrome (EGUS) in 201 horses in Denmark. *Equine Veterinary Journal*, 41.

32. Atkinson, D. and J. (2014). www. arabianhorse.co.uk/breedingaims. Producer: D.A. Atkinson. Retrieved 19 March 2015 from Seren Arabians: www.arabianhorse.co.uk.

33. *Ibid*.

34. Beck, *Horsonality*.

35. Papaioannou, S., Brigham, S. and Kreiger, P. (2013). Sensory deprivation during early development causes an increased exploratory behaviour in a whisker-dependent decision task. *Brain and Behaviour*, 3.

36. Hanggi, *The Thinking Horse: Cognition and Perception Reviewed*.

37. *Ibid*.

38. *Ibid*.

39. Keeling, L., Jonare, L. and Lanneborn, L. (2009). Investigating horse–human interactions: the effect of a nervous human. *The Veterinary Journal*, 181:70–1.

40. Kamiya, K., Fumoto, M., Kikuchi, Sekiyama, T., Umino, M. and Arita, H. (2009). Gum chewing evokes activation of ventral prefrontal cortex and suppression of nociceptive responses: involvement of brain serotonergic system. *European Journal of Pain*, 13.

41. McGreevy, P. and Mclean, A. (2010). *Equitation Science*. Chichester: Wiley-Blackwell.

42. Houpt, K.A. and Hintz, H.F. (1983). Some effects of maternal deprivation on maintenance behaviour, spatial relationships and responses to early novelty in foals. *Applied Animal Ethology*, 9:221–30.

43. Heird, J.C., Lennon, A.M. and Bell, R.W. (1981). Effects of early experiences on the learning ability of horses. *Journal of Animal Sciences*, 53:1204–9.

44. McGreevy and Mclean, *Equitation Science*.

45. Kiley-Worthington, M. (2005). *Horse Watch: What it is to be Equine*. London: J.A. Allen.

46. Teskey, T. (2005). *The Unfettered Foot: A paradigm change for equine podiatry*. Pearblossom Private School Inc., publishing division.

4 Diet and Nutrition

Equine nutrition is a huge subject and an area that generates much debate, particularly in regard to 'What is a suitable barefoot diet?' That barefoot horses need a special diet is something of a myth, as *all* horses need an appropriate high fibre, low sugar and starch diet with sufficient levels of vitamins and minerals. However, shoes mitigate some of the symptoms that stem from an inappropriate diet, which has given rise to the idea that barefoot horses need something different. Systemic Inflammatory Response Syndrome (SIRS), triggered by excessive sugars in the diet, increases sensitivity in the horse's feet and in the authors' experience is commonly why 'my horse can't cope without shoes'. Once a high fibre, low sugar and starch diet is provided, the footiness disappears.

Whilst full coverage of the topic is beyond the scope of this book, nutrition is a vital component in successfully working horses unshod, and therefore the key issues will be addressed.

The herd at Dinnet Equine Herd Project graze on a variety of plants.

THE OBESITY EPIDEMIC

'You are what you eat' is commonly understood to mean that if you want to be healthy, you need to eat a healthy diet. Conversely, if you are not healthy, then what you are eating could be contributing to that. This most certainly is the case for equines. In recent years obesity has become a significant problem, not only for humans but for horses too. A pilot study carried out by the University of Nottingham School of Veterinary Medicine and Science[1] found that owners were not accurately evaluating their horses' body condition. A total of 160 owners participated, reporting that one in five horses were overweight or obese. When the researchers took a random sample to evaluate and compare with the owners' evaluation, they discovered that the owners had significantly underestimated their horses' body condition. They believed the true prevalence of overweight or obesity was one in two horses.

Similar under-estimation of body condition by owners and vets has also been reported by other researchers,[2] supporting the estimate of 50 per cent of UK horses being overweight or obese.[3]

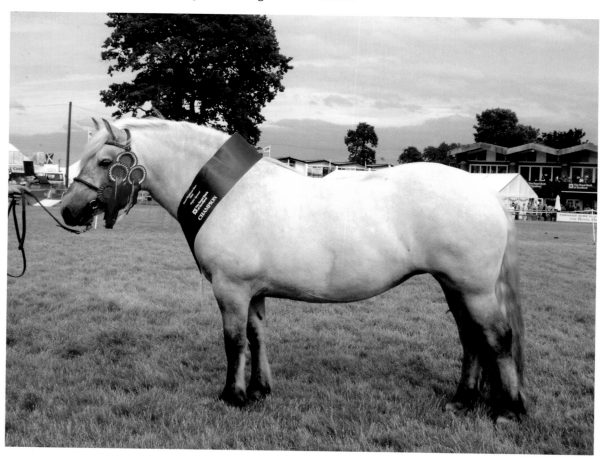

Obesity is a significant problem for modern horses. Image courtesy of Confuslefu at English Wikipedia (Transferred from en.wikipedia to Commons.) [Public domain], via Wikimedia Commons By Confuslefu at English Wikipedia (Transferred from en.wikipedia to Commons.) [Public domain], via Wikimedia Commons.

Research undertaken by the Animal Health Trust[4] over a two-year period looked to identify factors contributing to this worrying trend. Perhaps not surprisingly, one of the factors they identified was breed: in particular, UK native breeds, draught and cob types were significantly more likely to be obese compared to Thoroughbreds. What the horses did 'for a living' also played an important role, with pleasure horses being twice as likely, and non-ridden horses nearly three times as likely, to be obese as competition horses. The results of this study are also reflected in the authors' practice.

Obesity is linked with poor health status and chronic health conditions. Key conditions associated with equine obesity that are of particular importance to the barefoot horse are chronic inflammation (SIRS), laminitis, insulin resistance and equine metabolic syndrome, which will be looked at in more depth in Chapter 7.

AN EVOLUTIONARY PERSPECTIVE

Why is it so difficult to manage horses' weight to keep them in a healthy range? The simple answer is they are being fed too much, but years of working with clients to control their horses' weight reveals that it is somewhat more complex than that. Simply reducing the amount of food they have does not always solve the problem. The authors' experience shows that a horse's overall management, including what they eat, is as important as how much. To get a better understanding of why that is the case, it is helpful to take a look at the evolution of the horse.

Much of the evolution of the modern horse – including its speed, size, and intelligence – can be explained by diet and changes in diet . . . Like all animals, equids have chosen an ecological niche that allows them to avoid competition from other species. Their niche is the poorest-quality vegetation.[5]

The ancestors of modern horses first began to appear around 18 million years ago. The fossil record shows that prior to this time, equids were browsers. They ate the shoots and leaves of trees and other woody plants and were forest dwellers. As the climate changed, becoming cooler and drier, savannah and

Horses grazing.

grassland replaced large areas of forest. Equids adapted to this change in a variety of ways, two of which are of specific relevance to diet:

- Teeth. As equids moved over to eating grass, which is much tougher than browse, the action of their jaws and teeth changed from simple compression to side-to-side grinding. The jaw became bigger and more powerful, and eventually the teeth became ever-growing.
- Fermentation in the caecum. Cellulose provides the majority of available nutrients in grass. Unfortunately, mammals are unable to digest cellulose, therefore species for which grasses became their main food source had to adapt. In the case of the horse, cellulose is broken down in the cecum by bacterial fermentation into volatile fatty acids, which can then easily be taken up.

Although often overlooked, the teeth are an essential part of the digestive system: grinding food into fine particles creates a larger surface area for the digestive enzymes and bacteria to work on, making the feed more easily digestible. Fermentation produces at least 50 per cent of the calorie yield from an average equine diet.[6]

These two physiological adaptations remained throughout the rest of the equids' evolution into our modern-day horses, indicating that further dietary changes did not occur. Their niche remained 'the poorest quality vegetation'. A corollary to thriving on the poorest quality vegetation is the requirement for a significant amount of feeding activity in order to consume a sufficient amount of nutrients. That nature designed the horse to spend a great deal of time eating is also supported by the fact that horses produce stomach acid continually, whether there is food present in the stomach or not, which is particularly important in relation to ulcers. A

study of free-ranging Camargue horse feeding patterns identified that grazing activity was undertaken during every hour of the day, regardless of season.[7] The transit time for food to pass through the stomach varies between two and four hours.[8] With food being taken in on an hourly basis, digesta would constantly be present in the stomach of free-ranging horses.

THE HORSE'S DIGESTIVE SYSTEM – ARE WE WORKING WITH OR AGAINST NATURE?

It is helpful to understand how the horse's digestive system works and to use that knowledge as a guide to optimizing the diet. For the purposes of this book, the digestive system will be divided into four sections: the mouth and oesophagus; the stomach and small intestine; the large intestine; and the rectum.

The mouth and oesophagus

Food enters the digestive system through the mouth and initiates the first stage in the

Equine digestive system.

digestive process – grinding down the food into small particles. A horse with healthy teeth will generally grind hay and grass to less than 1.6mm in length. The majority of hay particles found in the stomach are less than 1mm.[9] Accompanying chewing is the production of saliva. This coats the particles and makes them easier to swallow. Saliva is also high in bicarbonate, which acts to buffer the digestive acid in the stomach. A horse produces 10–12 litres of saliva a day.[10] Once swallowed, the food passes down the oesophagus and enters the stomach.

The stomach and small intestine (foregut)

The stomach of an adult horse is small: by volume, it represents about 10 per cent of the gastrointestinal tract. The stomach is divided into two parts: an upper non-glandular part and the lower acid-producing section, which is protected by a mucosal lining. Along with contributing to the further breakdown of digesta, stomach acid also ionizes insoluble minerals into soluble ones, kills any bacteria that have been ingested, and activates pepsin, which starts the process of protein digestion. Lipase is also present in the stomach, which begins to break down fat. The small intestine is the primary site for digestion of the non-structural carbohydrates, sugar and starch. Transit time through the small intestine, in comparison to the rest of the digestive system, is very fast – only thirty minutes to an hour and a half. Some sugars – glucose, fructose and galactose – do not require digestion and can be simply absorbed across the intestinal cell wall. Although sugar and starch can also be digested via fermentation in the hindgut, this is far from ideal as the by-product of this fermentation is lactate. This gives rise to a drop in ph level and can lead to hindgut acidosis. The rapid transit time provides strong

physiological evidence that the proportion of sugar and starch in the diet should be small.

Large intestine – caecum and colon (hindgut)

Once the digesta enters the hindgut, the remaining fraction of the non-structural carbohydrates that could not be directly absorbed or digested enzymatically (fructans) and cellulose (structural carbohydrates) are fermented for anything up to fifty hours by billions of micro-organisms. Volatile fatty acids are the by-products of this fermentation, which are taken up by the horse. The volume of the hindgut is more than twice that of the stomach and small intestine combined. The large intestine measures up to 8 metres in length and therefore has to double back on itself several times in order for it to fit within the abdominal cavity. Due to these twists and turns, it is important that the particle size of the digesta is small and that there is an ample liquid component to avoid impaction colic.

Rectum

Once fermentation has been completed, the remaining fibrous material passes into the rectum and is expelled from the body. The properties of a horse's dung can reveal a great deal about the overall health and functioning of the digestive system. Dung should be firm, dry and formed into individual 'apples'. It should not have a particularly strong smell. The amount of dung passed each day should be fairly consistent. Rapid changes in the horse's diet often precipitate marked changes in the properties of the dung. Most horse owners have experienced the effects of new spring grass coming in where the dung resembles bright green cow pats. Just because this is a common experience does not mean that it is healthy. Loose and smelly dung is not normal for a horse and indicates a digestive system which is being significantly challenged. As with humans, if diarrhoea persists for more than a few days, seek medical advice.

MODERN HORSE KEEPING PRACTICES

Having outlined a general over-view of what and how horses have evolved to eat, let's contrast that with what the average domesticated horse experiences. Modern horse keeping practices typically prioritize convenience and time-saving measures, which are often at odds with the physiological evolutionary adaptations of the horse.

The vast majority of horse owners in the UK keep their horses at a livery yard. Individual liveries vary in the amount of turnout the horses are able to have but it is common practice for horses to be kept in for half of the day (often much more in the winter). Where horses are stabled for half of the day during the summer, the reason given is often to 'get them off the grass'.

Livery yards are generally either ex-farmland or part of an existing farm. Farmland has gone through significant changes in relatively recent years. During the Second World War the need to produce more food here in the UK saw many old meadows being put to the plough to grow food crops. Importing food, as had previously been the case, became increasingly problematic due to the targeting of the merchant navy by German U-boats. More recently, much time and effort has been

Feeding time.

spent by agronomists to develop grasses which produce high levels of non-structural carbohydrates to increase milk or meat yields in farm animals. Studies conducted by the Institute of Grassland and Environmental Research[11] looking at rye-grass established that 'the high WSC trait promoted increased production performance in terms of milk volume, milk protein yield and beef and sheep liveweight gain'. Dr Carol Micheal's article 'How safe is your grass for horses to graze?' in the Farmers Guardian in March 2015 reported that:

> The most popular grass sown in the UK at the moment is perennial rye (86 per cent) and since 2005 perennial rye-grass has been bred to have a high (80 per cent) fructan content, whatever the weather or environmental conditions.

Rye grass.

The desire to produce these rye-grass strains stems from the idea that the energy released by the high level of water soluble carbohydrates provides a better balance of nutrients for the microbes within the rumen to utilize. Great for cattle and sheep – but not horses. In recent years there has been a great deal of discussion about fructans in relation to laminitis (some types of fructan have been used experimentally to induce

laminitis) and the causal role they might play. Fructans are also often confused with sugar as fructans are carbohydrates, and simple sugars (also carbohydrates) do have a significant role in triggering bouts of endocrinopathic laminitis. The possible involvement of fructans in laminitis aetiology will be discussed subsequently; the focus here is on its potential nutritional (calorie) contribution.

> Non-structural carbohydrates (NSC) consist of three elements: sugars, fructans and starch. Forage analysis can be undertaken to identify how much and what types of NSC are present in forage. The results are broken down into:
>
> - WSC – water-soluble carbohydrates, which measures sugars and fructans;
> - ESC – ethanol-soluble carbohydrates, which measures sugars; and
> - starch – which is self-explanatory.
>
> In a forage analysis report, these values are expressed as a percentage.

Whether the pastures horses live on are converted arable land re-sown to grass or ex-dairy, beef or sheep land, they are highly unlikely to be the old-fashioned meadows of mixed native grass species and herbs which generally have far lower NSC levels. The dominance of nutrient-dense ryegrass in pasture – and as a consequence in hay and haylage – must surely be playing a part in the obesity and other associated health problems our horses are facing.

Stabling horses and providing meals in the form of bucket feed is also a far cry from the eating patterns horses have evolved to follow. Compared to obtaining a given weight of food from grazing, bucket feeds provide a vast quantity of food in a very

Rye grass hay field.

Horses make between 800 and 1200 chewing movements per 1kg of concentrates, whereas 1kg of long hay requires between 3000 and 3500 movements . . . Horses given a hay diet chewed 40,000 times/day compared with 10,000 times/day for those fed on pellets.[12]

Forage based bucket feed.

short space of time. Just think how long it takes a horse to eat a scoop of nuts weighing around 1.5kg and how long it would take it to crop the same weight of grass from its paddock. On average, a healthy weight horse needs to consume 2 per cent of its bodyweight in food (dry matter) per day, so for a 500kg horse that is about 10kg in total. Thus that scoop of nuts represents about 15 per cent of its daily requirement. Allowing a very conservative total grazing time per day to be twelve hours for a free-ranging horse, on average it would take that horse a little over an hour and forty-five minutes to consume 15 per cent of its daily intake. Chewing forage takes considerably longer than concentrates.

So why is this important? Under natural conditions, food trickles through the digestive tract in small amounts continually throughout twenty-four hours of the day. As a result, any nutrients that are able to be digested in the foregut, primarily sugars and starch, will also be released into the bloodstream as a trickle in small amounts. In a bucket feed, by comparison, a much larger amount of food arrives quickly. Even if the total quantity of sugar and starch in the diet is the same, the way in which the body receives it is not.

Confined to its stable, the horse does not need to expend energy in obtaining its food, nor is it likely to need to expend much energy after it has eaten it – it is common practice not to feed before exercise. The horse now has far more food energy available than it needs at that point in time. Depending upon the horse, this excess energy can translate into fizzy excitability or be stored as fat.

HOW SHOULD WE BE FEEDING OUR HORSES?

Clearly, optimal feeding will mimic what and how horses have evolved to eat. The question is, can that be replicated in typical domestic situations?

Native grasses require migratory grazing patterns. They cannot survive over-grazing, which is inevitable with horses confined to paddocks. Trying to reinstate native grasses into a sward is next to impossible, as they cannot compete with modern improved varieties which include Timothy. Seasonal changes also impact on the growing period for native grasses, whereas commercial rye-grass strains have been selected to have an extended growing period. Even if the field is ploughed up and re-seeded, over time modern varieties will begin to infiltrate the sward as seeds are blown in from neighbouring land.

Pasture management

Having been engaged in numerous barefoot social media fora for a number of years, it is apparent that there is a widespread understanding that most pasture is 'too rich'. In this context 'too rich' equates to too much NSC.

In an attempt to combat this richness, ceasing to use fertilizer is frequently recommended. The assumption behind this is that fertilization will make the situation even worse, with richer grass – but is this the case? Are sparse, weedy paddocks a better option?

Research looking at the effect of moderate fertilization on NSC levels showed that nitrogen application actually lowered the NSC percentage in the grass, although overall yield per acre was higher as grass density increased threefold.[13]

	NSC % dry matter	NSC lb per acre
35lb Nitrogen/acre	17.88	631
No Nitrogen	23.10	285

It is well known that pasture overrun with clover is lacking in nitrogen. This is a common sight in many horse pastures in the UK. The problem that this presents for the equine diet is that clover can contain up to 20 per cent NSC, mostly in the form of starch.

Another common outcome of not fertilizing pasture is the invasion of weeds, which can often be higher in NSC than grass, as Katy Watts explained at the

Clover is a common sight in horse pastures.

Barefootworks Pasture Management Seminar in 2015: 'Plantain, dandelions, thistles and the daisy family are all high in inulin.'[14]

Neglecting pasture does nothing to address the issue of it being 'too rich' but rather simply makes growth less dense and vigorous. The amount of NSC per bite is higher, but there are fewer bites to be had. In these circumstances, the number of bites to be had can be significantly influenced by the weather. Periods of drought further stress the grass and slow growth rate. Once the drought breaks, rapid growth resumes and NSC levels can rocket.

Overgrazing, either due to stocking density or to restricting the area of pasture available, replicates the symptoms of pasture neglect. In addition, it causes soil compaction and damages the grass due to excessive trampling from hooves.

PRO COMMENT

Many of my clients keep their horses at grass 24/7 during the spring and summer. In an attempt to maintain their horse's weight in a healthy range, this often means that they are on restricted grazing. The pasture is usually very short and often weedy. In north-east Scotland the summers are often quite dry and it is not unusual to have two or three weeks in a row with little or no rain. Problems with foot sensitivity are often encountered when the dry spell breaks and the very short, stressed and weedy pasture has a flush of growth.

Along with having higher levels of NSC accumulation in comparison to fertilized pasture, over time unfertilized pasture becomes progressively less healthy.

There are a number of factors that interact to regulate NSC levels. They can be expressed as a rough equation: genetic potential of grass type(s) × temperature × water level in the soil × soil nutrient status × light intensity × time of day × day length × zone of grass stem = NSC level.

Light and shade

NSC levels are dynamic and can change markedly from day to day as well as throughout the day. Of all these factors, at least in the UK context, light intensity and day length may be the most influential. Shade can significantly reduce the amount of NSC accumulated. Studies have found that four hours shading brought about a 19 per cent reduction in NSC levels.[15] Grazing horses amongst trees where grasses have to compete for light with the tree canopy can be a very effective way to help limit potential NSC intakes.

Undertaking soil sampling and providing appropriate fertilization to produce a dense, weed-free, vigorous sward seems counterintuitive, but in addition to the fewer NSC per bite as outlined above, dense sward maintained between 10 and 15cm in height casts considerable shade over itself, helping to minimize NSC accumulation.

Turning out during the hours of darkness can be an effective strategy to minimize levels of NSC accessible in the pasture.

It is important to stress that the total nutrient (calorie) value consumed needs to be managed. Although fertilized and longer grass may have an overall lower NSC level, there will be more of it so it may not be appropriate to allow unrestricted access to pasture 24/7.

Grazing under trees is an effective way of managing sugar intake.

Rye grass seed heads are highly calorific.

Ad lib feeding vs ad lib foraging

As an understanding of the digestive health needs of equines becomes more widely acknowledged and accepted in conventional horse keeping, a range of ideas and products have been put forward to stimulate 'slow feeding' – the consumption of forage feeds high in fibre and low in calories over an extended time period designed to replicate natural feeding patterns.

As previously described, the horse has evolved to be a trickle feeder, foraging throughout the day and night. Foraging is more than simply the rate of consumption: it

Horses eating bilberry plants.

status. Observation of horses in systems with feeders on tracks suggests that this kind of pressurized movement may expose them to unnecessary stress, and it becomes questionable as to whether using feeders in track systems sufficiently replicates equine feeding behaviour. However, managing consumption rates and forage wastage is difficult to achieve without using feeders, particularly in wetter environments where mud is a problem.

Evening hay delivery at Dinnet Equine Herd Project.

involves slow step-by-step movement through the environment, sorting through plants for edible materials.

Paddock Paradise and other track systems try to replicate this by the inclusion of a number of feeder units or stations in their design. The theory behind this is that horses are motivated to move around the enclosure from feeder to feeder, thus expending calories by making some movement between bouts of eating. Some feeders are even automated so that they allow access to an amount of food at timed intervals.

In grass-free track systems horses can only eat from the feeders, so they either share, move each other off the feeders, or wait for access, depending on their herd

Dispersal areas are an essential part of a track system for equines, but there may be times when you need to set up a grass-free system for horse health reasons, or if your property needs time to establish appropriate plant species on the land. In this case you need to provide several more feeders than horses, add other enrichments that encourage dispersed foraging, and carefully observe the herd for signs of bullying behaviour or stress. If stress is a problem even with sufficient numbers of feeding stations, adjusting the composition of the herd to exclude the bullies may be the only solution.

What kind of eater is your horse?

Research into human eating behaviour and obesity has found that humans can be categorized by their typical eating behaviour. Each category has several variables, including rate of consumption, attention to food items in the environment, emotional association with eating and hormonal balance. Observing the eating behaviour of horses on ad lib feeding systems, it becomes clear that horses also occupy distinct categories of eating behaviour. Research indicates that there is a significant link between hormones and consumption rates. Some horses will slowly eat small amounts of feed, stop when they feel full, and do not appear to gorge on ad lib feed. Other horses will stand all day at a feeder and consume food for much longer periods. Getting access to feeders appears to be much more important to these individuals, and they will aggressively move other horses away from them.

Scattering is a useful approach to take with food enrichment for horses when you want the whole herd to experience the food. Food can also be used in behavioural conditioning by feeding it as rewards – such foods can be fresh, frozen, dried and combined, and all produce different experiences when eaten. Horses like to dig, so burying a salt lick in the ground is another way of encouraging them to display species-appropriate behaviour.

Horses sharing hay.

HERD COMMENT

During the winter the herd enclosure has insufficient plant growth to sustain the herd, therefore we supplement the horses with hay from a local farm. In previous years the nutritional quality of the hay has been very high in comparison to the naturally occurring forage in the herd enclosure, resulting in digestive problems. Our response has been to provide the herd with ad lib straw and twice daily hay feeds distributed around the herd enclosure in the mid-winter months. This winter the calorific content of the hay was lower, so we introduced three feeding stations where we deposited round bales of hay in slow feeder nets inside ring feeders. Whilst this made hay feeding less time-consuming for the humans, it introduced increased stress levels for the herd due to resource guarding and proximity. Three feeding stations between nine horses somewhat mitigated the situation, but the majority of the herd gained a considerable amount of weight and started to show metabolic changes, including increased levels of thrush infection in their feet. It was clear when we returned to twice-daily hay distribution in March that the horses spent more time eating slowly at a comfortable distance from each other, and were foraging between hay feeds.

Scattering hay is a good way to reduce pressure.

Free choice minerals and herbs

It is worth considering the current practice of leaving a range of herbs or free choice minerals for the horses to eat when they choose. Currently there is little evidence to suggest that horses choose what to eat based on anything but taste and flavour. This is not to say that the horses will not benefit from this practice, as they have been provided with some new and possibly tasty experiences, but it is best not to rely on free choice to ensure they are getting sufficient minerals in their diet. Anecdotally, there are many reports of horses choosing foods that may be helpful in disease processes. For instance, cinnamon (potential metabolic support), linseed (omega fats), turmeric (inflammatory processes) and meadowsweet (digestion) are all popular choices. However, biscuits, polos and coffee could also be added to this list. In offering lots of different flavour experiences, it may be the novelty of the flavour that provokes the choice. In summary, horses will appreciate being offered a wide range of gustatory experiences but such experiences should be used for sensory enrichment rather than forage balancing.

A forage based combined feed.

CHOOSING A VITAMIN AND MINERAL SUPPLEMENT

All of a horse's bodily functions and health are dependent on appropriate levels of vitamins and minerals, which the horse has evolved to source from a wide range of plants or can synthesize itself from food sources. The main questions for the horse owner are what is the horse's existing diet delivering, and does it meet its health and performance needs?

Supplementing feed with vitamins, minerals and nutraceuticals.

An excellent online training programme with a specific barefoot focus is available for equine nutrition self-study at http://www.drkellon.com/coursedescriptions/nrcplus.html.

Feeding a horse properly isn't like building a house or putting together a puzzle. It's more like baking a cake. If you leave the baking powder out of a cake recipe, the results are catastrophic and you end up with a cracker instead of a cake. This is the equivalent of a full-blown nutritional deficiency. However, adding too much also has negative effects. To get the perfect cake, all ingredients need to be balanced. This dynamic approach, focusing just as much on balance as on intake of individual nutrients, is what I have seen to be the most effective – and also efficient – way to build a sound diet.[16]

It is impossible to tell the calorific or mineral value of hay without forage analysis.

Vitamins

A healthy horse on good pasture doesn't need supplemental vitamins, except for E if the horse is working very hard. Vitamins B12, D and K probably never require supplementation regardless of the diet. Vitamin A should be given as a supplement with caution, and only to horses being fed hay that is a year old or older... While it's likely that working horses would benefit from some supplementation of C and B vitamins when they are on hay and grain-based diets, precisely how much is a matter of guesswork... Requirements for vitamin C and the B vitamins may be increased in a variety of situations, including:

- injury or surgery
- antibiotic use
- heavy exercise
- allergies
- bowel problems, especially involving the small intestine
- liver disease
- lung disease.[17]

Minerals

The most accurate approach where possible is to arrange a forage analysis for grass and/

Mineral deficiencies are highly visible in hoof wall growth.

Mineral ratio	Comments
Calcium:phosphorus Between 2:1 and 1.2:1	An inverted ratio risks nutritional bone disease. Ratios as high as 6:1 can be tolerated for short periods.
Calcium:magnesium Estimates range from 3:1 to 2:1	Horses vary in their sensitivity to magnesium, with some horses showing a positive response in sensitivity and muscle tension, and others a marked sedation response.
Copper:iron Ratio 1:4 NRC recommended minimum intake	High levels of iron in UK forage make iron supplementation rarely necessary, but balancing copper is required in many areas.
Copper:zinc:manganese Ratios 1:3:3 to 1:5:5	An excess of any trace mineral can interfere with absorption channels of other minerals.

or the horse's main forage source. A forage analysis will identify the constituent vitamins and minerals in the horse's diet, and a custom-made vitamin and mineral balancer and diet plan can be produced to make up for any deficiencies. Free diet analysis offers from feed companies will be unlikely to advise anything except their branded products, and while these may provide a daily intake level, they are unlikely to focus on the ratio of minerals, which is where the balancing part comes in. Doing

the maths for mineral balancing is possible, but it can be complicated. There are forage analysis companies who will work up a diet plan for a reasonable fee.

If a forage analysis is not possible (due to hay or haylage stores being purchased from varying sources), forage balancers are now available that base their contents on average levels of vitamins and minerals found through forage analyses. There are many products to choose from in the feed store, and a lot of marketing hype. When choosing an off-the-shelf product, read the label carefully and avoid any type of sugar or glucose, and fillers.

EMERGENCY DIET

At times when the onset of a laminitic episode or other illness is suspected, an emergency nutritional plan is useful.[18]
Recommendations:

- Base diet: grass hay, with starch and sugar levels less than 10 per cent. Soaked in copious clean water for an hour if sugar intake is a serious concern. Start by feeding at 1.5 per cent of the horse's current bodyweight, checking weekly for changes.

Sea salt.

- Soaked un-molassed beet pulp as a carrier for supplements. Beet pulp should always be thoroughly rinsed before soaking to remove remaining molasses and dirt, until the rinse water runs clean.
- 50–150g ground, stabilized linseed will provide essential fatty acids. Its omega 3 to omega 6 ratio most closely resembles grass seed, and it is high in anti-inflammatory omega 3 fatty acids.
- 2000IU of vitamin E. Some feed suppliers are selling this in powdered form with an oil carrier.
- Forage-balanced mineral supplement. Well researched forage balancers are available specifically with the barefoot horse in mind. Avoid supplements containing unknown fillers, iron or additional sugar or glucose in any form.

Horses sharing a salt lick.

- Avoid any bagged feed that contains molasses, glucose, any syrup, grains or grain flours.

TREATS AND REWARDS

Many horse owners choose to hand feed their horses, either as treats or as food reinforcement during behavioural training. Commercial bagged treats are often high in sugar, and when used for high frequency food reinforcement the horse can consume enough sugar to give them a temporary sugar 'rush'. This amount of additional sugar could be dangerous for horses with EMS, insulin resistance or laminitis. Feed stores often sell sugar-free alternatives, or regular fruits, vegetables and sunflower seeds can be used instead.

Likewise, licks (unless pure salt) are usually made from molasses or other forms of sugar that are dangerously unhealthy for horses. The authors have experienced having empty treat balls thrown at them by frustrated horses, and horses who have become so 'sugar high' from molasses licks that they aggressively defend them from other horses and humans, and even roll on them.

KEY POINTS

- An estimated 50 per cent of horses are either overweight or obese.
- Owners tend to significantly under-estimate body condition.
- Domestic pastures are best considered as 'rocket fuel'.
- The horse's breed and level of work significantly influence its risk of obesity.
- Horses have evolved to eat little and often throughout the day and night.
- Many forages and pastures are deficient in minerals.

- Vitamin and mineral balancing is the gold standard.

REFERENCES

1. Stephenson, H.M., Green, M.J., Freeman, S.L. (2011). Prevalence of obesity in a population of horses. *UK Veterinary Record*, 168(5):13.
2. Johnson, P.J., Wiedmeyer, C.E., Messer, N.T., Ganjam, V.K. (2009). Medical implications of obesity in horses – Lessons for human obesity. *J. Diabetes Sci. Technol.*, 3(1):163–74.
3. Argo, C.McG. (2010). *Management of Equine Obesity*. World Horse Welfare, www.worldhorsewelfare.org/Right-Weight (accessed 28.1.15).
4. Robin, C.A., Ireland, J.L., Wylie, C.E., Collins, S.N., Verheyen, K.L.P., Newton, J.R. (2014). Prevalence of and risk factors for equine obesity in Great Britain based on owner-reported body condition scores. *Equine Veterinary Journal*. doi: 10.1111/evj.12275.
5. Budiansky, S. (1998). *The nature of horses: Their evolution, intelligence and behaviour*. London: Phoenix, 18–27.
6. Kellon, E.M. (2008). *NCR Plus*. Retrieved 15 July 2015 from drkellon.com: http://www.drkellon.com/coursedescriptions/nrcplus/html.
7. Mayes, E., Duncan, P. (1986). Temporal Patterns of Feeding Behaviour in Free-ranging Horses. *Behaviour*, 96(1/2):105–29.
8. Kellon, *NRC Plus*.
9. Frape, D. (2010). *Equine Nutrition and Feeding*. Chichester: Wiley-Blackwell.
10. Kellon, *NRC Plus*.
11. Institute of Grassland and Environmental Research. (2005). *High-sugar ryegrasses for improved production efficiency of ruminant livestock and reduced environmental N-pollution*. Final Report, IGER.
12. Frape, *Equine Nutrition and Feeding*.
13. Watts, K.A. (2009). *Advances in Equine Nutrition*, vol. IV. Kentucky: Kentucky Equine Research, 37–8.
14. Watts, K.A. (2015). *Pasture Management*. Author's personal lecture notes. Barefootworks Seminar, Aberdeenshire, Scotland.
15. *Ibid*.
16. Kellon, E.M. (2008). *Horse Journal Guide to Equine Supplements and Nutraceuticals*. Guilford, Connecticut: Lyons Press.
17. *Ibid*.
18. Kellon, *NRC Plus*.

5 Equine Biomechanics and Functional Anatomy

As Chris Pollitt so eloquently says, 'the forces of evolution have in the equine foot produced a miracle of bioengineering'.[1] The locomotor system of equids is unique, as they are the only animal to walk on a single digit. The significance of this is such that it bears repeating: *equids are the only animal to walk on a single digi*t.

Whilst this confers significant evolutionary advantages to them in terms of speed, in domestic circumstances it also makes them remarkably fragile for such large animals. Their tolerance for operating outside of optimal is often low and all too often things go wrong. Whilst occasionally this may be due to an acute injury, more commonly the problem develops

Registered Irish draft gelding Rossi as a six-year-old.

slowly over time and is in fact a repetitive strain injury.

The terms *sound* and *lame* are often viewed as the opposites of each other – thus, if a horse is not lame, then it is sound. *The Merck Veterinary Manual* defines lameness as follows:

> Lameness is… an abnormal stance or gait caused by either a structural or a functional disorder of the locomotor system. The horse is either unwilling or unable to stand or move normally… The most consistent and easily recognized clinical signs of lameness are the head nod associated with forelimb lameness and the sacral rise, also called a pelvic rise or hip hike, associated with hindlimb lameness.[2]

However, lack of head nod or sacral rise does not necessarily translate to sound movement. Frequently the more subtle signs of abnormal stance and gait are overlooked – indeed, many of them are so commonplace that they are not viewed as anything out of the ordinary, nor as cause for concern, for example a horse which:

- is unable to square up;
- excessively lands on the toe or heels of the foot;
- is prone to trip and stumble;
- plaits in front or brushes behind; and
- is not able to walk backwards in a straight line.

Understanding functional anatomy and how

The integrated horse and rider – Johanna Pelling and her PRE Stallion Jensen. Image courtesy of Richard and Johanna Pelling.

it relates to movement, sound or otherwise, is essential when considering any horse, whether shod or barefoot. Given that for the most part we intend to ride our barefoot horses, it is also important within this context to consider the horse/tack/rider/training combination as a whole, and how those component parts interact and influence one another.

In this chapter we will discuss why and how optimizing equine biomechanics is the key to long-term soundness and performance. At the time of writing, 'biomechanics' is the current hot topic in equine sports physiology. Reading the equestrian press, or attending conferences, you will see many references to biomechanics. But what does biomechanics mean, and how does it relate to hoof function?

A medial flare on a standardbred mare.

BIOMECHANICS IS:

- the study of *the action of external and internal forces* on the living body, especially on the skeletal system;
- the study of *the mechanical nature of biological processes*, such as heart action and muscle movement; and
- The study of *mechanical laws and their application* to living organisms.

Flares need to be appropriately managed.

A biomechanical approach occurs when we take proven laws of physics, as established in the engineering sciences, and apply them to the structures and processes existing and operating within living organisms. Let's take an example: hoof wall flares. Flares are deviations in the relationship between the angle of wall growth and the angle of the profile of the adjacent pedal bone, and are a common characteristic of the equine hoof wall which trimmers and farriers observe in their practice every day. What occurs biomechanically when they are formed?

Shod flare in an overweight warmblood gelding.

When the horse steps on and loads the foot, the peripheral hoof wall meets the ground. The ground exerts a *reaction force* on the hoof wall via *leverage*, which will then imperceptibly and temporarily *distort in shape* until the leverage is removed as the hoof follows through its flight pattern and leaves the ground again. So long as the ground reaction force does not exceed the internal *resistance* of the laminar connection, the pressure will not cause the hoof wall angle to deviate for long enough to cause any internal damage. If the wall is long or at a shallow angle, however, it will lever against the laminar connection like a human nail being bent backwards. This causes the leverage from the ground reaction force to *distort* the adjacent wall more powerfully, and as the distortion will take longer to retract, the chances of localized *material destruction* increase. Gradually the wall will be levered away from the adjacent pedal bone, maintained by the excessive wall length, and will cause a flare. Eventually, depending on what substrate the horse experiences on a daily basis and the quality of the connection interface provided by the laminae, *material degradation* will occur from the pressure exerted on the flared wall. This could take the form of *abrasion*, horizontal *splitting* inside the wall, vertical *cracking* (either partial or full thickness), and in extreme circumstances parts of the hoof wall may break off completely. If it does not break off, the flared hoof wall will then start to become a lever itself. If the flare persists, at the region of angle change between the flared hoof wall and the more firmly attached hoof wall higher up, *folding pressure* will damage the soft tissues underneath which will become anaemic and potentially necrotic, and the laminae below the fold will become excessively thin and stretched. Over time the pedal bone will also respond to the excessive leverage by losing density and becoming thin and crumbly around the margin adjacent to the flare (osteoporotic).

This example applies several different scientific laws to help understand and model a biological process, including *compression, ground reaction forces, leverage and material degradation and destruction*. Other scientific principles used to help understand the internal functioning of the hoof include:

- fluid hydraulics – giving a better understanding of the internal processes occurring during locomotion, and a more comprehensive model for laminitis;
- strain theory – understanding how strain theory applies to the musculo-skeletal system helps us develop and support the system to become strong enough to withstand injury. Understanding the strain within a system allows an assessment to be made of what that system's tolerance to strain is, i.e. when the DDFT is subjected to too much leverage by jumping a horse with excessively long toes, the tendon's stretch tolerance exceeds its elastic resistance;
- gait analysis – the systematic study of movement and how it deviates from what is perceived as normal. In veterinary diagnostics computer-based gait analysis systems are now being used more frequently to detect subtle gait abnormalities that may be producing mild clinical signs or affecting multiple limbs. The University of Glasgow is the first in the UK to introduce the Lameness Locator® system, which uses a non-invasive sensor system that transmits data wirelessly to a PC. Such systems are more accurate than the human eye and potentially detect gait changes before they become catastrophic;
- plasticity – a very relevant model for the equine foot, plasticity refers to the adaptability of the hoof to respond to changes in its immediate environment. Neuroplasticity is another useful term which describes how neural networks develop

and change as the brain reorganizes itself throughout the lifetime of the organism;

- elasticity – particularly useful when talking about the function of tendons and ligaments, elasticity refers to the ability of an object or material to rebound and resume its normal shape after being stretched or compressed; stretchiness;
- visco-elasticity – visco-elastic materials exhibit viscous and elastic characteristics when exposed to deformation, which means they will return to their original length when the load is removed. Ligaments are visco-elastic, and the extent of any potential damage to them depends both on the speed of the change in length as well as on the force they receive;
- mechanism analysis – in the biological sciences, a mechanism is a system of causally interacting parts and processes that produce one or more effects. When explaining a complex system such as a body, it is useful to be able to explain what part of the system causes what function and how; and
- contact mechanics – the science of contact mechanics examines how solid objects deform on contact. In equines, this is especially relevant to the function of the hoof capsule and how it responds to pressure, and the friction, wear and lubrication of joints.

A key point to remember is that *all* of these principles apply *to every single horse (and human)* organism. In the previous example regarding flaring, there is no evidence to suggest that this situation is anything but the body responding to imbalances in its biomechanics. Explanations that the horse might 'need' such a serious hoof wall deviation to be sound are often based on misunderstandings stemming from other contexts. For instance, flying buttress tree roots and outrigger canoes are often used as analogies to explain why serious deviations should be disregarded. But a horse with this level of deviation is unlikely to be properly sound even if they move 'OK', and will very likely be compromised and in chronic pain from more than one origin.

Understanding how the laws of biomechanics apply can help us differentiate between what is normal and what is common, can allow us to develop training and management approaches to optimize performance, and can enable us to prevent and rehabilitate horses from injury.

Continuing with the engineering theme, the horse's basic conformation has a considerable impact on its biomechanical performance. Full-time hoof care professionals see hundreds of horses every year and, with insight from biomechanical research, can reflectively observe and evaluate their function, allowing them to predict and manage their hoof care with more accuracy. The rest of this chapter will consider some of the wider themes where it is important that the rider and horse owner understand biomechanics, including conformation, riding, saddling and training approaches.

FUNCTIONAL ANATOMY

Anatomy is fascinating and is the subject of many books. As this book is about barefoot hoof care, this section will focus on the equine foot and how locomotion happens. A list of further reading is provided at the end of this section, and the authors strongly urge all horse owners and care providers to delve deeply into the subject. Some hoof care practices offer owners and other professionals the opportunity to attend dissection clinics. These can give a fascinating insight into the function of the horse's limbs and feet, and can significantly increase understanding beyond the written page.

ANATOMICAL DIRECTIONAL TERMS – WHERE IS EVERYTHING?

Proximal	closer to the body or head
Distal	further away from the body or head
Medial	the inside (towards the midline)
Lateral	the outside (away from the midline)
Dorsal	the front surface of the lower leg and hoof
Palmar	the back surface of the lower foreleg and hoof
Plantar	the back surface of the lower hindleg and hoof
Anterior	towards the front
Posterior	towards the back/rear
Ventral	the front side of the body, also known as anterior
Caudal	towards the rear
Cranial	above or near the head
Solar/volar	the surface of the sole of the foot

Anatomical directions.

THE HOOF

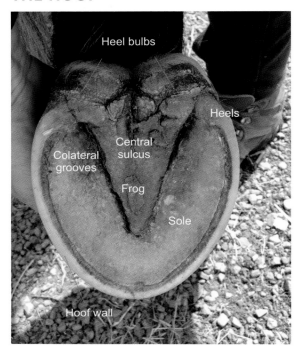

The hoof – solar view.

The hoof – lateral view.

Left front foot – Arabian gelding. Uncontracted and functional foot.

Right front foot from the same Arabian gelding. This foot is more contracted due to the presence of an abscess and central sulcus infection present.

Structure	Description	Function
Hoof wall	Hard horny outer casing of the dorsal hoof. It is comprised of tubules and intertubular horn.	Protects the internal hoof structures, most directly the pedal bone and co-lateral cartilages. Provides structural support for the hoof and contributes to the weight-bearing surface area (both in terms of suspension of the coffin bone via the laminae and at ground level).
Sole	Hard horny outer casing for part of the underside of the hoof.	Protects the internal hoof structures, most directly the pedal bone and lateral cartilages. Contributes to the weight bearing surface area of the hoof.
Frog	Flexible, folded triangular structure of rubber-like consistency located on the underside of the hoof. The central sulcus is a groove located towards rear of the frog.	The flexible nature of the frog allows the heels to widen upon loading and to some degree allows independent movement of each heel and quarter. It plays a significant role in shock absorption and traction, and contributes to the weight-bearing surface area of the hoof. It provides protection for the underlying coria and digital cushion and together they provide support for the coffin joint. It is also a neurosensory organ containing pacian and ruffini corpuscles which are involved in proprioception.
White line	Located between the periphery of the sole and the hoof wall. The white line is produced by the terminal papillae of the dermal laminae.	Bonds the hoof wall and sole and mediates between the different material properties of the semi-rigid hoof wall and the more flexible sole. Contributes to the weight-bearing surface of the hoof.
Bars	Continuation of the hoof wall and white line from the heels to approximately half way along the length of the frog where they blend with the sole. Contains laminated and unlaminated portions.	Provides structural support for the caudal foot. Contributes to traction and dissipates ground reaction force to the lateral cartilages and digital cushion.
Coronary band and periople	Positioned at the border between the top edge of the hoof wall and the skin of the pastern.	Provides a flexible interface between the hard hoof wall and the skin of the pastern. It over-lies and protects the coronary corium from where the hoof wall is produced. An injury to the coronary band often results in a permanent defect in the hoof wall immediately below it. The periople can be compared to cuticles on fingernails. It is only a few cells thick and typically extends 1–2cm down the hoof wall.

These external structures of the hoof form a dynamic, integrated system that is continually responsive to both the external environment and the horse's own internal environment. The nature of this interaction can often be overlooked, especially in relation to the effect it can have on the whole horse.

Let's take the common example of thrush left untreated in the central sulcus of one front foot. Due to the discomfort, the horse avoids fully loading the back of the foot. This in turn causes the heels to grow higher, placing more pressure on the toe and changing the angle of the hoof pastern axis.

As the heels get higher, they reduce the loading the frog experiences and it begins to atrophy due to under-use, becoming less able to contribute to the shock absorption mechanism and weight-bearing area of the foot. The stride length shortens and the change in stance alters the angle of the scapula. Now the horse has asymmetrical movement (or more likely a more exaggerated asymmetrical movement) that will impact upon the entire spinal column

Structure	Description	Function
Coronary corium	Located underneath the coronary band and within the coronary gasket groove at the top of the hoof wall, it is a soft, cushion-like band.	Produces and nourishes the hoof wall. Biomechanically it operates a little like a gasket or seal in terms of balancing out pressure differentials within the top of of the hoof.
Epidermal laminae (although not strictly an internal structure, their true nature is only visible upon dissection, hence inclusion here)	The epidermal laminae form the internal surface of the hoof wall. There are approximately 600 primary laminae around the perimeter of the hoof wall. The surface of each lamina has finger-like protrusions – secondary laminae – which greatly increase the overall laminar surface area.	Together with the dermal laminae, they interdigitate, a little like a multiple complex dovetail joint, to bond the hoof wall to the pedal bone. They contribute to maintaining the position of the pedal bone within the hoof capsule and play a role within the shock absorption mechanism of the foot. The epidermal laminae are not vascularized and are insensitive.
Dermal laminae	Located on the dorsal surface of the pedal bone. They mirror the form of the epidermal laminae.	Function as for epidermal laminae. Unlike the epidermal laminae, they are vascularized and sensitive.
Solar corium	Mirroring the shape of the sole, the solar corium is located under the coffin bone and extends to the caudal foot at the heels. The entire surface of the corium is covered with papillae which slot into tubules in the sole.	Produces the external sole horn.
Frog corium	Located immediately under the frog.	Produces the external frog.

as it tries to compensate. The feel of the horse to the rider, and even potentially the fit of the saddle, will be altered and it may start to twist or drop to one side, creating uneven pressure on the lumbar area. The difference in stride length and lumbar pressure will impact on how the horse weights its front feet on circles, and training issues may emerge. Now the horse has not only a sore foot but also a sore body, and a reluctant attitude towards stepping on the damaged foot. From the owner's perspective, they may start to address the problem from any one of the angles above, and may face a complex, expensive, time-consuming and frustrating task working out where the original cause of the problem lies.

Internally the hoof capsule consists of a number of sensitive coria and the laminae of the hoof wall.

THE FOOT

The horse's foot is made up of both hard bones and soft tissues. The bones of the foot form a hinge joint, which is designed to extend and flex (open and close) backwards and forwards. It is not designed for movement through the medio-lateral (side to side) plane, in the

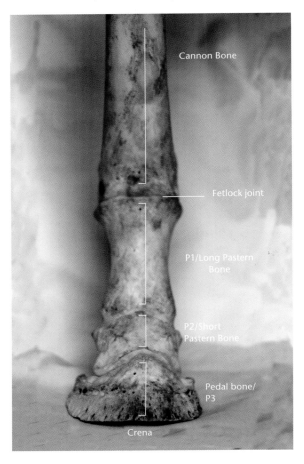

Lateral view of the bones of the digit.

Dorsal view of the bones of the digit.

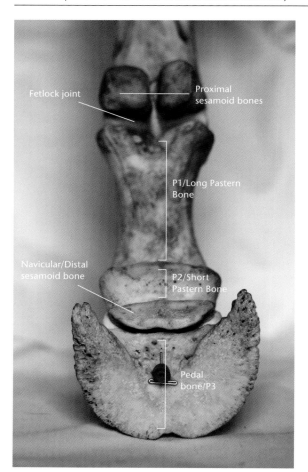

Caudal view of the bones of the digit.

way that ball and socket joints can. This is particularly important to bear in mind when considering the balance of the horse's hoof.

Bones

The bones within the foot are:

- the pedal bone, also known as the coffin bone, third distal phalanx or P3;
- the navicular bone, also known as the distal sesamoid bone;
- the short pastern bone, also known as the second distal phalanx or P2; and
- the long pastern bone, also known as the first distal phalanx or P1.

The interface between the first three bones listed here forms the distal inter-phalangeal (DIP) joint, also known as the coffin joint.

Tendons

The deep digital flexor tendon inserts onto the semi-lunar crest on the solar surface of the

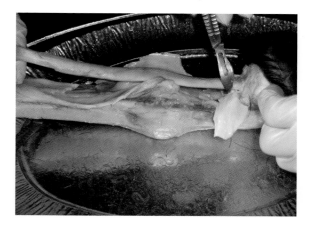

Distal limb dissection showing the deep digital flexor tendons.

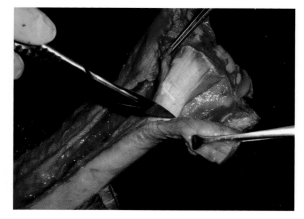

Distal limb dissection showing the division of the check ligament.

Tendons are the tissues that connect muscles to bones. They are made up of bundles of parallel collagen fibres encased in lubricated sheaths and are largely inelastic – i.e., they do not stretch. Functionally, their primary purpose is to facilitate the movement generated by muscle contraction, but they also provide some structural support to the body.

Ligaments are the tissues that connect bones to bones. Like tendons, they are made up of parallel collagen fibres, but ligaments are visco-elastic, meaning that they can stretch under load and return to their original length (rebound). However, there is a limit to the amount they can stretch. Sudden extreme loading at speed can exceed their tolerance and damage will occur. Functionally, their primary purpose is to support the joint and in some cases limit the range of movement in the joint.

Tendons and ligaments are strengthened with movement. As the horse repeatedly loads and unloads each limb, small stresses occur and the body responds by increasing the density and strength of the structure. It is essential that young horses are allowed to develop the strength of their tendon and ligamentous structures slowly, through regular sustained movement and by living on variable and undulating terrain. Good hoof balance is critical to ensure that the tendon and ligament system is not overstretched and does not exceed appropriate tolerance limits.

Both tendons and ligaments have a poor blood supply so healing tends to be very slow but it can be supported by managed rehabilitation, which may include controlled exercise, cold laser or shockwave therapy. The healing process can be disrupted by subsequent micro-injury to the repair tissue and the parallel nature of the collagen fibres is often lost. Repaired tissue does not regain the same pre-injury tensile strength. Ultrasound scans are often used for diagnostic purposes with tendon and ligament injuries. When scanning a healing structure, vets are looking to see how the collagen fibres within the structure are healing. Straight, even fibre development denotes improved functional strength.

pedal bone. It is responsible for drawing the foot up and back. The extensor tendon inserts onto the extensor process of the pedal bone and the dorsal surface of the short and long

The Pedal Bone.

pastern bones. It is responsible for extending the foot forwards.

Cartilages

Two hyaline cartilages are attached to either side of the coffin bone at the palmar processes, also known as the lateral cartilages (LCs) or ungulate cartilages. They create a flexible wall on either side of the digital cushion, which allows the back of the hoof to expand and contract, whilst providing structural support to the caudal foot. There are four pairs of ligaments, which variously connect the cartilages to all the bones of the foot.

For many years it was thought that the

lateral cartilages were usually narrow and had little blood supply, but from the work of Dr Robert Bowker we now know that in a healthy foot they are thick and have a network of blood vessels, which over time become greater in number but with a smaller diameter. This vascular network contributes to shock absorption via *haemodynamics*. The smaller the blood vessels become, the more energy it takes to squeeze the blood through them, which produces a greater damping effect.

Ligaments

Ligaments originating within the foot:

- the capsular ligament of the coffin joint surrounds and seals the joint and produces synovial fluid;
- the distal interphalangeal ligament joins the pedal bone and short pastern;
- the suspensory ligament of the navicular bone joins the navicular bone and the short pastern;
- the impar ligament joins the navicular and pedal bones;
- the chondroungular ligament joins the LC to the pedal bone;
- the chondrocoronal ligament joins the LC to the short pastern;
- the chondrocompedal ligament joins the LC to the short pastern;
- the chondrotendinous ligament joins the LC to the extensor tendon and as a consequence, the pedal bone.

Ligaments terminating within the foot:

- the extensor branches of the suspensory ligament merge with the extensor tendon and join the pedal bone with the fetlock joint;
- the distal annular ligament maintains the deep digital flexor tendon's position along

the palmar/plantar surface of the short pastern.

Digital cushion

The digital cushion (DC) is wedge-shaped and fills the space between the lateral cartilages.

Located distal to the deep digital flexor tendon, it extends forward underneath the short pastern and in a healthy, well developed foot, passes under the coffin joint and

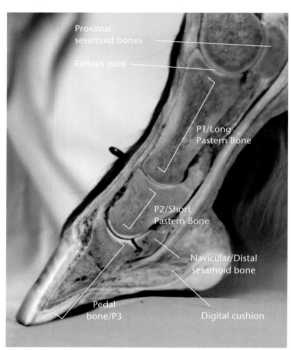

Lateral view of the distal limb.

terminates at the insertion point of the deep digital flexor tendon. The DC plays a significant role in supporting the back of the foot, along with the heels and LCs, helping to maintain the palmar/plantar angle of the pedal bone. During locomotion, it is compressed as the bodyweight of the horse loads onto the foot. As the pastern descends, the DC is squeezed, which in turn causes the frog to expand and pushes the LCs and heels apart. A strong robust DC feels rounded and firm and has the resistance of a warm squash ball. It supports the function of the suspensory ligament in limiting the descent of the pastern. It dissipates shock and protects the underlying bones.

Further research by Dr Robert Bowker suggests that there may be a specific developmental period for the hyaline cartilage within the digital cushion. Rehabilitation experiences find that it may not be possible to restore the digital cushions in the feet of a horse over the age of about fourteen

years. This is not to say that they cannot be improved, but it may not be realistic to expect them to become as thick and solid as they could have been had the horse been appropriately managed and exercised in its youth.

A further word on tendons

The quality (speed, direction, length and flow) of the movement of the limbs, and the placement and unrolling of the feet, are controlled by large ventral muscles within the body and upper limbs of the horse. There are no muscles in a horse's legs below the carpus or knee, and tarsus or hock. The extensor and flexor tendons, which can be thought of

Under developed heels and weak digital cushion.

Well developed heels and supportive digital cushion. The frog is preparing to defoliate.

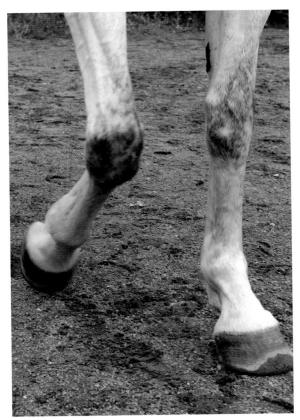

Swing phase and stance phase.

PRO COMMENT

Diagnosis of soft tissue damage is a common reason why new clients get in touch to have their horse's shoes removed. These typically fall into one of three categories:

- middle-aged leisure horses which, although not performing at a high level, have clearly had a long-standing hoof imbalance issue;
- young sports horses which have done a lot of jumping with immature bodies and under-developed feet;
- specific breeds – Warmbloods and Quarter Horses – which, in comparison to their body size, have small feet and fine lower limbs.

Upon initial evaluation, all these horses present body soreness and their owners report they were 'just not right' for a while before they went lame. Bodyworkers would unlock tight areas commonly in the pectorals, shoulders, withers and lumbar spine, psoas and hamstring muscles, but the problems would return. Following transitioning to barefoot management, and with sympathetic rehabilitation, owners of these horses report improvements in body comfort, and chiropractors see less frequent requirements for treatment and adjustment.

Due to climate change, in recent years the UK has experienced more prolonged dry spells. The resulting changes in average ground resistance mean that horses have been exposed to harder ground in turnout areas as well as during planned hard surface exercise such as road work and hacking. This exposure has increased the firmness and general functionality of many of our clients' horses' digital cushions.

somewhat like puppet's strings, activate the movement of the lower limbs and feet.

The sequence in which the hoof makes impact with the ground has a significant role to play in maintaining healthy tendons. The horse's stride is divided into two phases, the stance phase, where the hoof lands, is maximally weight-bearing in mid-stance, then breaks over, and the swing phase, where the limb is lifted in the air in preparation for the next step.

When the horse is moving in a relaxed posture, such as when walked up in hand, entering the stance phase the healthy hoof impacts the ground heel first. This can be very subtle and only visible using high definition slow-motion video. To the naked eye it may appear that the foot lands flat or on the mid-sole. Initial ground contact triggers deceleration of the limb, followed milliseconds later by the bodyweight loading onto the limb until it reaches maximal load at mid-stance. As the foot moves from heel contact to become flat on the ground, the tension on the deep digital flexor tendon is smoothly increased along a gradient as the bodyweight of the horse causes the pastern to descend. At speed, if the toe makes ground contact first, the tendon does not experience a smooth increase in load but a sudden jerk as the heels slam down, which can over-stress the tendon. Rooney suggests that this jerk or third order acceleration causes friction,[3] abrades the tendon sheath and eventually causes lesions in the tendon itself. The function of the navicular bone is to ensure the angle of insertion of the deep digital flexor tendon remains the same throughout the stride. A heel-first landing ensures that the pressure exerted on the navicular bone by the DDFT increases and decreases smoothly. The jerk of third order acceleration caused by fast impact toe-first landing is also transmitted to the navicular bone and coffin joint, which over time can become damaged.

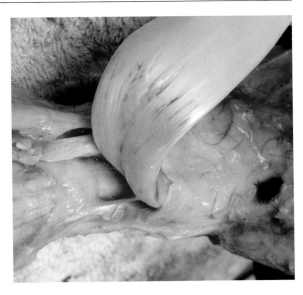

Some lesions fully transect the tendon.

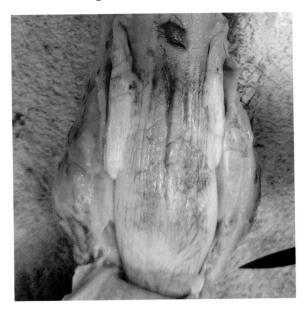

Lesions on the outer surface of the deep digital flexor tendon.

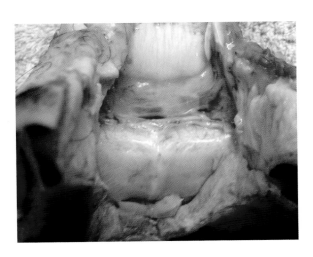

Areas of damage evident on the navicular bone and P2 after the deep digital flexor tendon was removed.

POSTURE AND LANDING – HEEL FIRST OR OTHERWISE

One is unlikely to have come across any information on barefoot trimming and functional anatomy without stumbling across the subject of heel-first landing. Stemming from physiological research into hoof function, and based on observations of the flight and landing patterns in wild and feral horses, heel-first landing has become something of a barefoot mantra. However, there is more to understand in relation to the theories just discussed. Observation of the same horse walked and trotted up in hand, and ridden in basic self-carriage or in collection, tell a more nuanced story about landing.

It is normal for healthy barefoot horses walked and trotted up in hand, or moving around in a relaxed attitude, to place the feet down at the end of the flight phase visibly heel first. In these circumstances the muscle tone in the rest of the horse's body is low, it is in an efficient neutral posture, and is not required to carry a rider's weight. Horses that do not land heel-first when walked or trotted up in hand but still have a relaxed posture either have pathology somewhere in the foot, limb or body that is causing them pain, or have weakly developed digital cushions and caudal feet. As horses are commonly observed by professionals walked or trotted up in hand, or in their living environment, heel-first landing has become what we commonly expect to see. It does not mean, however, that heel-first landing is normal in every context. Even watching a healthy horse grazing, you will be able to observe that toe-first foot placement is common, and is not a sign that the horse is in pain or is damaging itself.

There are times when a toe-first landing is absolutely appropriate – for example, when a horse is grazing it will take individual slow steps as it gradually progresses and forages. It will also land toe-first when going uphill or when highly aroused and 'on its toes'; these are all normal landings. When a horse is trained to change its posture during collected ridden work, its strides get higher and shorter, the 'tensegrity' (*see* below) of its body will hold more spring and its footsteps become more controlled.

In very collected movements, flat or toe-first landing is also possible, but the effect is mitigated by the low speed, control and trained tone of the horse's body. It is

Dorothy Mark and Anglo Arabian gelding Solo ridden in neck extension.

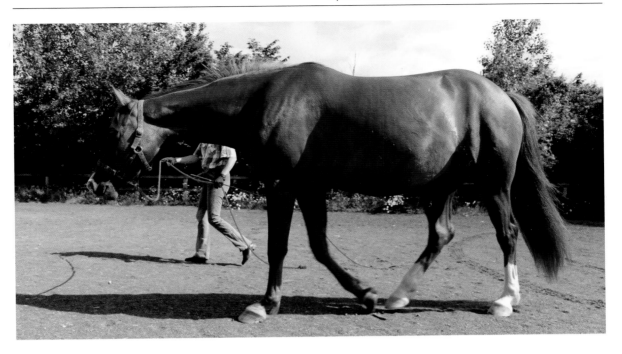

Arabian X Saddlebred gelding Tango in a relaxed posture, commonly seen when walking up in hand.

important to consider the force and duration of these toe-first landings in comparison to the slamming toe-first landings experienced by a horse landing after a big fence. If every horse learned to control its steps through being taught basic ridden collection, it would improve the function of the horse's landing. Pounding around a course of show jumps on a horse with a dropped back and with low abdominal tone, or galloping across country on an excited and adrenalin-filled horse jumping big hedges after hounds will not teach them this.

It is rarely noted by hoof care professionals but correct biomechanical training can considerably increase the control a horse exerts on its limb movement. Both in hand and under saddle, the horse should be encouraged to

Dorothy Marks and Arabian X gelding Tango toned up and performing school walk.

Dorothy Marks and Solo demonstrate how training the horse to rock back over its legs trains the horse to centralise its balance over its feet.

be aware of, and actively control, how it balances its body over its feet, how it tones its muscles to achieve this and how it loads and unloads the limb. Observations from healthy barefoot horses suggest that when the horse is ridden and developed in collection, the flexion of all the limb joints is increased and the flight pattern of all the limbs is higher and longer in duration. In neck extension, where the horse lifts and telescopes its neck away from the body, with the head in front of the vertical, stabilization of the trunk and spine is achieved by the upper body musculature. The horse can then extend the flight phase of the stride, move its limbs more precisely and will deliberately aim the mid-foot towards the landing point.

Slow systematic training can teach the horse

Training the horse to accept changes in the vertical flexion of its head and neck gradually activates core abdominal muscles. Dorothy Marks and Solo in high position.

to centralize its balance around its mid-foot more effectively, rather than leaning forward and weighting the toe, as is commonly seen. It starts with training the horse to change its balance caudally by rocking back over the legs.

Training the horse to accept changes in the vertical flexion of its head and neck between high, low and extended positions, and in lateral flexion with an open poll, gradually activates and strengthens the core abdominal muscles. Over time the horse also learns to weight and flex the joints of the hind limb, to carry more weight and energy in the quarters, and to stabilize its spine and trunk. The resulting postural change gives the horse

Dorothy Marks and Solo demonstrate how teaching a horse to extend its neck activates core abdominal muscles.

the potential to lift and stabilize the rib cage between the shoulder blades, and to move the front limbs slowly in response to the rider's seat aids to reach and deliberately place the front feet further forward without losing balance.

How can both heel- and toe-first landing be 'normal' landing options for the same animal? Let us introduce another fabulously useful biomechanical model: 'tensegrity'.

Defined by R. Buckminster Fuller in the 1940s, the term tensegrity is a contraction of 'tension integrity'. It is defined as a structural relationship principle by which structural shape is defined by continuous tension around localized compression within an independent system.[4] In the horse's body, the tension within the system normally varies in relation to its emotional state through the myofascial network – a relaxed horse equals lower myofascial tension and a lower toned body, while an aroused horse equals higher myofascial tension and a collected or highly toned body. In the natural state collected postures equal aroused emotional states, which will encourage the horse to tone up its body for excitement in play, flight in fear or sexual activity. All of these activities require the body to be in high tensegrity, balanced for split-second manoeuvrability, to protect the body from harm. In the highly toned horse, mid-foot or toe-first landing equals acceleration and manoeuvrability. If you

Excited Russian feral horses in natural collection. Their hoof morphology is adapted to a soft environment. Image courtesy of Artur_Baboev (Own work) [CC BY-SA 3.0 (http://creativecommons.org/licenses/by-sa/3.0) or GFDL (http://www.gnu.org/copyleft/fdl.html)], via Wikimedia Commons.

PRE Stallion Barquero JF and his rider Rebecca Brennand in passage. Image courtesy of Manolo Mendez Dressage.

PRO COMMENT

Listening to a horse's footfalls can often give clues as to how controlled their landings are. A balanced horse will be very quiet, almost silent, as it progresses over the ground. A physically or emotionally unbalanced horse will be loud and its footsteps will resound. On a conformable surface the balanced horse will leave shallower footprints. Deliberate placement of the limb makes its feet in the mid-stance phase appear to be very grounded.

Arabian X gelding Tango demonstrating controlled footfalls in hand.

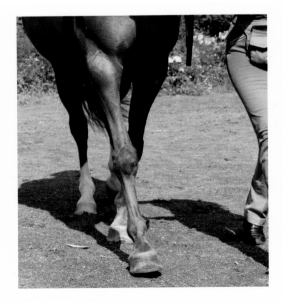

have ever followed in the footsteps of a horse which is running away, you will see very little impression at the heel but a big dig-in at the toe. Heel-first landing in the highly toned horse equates to deceleration: think of the big, wide, heel slide marks excited horses make when they are playing and they run out of field. When the horse's body is in tensegrity and balanced, it allows the horse to distribute pressure evenly throughout the tensile network and bone

structure, so mid-foot landing distributes pressure most evenly around the distal interphalangeal joint.

The goal of sympathetic training is to achieve artificial collection by engaging the horse's muscular system without triggering the emotional arousal mechanisms. After all, even though it might be a thrilling experience for some, no sane person wants to ride a horse which is seriously thinking about mating or actively running away. The postural changes

French Thoroughbred Stallion Nepal. Image courtesy of Haras national suisse HNS (Haras national suisse HNS) [GFDL (http://www.gnu.org/copyleft/fdl.html) or CC BY-SA 4.0-3.0-2.5-2.0-1.0 (http://creativecommons.org/ licenses/by-sa/4.0-3.0-2.5-2.0-1.0)], via Wikimedia Commons.

that are the goal of correct training actively teach horses to balance their bodies in high tensegrity with a rider. Through gradual training, based on positive reinforcement, the horse learns to maintain its emotional balance and co-operate even when in a highly toned state.

The bottom line where landing is concerned is that the horse needs to be able to be comfortable, balanced, toned and confident enough to place the foot down from any angle and keep the strain within the system within tolerance.

DEFINING CONFORMATION AND GOOD POSTURE – *THE HORSE WHICH STANDS BEFORE YOU*

Specialist knowledge, or 'an eye' for good conformation, has become something of a lost art, subsumed by fashion in modern horse breeding. A horse's conformation impacts upon its ability to stay sound throughout its life, how it will use its feet during locomotion and how it will feel to ride, and can significantly influence the overall structure of the foot and hoof. Biomechanics can be used to analyse the basic principles behind what made traditional conformation evaluation criteria sensible ones. Conformation of riding horses will be principally discussed, as riding is the predominant activity that horse owners currently choose to engage in. The criteria outlined here for riding horse conformation does not specify a particular breed, as there are also many horses which are the products of cross-breeding and are very adaptable riding horses.

Conformation can sometimes seem a daunting and exclusive topic, reserved for the breeders of racehorses, stallion owners or top performance horses, but an eye for conformation is a skill that can be developed. When looking at a potential horse, try to remain objective and do not be influenced by the words attached to any animal, attractive sales banter or glossy advertising.

Dr Deb Bennett, in her classic text

PRO COMMENT

When I evaluate the posture and feet of a ridden barefoot horse, I can often tell how its training and recent activity have influenced its posture and conformation. The most obvious sign is the wear pattern, but there are other, more subtle, indications. I have had clients tell me their obese horse has been busy, when clearly, from its unworn feet, it hasn't been out of the field for a month, but at the other end of the scale fewer than 5 per cent of my clients' horses exhibit the signs of balanced loading I would like to see in the feet from effective postural training. All horses are to varying degrees asymmetrical, but with close attention to training for straightness, asymmetry can be significantly improved. It takes education, time and a training plan that is responsive to the horse's fitness and ability, but it is a shame that more people don't invest the time learning how to do it. In these horses I see their wear and loading patterns becoming more symmetrical, with better development of digital cushions and concavity corresponding to a hoof where compression and leverage stay within tolerance, which both helps and prevents tendon and ligament strain.

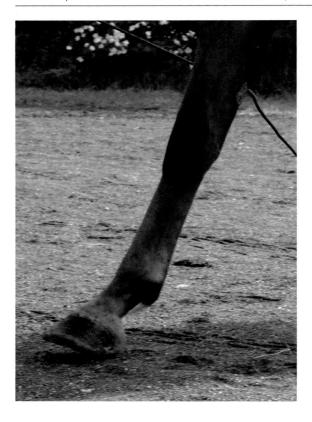

Heel first landing is normal in the relaxed horse.

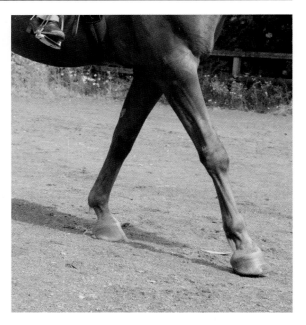

Arabian X gelding Tango demonstrating how tensegrity helps him control his landing and balance around his midfoot.

Principles of Conformation Analysis (vol. I), makes a very sensible comment: 'Even if the horse of your dreams has a pedigree as long as your arm, when signing a breeding or purchase contract you are not buying his breed. Instead you are buying the individual horse who stands before you'.[5] The following quotes illustrate two of the crucial points which need to be understood when considering where to start with conformation:

> The conformation of an individual horse largely depends upon his *bone structure*. The remainder depends upon the muscle type he has, the amount of body fat he is carrying, and how fit he is… while all horses possess the same bones, the proportions of each skeleton are different.[6]

Conformation is a *point in time*, both hoof and bone change with time depending on how they are loaded. It takes years to go through, but the loading pattern will gradually change.[7]

Each horse has its personal genetic blueprint, but its conformation and bone structure can and will change in response to many aspects of the horse's life, including development, environment and training. Close examination of a horse's body can give many clues as to how it has been altered by human intervention and use. It is possible to rehabilitate a damaged horse, but it can be a heart-, back- and wallet-breaking business. Potential horse buyers need to understand, and have a realistic attitude to, what they are starting with.

As introduced previously in relation to foot landing, the horse's ability to use its body in a balanced way can prevent unsoundness even when the horse is less than perfect in terms of conformation. Even if the skeleton is not structured in a way that biomechanics experts would consider ideal, it is important to understand how everything is connected and integrated, in order to help a less well conformed horse learn to balance. How do all these complex parts harmonize into the beautiful expression of equine movement that attracts us so powerfully?

THE PURPOSE AND EFFECT OF SELECTIVE BREEDING

During the last 5,000 years, as humans selectively bred horses to use for a range of different tasks, understanding of the benefits and disadvantages of different points of conformation developed with equestrian culture into a specialist area of knowledge.

> Over the years, breeding has gravitated towards the production of certain ideals associated with speed, strength, temperament, movement, etc. This, naturally, has related to the type of use for which the particular horse was intended. Judges tend very often to have their own idea of what is best, but there are people in existence whose ability to judge a horse for a specific purpose has marked them as masters of the art.[8]

In the early twentieth century stock judging was in its heyday. At this time the American Horse Shows Association (AHSA) had three purposes for halter classes:

- to identify the horse that was likely to stay soundest for the longest time whilst doing the job it was bred for;
- to identify the horse that moved the best relative to its intended purpose, whether draught, carriage or saddle horse; and
- to certify the winners as bloodstock.[9]

The purposes of halter classes then were clearly practical. Unlike modern showing, there was no emphasis on colour, extreme movement, glitz or show-ring glamour. Horses were considered working animals and were expected to be able to perform efficiently in their intended tasks for the longest time possible. Selecting larger horses with good feet, lots of bone and strong limbs was clearly understood to be practical if you wanted to employ them in jobs that involved pulling, or rather pushing, heavy weights such as canal barges, logs, ploughs and heavy wagons. In the past a draught horse would not have been chosen for a ridden career. Stock judges would not consider these horses to have optimal conformation for riding, as their sheer size makes it virtually impossible for a rider to match the forces generated by the horse's body, but they were clearly fit for the purpose for which they were bred.

In an era when many people could anticipate long hours in the saddle if they wanted to travel any distance, riding horses were selectively bred for characteristics that make them comfortable to ride. Ridden horses needed to comfortably match the human body, and their way of going to confer as smooth, comfortable and efficient a riding experience as possible. Their height, size and weight had to be small enough for the average-sized rider to match the forces they produced, so riders could influence their horses' posture and make them rideable without exhausting themselves.

Since the 1920s humans have no longer used horses extensively for work purposes, and keeping horses has predominantly become a leisure pursuit. During the last thirty years many more people have become horse owners than would have been previously. Many modern leisure horses are small cross-bred draught breeds, or very large horses, sold now for colour and points,

Clydesdale gelding Bucket, at seven years old. An example of a draft horse.

mane and tail, and leg feathering rather than conformation. This paradox results in owners often being challenged by saddling, postural, riding, gait and hoof balance difficulties.

Some of the key points of conformation that old horse masters prioritized in purchasing or breeding a riding horse are sensible features to bear in mind when assessing a horse intended for riding. This list is not exclusive, and limb conformation will be covered in more detail subsequently:

When purchasing a shod horse with clear limb misalignment, it may be tempting to believe that taking its shoes off will allow the horse to 'naturally' correct the misalignment. If the horse is more than five or six years old, there may be little that can be permanently changed, however, without doing more than balanced trimming and exercise. You may be encouraged to allow the horse to go along 'comfortable in his own asymmetry', but there are very likely to be internal compensatory mechanisms at work that will lead to difficulties later on. This is particularly the case in larger horses, where arthritis is commonly diagnosed at an early age.

Conformation point

Size

Miniature horse. Image courtesy of DanDee Shots (Guide horse) [CC BY 2.0 (http://creativecommons.org/licenses/by/2.0)], via Wikimedia Commons.

Dictator. The photos illustrate size extremes on a continuum.

From selective breeding in many domestic animals we have produced unnatural extremes of size. Miniaturization leads to many physical problems, as does breeding for extremely large sizes. To maximize soundness the most appropriate size for a riding horse is 16.2hh or less with a weight of around 600kg. Wild horses are mainly pony-sized. Modern feral herd heights average at 14–15hh, and larger domestic horses suffer a greater frequency of joint problems, therefore it is sensible to assume that a lower height range is optimal for the species.[10]

Head

A well proportioned head.

Any extremes in terms of facial proportions may indicate the potential for problems. The head should be of a size proportionate to the body, with a wide and flat face line, and good jaw width with well-aligned teeth, not over- or under-biting, and large nostrils. There should not be too great a dished appearance to the face. The eyes need to be large, prominent and clear with no discharge. The ears should be well placed and alert, ready to move at the slightest sound.

Neck

The angle at which the head is set on to the neck needs to be open, as this allows the horse to breathe and eat comfortably. The neck needs to be set on to the body not too low or too high. For example Quarter horses can be distinctly 'downhill', and Friesians can have a neck set so high it places the rider at a disadvantage in staying forward enough to keep up with the movement. A well set neck confers a distinct biomechanical advantage in training the horse for riding.

A well set neck with good length and curvature.

Shoulders

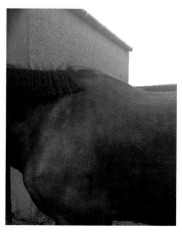

An upright shoulder.

A well angled shoulder.

A sloping shoulder conveys efficient shock absorption and a longer, smoother stride. Many draught breeds have steeper shoulders which maximizes their 'pushing' ability, but will therefore have shorter, choppier strides, making riding more uncomfortable. The pasterns are likely to follow the pattern of the horse's shoulder. If they don't, this may indicate a hoof care approach that does not biomechanically advantage the horse.

Withers

Without muscular atrophy, the withers need to be well defined and to slope away gently from top to bottom, known as the upslope. Where the upslope is short, saddling needs to be extra precise, as it is more difficult to position the rider in the most biomechanically efficient riding position. The length of the upslope can be changed over time with postural training. Flat or non-existent withers mean the rider may need to ride more skilfully to keep the saddle from moving forwards, backwards or sideways.

Back, girth and ribcage

The back needs to be short and broad, with a good bearing surface to take the weight of the rider. A long-backed horse may require more precise and extensive training to adequately strengthen the ring of muscles that allows them to lift and broaden their back under a rider. The girth groove needs to be well placed or the saddle will be inclined to move forwards. Horses with flat withers and a forward girth groove are very difficult to saddle well, as essentially this is small draught horse conformation. The ribcage needs to be round and well sprung, with adequate muscle development to support a saddle and rider.

Loins and hindquarters

The ability of the lumbar sacral junction to flex and bend is essential in the ridden horse as it corresponds with its ability to carry weight. The loins should be short and well muscled, with the tail set on not too low or too high. A well carried and relaxed tail suggests that the horse is using its body effectively. The horse must be capable of coiling its loins (like a human doing a crunch) to be biomechanically efficient in moving and carrying a rider. The hindquarters need to be strong, muscular and well developed.

Forelegs

The forelegs should be well set and aligned underneath the body. Foreleg conformation is more difficult to assess as the forelegs are subject to how the soft tissues around the shoulder attach the limb to the body. Narrow – as in 'both legs coming out of the same hole' – forelegs can mean the horse is immature, weak or has pain somewhere in its pectoral muscles, legs, feet or somewhere else in the forequarters. The elbow should stand out from the body, enough to fit a loose fist between the elbow and the ribcage.

Knees

The old masters loved a big, flat and well aligned knee that didn't go before or behind the vertical when looked at from the lateral side. Sensibly, this allows the weight of the horse to be more evenly distributed down the joints and bones of the limb and through the foot.

Bone and 'clean legs'

A good cannon bone measurement would be 7–9 inches to just below the knee, and suggests the horse would be strong enough to cope as a riding horse. Interestingly, Dr Bennett indicates that the amount of 'bone' in the average modern riding horse has decreased by approximately half as a result of domestication and selective breeding. She writes: 'in nature, the weight of a mammal predicts its "bone" circumference... The Plains zebra and the Przewalski horse (*Equus caballus przewalski*) possess twice as much bone per pound of body mass as domestic horses'.[11] Ensuring that the horse has sufficient bone to accommodate its weight is absolutely critical to soundness. If a large heavy body is supported on insufficient bone, as in some of the extremely tall dressage horses we see today, it may look 'elegant' by modern fashion standards, but there is very likely to be an enhanced chance of structural breakdown when the stress in the horse's system exceeds its tolerance limitations.

On a healthy limb, below the knee or hock the skin should fit well and you should be able to feel all the tendon and ligament structures clearly. Any swellings, thickenings or scarring may indicate a problem. Wind galls are soft and are often overlooked, but they are common symptoms of prior or existing lower leg congestion – i.e. laminitis.

GOOD POSTURE IS GOOD FOR BODIES, GOOD FOR FEET

In human athletes it has been proven scientifically that strengthening of the core stabilizing muscles enhances athletic performance and reduces injuries. The same benefits are desirable in equine athletes regardless of whether they are used for pleasure or competition.[12]

Good posture allows the body to function in a way that is most energy efficient and least likely to suffer damage either from interaction with the environment or from internal physical imbalances. Explaining the importance of posture and collection, coach, equine chiropractor and clinician Dorothy Marks describes good posture as putting the joints in a neutral and consistent place from which they have full range of motion. 'Good posture is neutral for the joint, it supports equal spacing throughout the joint, and it allows muscles to work in a balanced and efficient way. Good posture allows the animal to move as freely and safely as possible, putting the minimum stress on the joints, ligaments, tendons and muscles,

reducing the potential for falls and injuries, and makes the horse safer and more comfortable to ride.'[13]

Good posture.

The twenty-first-century horse world has mainly forgotten the why and how of correct postural training. In recent years there has been a backlash against modern training methods such as Rollkur, which has led to confusion for the average horse owner about where to turn for 'correct' training that will genuinely help their horses become stronger. Concerns about unethical, punitive and destructive training, and a lack of awareness of the alternatives, can lead horse owners to dismiss all modern training. As a result there has been an upsurge in 'natural' horsemanship and a belief that this kind of training is 'better'. Unfortunately natural horsemanship approaches, as they are mainly practised, do little to develop good posture and do not adequately address straightness or asymmetry.

Poor posture.

There are, however, a number of training systems which do support biomechanically correct posture, are robustly structured to include the science of equine learning, and are ethical. When choosing a training system, make sure the baby is not thrown out with the bathwater.

THE BIOMECHANICS OF TRAINING: HELPING YOUR HORSE DEVELOP GOOD POSTURE

From speaking with many horse owners over the last twenty years about what they 'do' with their horses, it is clear that several categories exist: there are people who compete and people who don't, people who 'do dressage' and people who don't. The former distinction is understandable: not everyone is competitive and many people simply enjoy riding without feeling the need to enter competitions. The latter choice regarding 'doing dressage' seems to be based on lost information about why people did it in the first place.

In human sports science, considerable attention has been given to developing knowledge about how to support the human body to be strong enough to resist injury and maximize performance in competitive sport. Even at the most basic level, taking a little bit of this knowledge and applying it to horses is a sensible thing to do, assisting them to live a long and pain-free life, even if there is no intention for them to become competition horses. Work on posture, fitness, form and attitude are essential elements of athletic development, and there are a growing number of ambitious leisure riders who

Free jumping.

Dawn Saunders and Loke enjoying the view.

Katja Voigt and Robin Hood completing an obstacle at a Trec competition. Image courtesy of Dave Cameron Photography.

Dorothy Marks encouraging Solo to extend his neck frequently but keep his spine lightly arched, to enable him to carry her efficiently during ridden work. Image courtesy of Horse & Rider magazine.

A horse ridden on a loose rein with 'natural' posture and spine 'dropped', is less biomechanically efficient than riding with a gentle abdominal tone and spinal arch.

are keen to help their horses develop their fitness for riding as much as they can. Going back to the 'why' of dressage, Dr Bennett explains: 'the effect of all dressage exercises is, in whole or in part, to strengthen the rectus

abdominus muscle of the horse's underline. A horse with deep, strong belly muscle – a horse whose groin depth nearly equals his girth – can bascule, engage his hindquarters, achieve collection and carry you athletically.'[14]

Establishing the basics of good posture is extremely useful for horses, especially when they are asked to carry a rider's bodyweight – something that is outside the scope of equine activity and evolution. With a sound knowledge of the biomechanics involved in carrying and moving with a rider, training can assist the horse to do this in the least stressful way possible.

THE SUSPENSION BRIDGE THEORY AND THE RING OF MUSCLES

The horse's body has often been described as corresponding to the structure of a suspension bridge, with the front and hind pairs of legs as two sets of stanchions. The horse's spine – equivalent to the bridge floor – has a slight upward arch, with the vertebrae supported by the interconnected cable-like structures of the dorsal ligament system. This ligament system is unique to equines and extends from the poll to the hock, with the principal cable structures positioned above the spine and held under tension. As the muscles underneath the spine contract, tension on the cables is increased and, as long as the back muscles can relax sufficiently, the back of the horse arches and the horse can collect its body and move efficiently.

The Ring of Muscles theory describes how the horse's body acts a little like a spring, coiling and storing energy under compression, which can then be effectively transformed into propulsive force. Dorothy Marks effectively describes what a horse's body needs to do to enable it to engage its ring of muscles, and comfortably and efficiently carry a rider's weight.

It is particularly important to train the 'collection' system, expanded as effective loin coiling, freespan arching and neck extension, because some of the muscles involved in these processes are small muscles, situated below the spine and deep within the body. They are easily overpowered by the larger upper body muscles: the trapezius, rhomboid and longissimus dorsi, lying above the spine. These muscles, when contracted, are involved in inverting or hollowing the spine. The ridden horse needs to be enabled by effective training, sympathetic saddle fitting and riding to relax its strong upper body muscles so that its collection muscles can contract and help it carry its body in a 'cat-like' arch. Once the collection system

Dorothy Marks encourages Solo in his gymnastic ability by adjusting the vertical posture of his neck, and using lateral flexions.

The lumbo-sacral junction in the hindquarters needs to be able to flex, leading to loin coiling and the hind legs coming under the body. The lumbo-sacral joint is the one joint in the lumbar spine that has significant ability to bend and flex. The 'free span' of the back, or the thoracolumbar spine, must lift and arch gently, which allows the horse to move its limbs more freely and makes it easier for it to carry the weight of a rider. The root of the neck must then lift, from the contraction of the scalenus and longus colli muscles, leading to the neck telescoping forward and away from the body as the horse reaches forward into the bridle.[15]

is functional, the longissimus dorsi muscles are effective as a cantilever, so long as they do not overpower the ventral muscles.

> In the broad sense of the term, 'dressage' is therefore all of the principles, methods and processes used to optimize the horse's capabilities, whatever the breed and whatever the discipline.[16]

Being able to carry the body in gentle collection or basic self-carriage can be systematically trained in the young horse and was in the past considered a basic essential for every ridden horse. Learning the skills and taking the time to teach this will allow the horse's tendon and ligament system throughout its body to balance the stresses of carrying a rider, to enable it to be responsive and comfortable to ride, and to live a longer and sounder working life.

Biomechanical horse training

> How can I train my horse without gadgets or force or pain even if I only want to ride my horse around the block? I also want to stay safe. What I've found from this work is that it mentally relaxes them, and means I can rely on my horse to respond to me even when the chips are down.[17]

Instead of spending money on training gadgets, invest in lessons in developing skills as a trainer. With a good coach and an effective training system, it is possible to learn to develop the horse using learning theory through observation, feel and timing. There are many principles in classical training, which will gradually develop postural strength and balance and benefit the horse's entire body and mind. A good trainer can show their own horses and how such training has improved their posture, comfort and way of going, and will be able to customize training to suit each individual horse and rider.

> Even though I don't want to compete at a very high level in dressage, I want my horses to be as sound as possible for as long as possible, and make it as easy as I can for them to carry me.[18]

With sympathetic hoof care and horse keeping, biomechanical training can significantly strengthen any horse's feet and legs, as well as building digital cushion.

It is important to emphasize that the best systems focus on gymnastic development and straightness, and respect each horse as an individual. Responsive and iterative training integrate ground and ridden work systematically. The authors refer clients to the following sources:

- Licensed trainers from the School of Légèreté: www.philippe-karl.com/423/english/school-of-legerete
- Straightness training: Bent Branderup: www.bentbranderuptrainer.com
- Straightness training: Marijke de Jong: academicartofriding.com/marijke

It is worth noting that learning in these systems also requires the rider and handler to develop their own cognitive and physical abilities, so the training will benefit both horse and owner.

Research into the effects of neck posture suggests that systems which alternately train neck elevation and extension with the nose in front of the vertical, rather than those which teach extension alone or encourage the horse to have its nose behind the vertical, teach the horse to transmit weight onto the hindquarters most effectively and affect functionality.[19]

SADDLES, TACK AND TRAINING 'AIDS'

It would have been useful if the horse had evolved symbiotically with the human in a way that allowed a rider to harmoniously 'slot into place' on the horse's body. Domestication and selective breeding have moulded the 'riding' horse as a set of conformational norms, but there is still a requirement for specialist equipment with which to support the human–horse interface. Whilst bareback and bridle-less riding is often romantically seen as the 'ultimate' in horsemanship, there are very good reasons why a saddle and bridle are a more appropriate choice for the majority of riders.

A saddle is a significant purchase for most horse owners. In recent market research on saddles to horse ratios, AJ Equestrian found that many horse owners own more saddles than horses. Many of these expensive pieces of equipment were redundant, in that they had been bought for a previous horse, the horse had changed shape or grown, or they were uncomfortable for the rider to ride in.[20]

Returning to the Ring of Muscles model, imagine a horse moving in basic collection. The rider is trained to carry their bodyweight in their joints and in their thighs, and can encourage the horse to engage its abdominal muscles to raise its ribcage and spine. In a well fitted treed saddle, the weight of the rider is distributed through wide saddle panels resting on the sprung cylinder of the ribs. The panels are appropriately angled by the saddle tree to match the lifted profile of the moving back, with all contact areas well padded to encourage the horse to lift. The seat of the saddle allows the rider to position themselves above the upslope of the horse's withers. When riding bareback, the pressure of the rider's seat is centred on the seatbones and thighs, which rest in the visibly lowest part of the back. The rider needs to be very strong to stay over the upslope of the withers and out of the horse's 'manhole'.

What would be the difference in pressure under the seats of the two riders? How easy would it be for each horse to lift its back? How long could each rider maintain a posture that

is not going to put excessive pressure on the most vulnerable part of the back?

The saddle (and here the authors also include saddling systems that use pads and other pressure distribution systems, such as independent panels) needs to:

- be wide enough to accommodate the horse's lifted back in basic collection;
- distribute pressure through uniform contact over the widest available area (the critical pressure is less than 1.5psi, but in practice there are very few opportunities to measure this);

Lateral back assessment.

Dorsal back assessment.

- assist the rider to encourage the horse to lift through the freespan of the back;
- enable full rotation of the shoulders along the rib cage; and
- maximize the effect of the ring of muscles.

The majority of saddle problems from the horse's perspective are caused by the tree of the saddle being too narrow to accommodate the actual shape of the moving horse. This is particularly critical in the area where the saddle is intended to sit, just behind the horse's shoulder, close to the upslope of the wither.

Traditional saddle fitting misses the biggest picture: the shape of the body in the area of the thoracic vertebrae in the *static* horse does not often reflect the shape of the area of the thoracic vertebrae in the *moving horse in basic collection.*

On most occasions the saddle fitter tries very hard to find a saddle in their stock, or to make a custom-made saddle, that matches the sometimes very detailed profiles taken from the horse's back when it is standing still and the ring of muscles is not in play. With a saddle fitted to the static shape, when the horse tries to move it is prevented from appropriately lifting the freespan by the restrictive width of the saddle, so is forced to remain in a dropped back posture. In the long term the horse will adapt its way of going to try to accommodate the situation. It is common to see over-developed brachiocephalic muscles, tension in the cervical area of the trapezius muscle and weak trailing hind quarters accompanying a sway back as the horse has hollowed away from the pain and restriction and hauled itself along by its front end. Even if the saddle fitter has done an accurate fitting job, the angle of the points of the tree will snugly fit the body behind the shoulder, therefore preventing the shoulder rotating back and under the saddle. The shoulder cannot move backwards over the ribs, resulting in the horse taking shorter strides with the front legs.

Limb action and foot placement are responsive to the dynamics going on higher up in the body. In the balanced horse, whose saddling and riding assist activation of its basic collection system, the loins can coil, the spine can lift through the freespan and the shoulders can rotate fully and glide along the ribcage. The loads exerted by the body can be evenly distributed through the joints in the limbs and feet, which can remain in alignment and breakover close to the centre of the toe. With a horse moving in a saddle that is narrower than its lifted shape, hollow backed and hind limbs trailing, it is common to see the elbows held in close to the body and toes turned out, providing excessive loading and crushing to the medial heels. An excessively lateral breakover and potential for lateral flaring completes the picture for the front feet. In the hinds the trailing legs result in a leverage situation on the hind toes. With each step the breakover drags the toe forwards, resulting over time in the hoof wall and sole migrating forward of the frog.

Have a saddle fitted by someone who can explain the biomechanics of equine movement. There are saddle fitters who can do so, but attendance at a course by the Society of Master Saddlers does not guarantee that

Lavinia Mitchell Riding Club GP saddle fitted with shim pads.

they provide the 'best' service. The authors recommend several saddle companies:

- Lavinia Mitchell Saddles:
  www.laviniamitchell.com
- Balance Saddles:
  www.balanceinternational.com
- Free 'n' Easy Saddles: www.fnesaddles.com
- Schleese Saddles: www.schleese.com

These companies train their fitters to go into much greater biomechanical detail than the SMS training entails, and they are required to produce case studies before they are approved. It is important to bear in mind that, with a saddle fitted by a specialist company or their representative, other generic fitters may not be able to offer an appropriate fitting service for the saddle.

The authors have also used Total Contact saddles (www.total-contact.co.uk), which

Total Contact saddle with owners pads.

provide a minimal saddling system and approach. They advise that these saddles can leave unbalanced riders feeling vulnerable, but they are an excellent product for technical riders with a good independent seat.

Arrange as a minimum six-monthly saddle checks, and checks before recommencing a work programme. On a regularly used flocked saddle, the panel should be dropped out of the tree and the flocking should be completely replaced every eighteen months to two years. Top stuffing is the addition of a small amount of flock at strategic points in the panel but does not equate to a re-flock.

Pads and numnahs

Very often, when talking about saddles and pads, people will say 'a well fitted saddle should fit without a pad underneath' and 'using pads just makes a saddle tighter'. This opinion is out of date and usually based on a misunderstanding of modern saddle design. Remember the static and lifted back discussion? For many years saddlers have put a considerable amount of effort into creating a product that precisely matches a static back shape. Now imagine putting on a thick pad and girthing up a saddle that snugly reflects the planes of the body. Using a thick pad in this situation may result in excessive compression and damage to the back muscles. It will actually make the saddle tighter, a bit like adding multiple pairs of socks to your own feet within your current shoe size.

However, the use of pads with a saddle is completely appropriate as long as the saddle tree is *bigger than the lifted shape* of the horse's back and is fitted and balanced appropriately by someone approved in using pad and saddle systems. Note the use of the word *bigger* – using a bigger saddle does not simply mean buying a saddle with wider points. The width needs to be designed throughout the saddle. Widening the points alone can result in changes to the angle of the panels further back in the saddle that affect pressure distribution. Conversely, if the saddle has been fitted to the lifted shape of the back, and was sold as a pad and saddle system (such as Lavinia Mitchell Saddles and Balance Saddles offer), randomly removing the pads 'because a well fitted saddle shouldn't need a pad' negates the effect of the system and will completely unbalance the saddle. Be aware that there are some trainers who do not understand these two different fitting concepts and will attempt to remove balancing or shim pads simply because it is outside their own education.

Rehabilitation

Shim pads and adjustable riser pads are very useful when rehabilitating a damaged back. An experienced fitter should be able to approach fitting for rehabilitation by anticipating where the horse needs to develop its body after muscle atrophy or underdevelopment, and should be able to advise on a rehabilitation work programme or refer to a suitable trainer who can help.

A tried and tested technique is to fit a wider saddle with a shim pad, and build up padding adjacent to the damaged area which can support the saddle but provide sufficient stimulation and space for the horse to push into. Horses can change very rapidly, sometimes in weeks, so the rider needs to be confident in assessing saddle balance and adjusting shimming appropriately. In a rehabilitation situation it is sensible to discuss saddle changes with the hoof care professional, and ask them to report any changes occurring at the hoof level that can indicate postural change.

Pads and numnahs need to be designed to reflect the shape of the thoracic area – high wither numnahs are particularly useful as they remain up in the gullet of the saddle and are less likely to compress over the withers. The pad needs to comfortably extend beyond the margins of the saddle panel, making sure there is no binding sitting underneath the edge of the panel that could cause chafing.

Pads and panels should not be harder in feel than the muscles of the back, but they should be firm enough to hold their shape and not squash or ruck up. Closed cell foams, such as Prolite, and some memory foams provide very acceptable 'feels' and encourage the horse to push their backs into the pad. Good flocking should also do this, and should be replaced if it starts to feel hard, 'felt like' or compressed. Horses enjoy the feeling of sheepskin pile next to the skin, and it is remarkably good at wicking. When the sheepskin starts to 'clump' with use, use a small wire-tined brush after washing to remove hairs and separate the clumps.

Training aids

The use (and misuse) of training aids is currently a hot topic in equestrian training circles, despite the fact that there is little evidence for their effectiveness. Many designers have invented systems that purport to assist the 'correct' development of muscles, action and particularly topline. Some vets are advising the use of training aids to rehabilitate from injury or strengthen a weak body. It can be tempting to incorporate a gadget, particularly with time pressure and the drive for quick results, but there are some basic principles to consider.

Things take time – back to that old chestnut again. Packing muscle is not the same as strengthening muscle; to develop strength, the body needs to be gradually stressed but also to use its posture correctly and effectively. Going back to the Ring of Muscles concept, any training aid that prevents a horse from achieving correct biomechanical posture is working against this. Most training aids connect the horse's body to its mouth or head. As the pressure increases on these sensitive areas, the horse will learn to avoid the contact provided by the aid, and will compress its body behind the pressure as much as it can, thereby preventing the forward, down and out action of the head and neck and increasing physiological and psychological stress. It is easy to see how horses used to training aids learn to break their neck posture in the upper cervical area so they can avoid the contact. Remember, as yet there are no equine training aids or gadgets with good research evidence of biomechanical effectiveness.

The biomechanical rider

In our work it is as if we give each rider a tool kit, or refine the tool kit that she already has. This 'first tool kit' concerns her body, for its position and texture; its asymmetry; and its stability (or lack of it), affect the horse profoundly. In both you and your horse there are places where movement 'goes through', and places where it is blocked, deadened, dissipated or disorganized. As you affect him and he affects you, the influence of your body mechanics, for good or ill, is enormous – but this is rarely acknowledged. Many trainers, for instance, ignore the rider's way of sitting and think only of teaching her to ride the school movements. These form the rider's 'second tool kit'; and when done correctly (from a body that functions well) they undoubtedly have profound training effects. But we cannot afford to negate the exquisite sensitivity that horses have to our body mechanics.[21]

The aim of many horse owners is to enjoy their riding, but this is often explained with a little guilt behind it, as they are aware and concerned that they are not 'the best rider' for their horse. By 'best rider' people often

Dorothy Marks demonstrates how an effective rider carries their own weight to encourage the horse to bascule – seat 'down'.

Dorothy Marks demonstrates how an effective rider carries their own weight to encourage the horse to bascule – seat 'lifting'.

mean talented and/or successful, but with an intelligent, disciplined approach to riding practice, and with individual coaching, every rider can learn good basics that will allow them to carry their own weight as a rider. Mary Wanless has spent many years researching and coaching riders of every level of ability, and her Ride With Your Mind rider coaching system helps riders to unpick and practise exactly what they as individuals need to do to unlock their riding ability. Ride With Your Mind brings the principles of neuroscience and psychology to the coaching arena, linking the rider's personal perceptions of their lived riding experience with their ability to influence the horse's posture and biomechanics. The basic principles taught gradually refine the rider's awareness of alignment, tone, connection or 'plugging in', application of core strength, balance and symmetry, and integrate learning theory, rider fitness, expert performance theory and mindful riding.

Riding style and its relationship to hoof function is difficult to study owing to the number of confounding variables present in the ridden context. However, in 1998 a Canadian study found that training horses for riding may have implications for their hoof form and balance. The study tested how much basic riding style affected the scale of hoof deformation and how the pressure forcing the deformation was distributed around the hoof wall. The study was conducted on very small numbers of horses, but the authors discussed some interesting findings:

- the addition of a rider caused a marked and significant decrease in strain at the quarters in the front feet, bringing the forces coming down the leg into closer alignment with the hoof tubules. The authors suggest that this is possibly due to the trained horses used in the study compensating for the weight of the rider by taking more of the combined load on the hind feet, perhaps by placing the feet further underneath the body.
- the same ridden trained horses redistributed the forces transmitted during the stance phase of the stride from the quarters and heels more along the length at the toe, leading to less flare at the quarters.

It is probable that the repeated deformation of the wall during many strides influences the change in hoof shape over a period of weeks or months, perhaps mediated by a cellular response in the germinative layers at the coronary band and secondary lamellae.[22]

In conclusion, to ensure that horses are prepared for the life their humans want them to lead, and stay as healthy and sound as possible throughout their lives, it is vital to establish an understanding of how to best support them. Biomechanics will always provide a range of models that help interpret correct function and unpick potential problems. If it looks like a stick and feels like a stick, it probably is a stick. Both humans and horses are complex and fascinating organisms, but none of the way they function is magic or beyond interpretation. Biomechanics allows cross-referencing between disciplines, and challenges one to think laterally, which can be extremely effective in illuminating dark corners.

REFERENCES

[1] Pollitt, C. (1992). Clinical anatomy and physiology of the normal equine foot. *Equine Veterinary Education*, 4(5):219–24.
[2] Merck. (2015). *Merck Veterinary Manual*. Retrieved April 2015 from http://www.merckvetmanual.com/mvm/musculoskeletal_system/lameness_in_horses/overview_of_lameness_in_horses.html.
[3] Rooney, J.R. (1998). *The Lame Horse*. Neenah: Russell Meerdink Company Ltd.
[4] Myers, T.W. (2009). *Anatomy Trains: Myofascial meridians for manual and movement therapists*, 2nd edn. Toronto: Churchill Livingston Elsevier.
[5] Bennett, D. (2012). *Principles of Conformation Analysis*, vols I–III, ed. E.M. Prinz. Boulder, Colorado: Equine Network.
[6] *Ibid.*
[7] Bowker, R. (2008). *Contrasting Structures of Good and Bad Feet*. Author's personal lecture notes, Barefootworks Seminar, Aberdeenshire, Scotland.
[8] Codrington, W.S. (1955). *Know Your Horse*, 7th edn, ed. P. Gray. London: J.A. Allen.

9. Bennett, *Principles of Conformation Analysis.*

10. *Ibid.*

11. *Ibid.*

12. Stubbs, N.C. and Clayton, H.M. (2008). *Activate Your Horse's Core: Unmounted exercises for dynamic mobility, strength and balance.* Lansing, Michigan: Sport Horse Publications.

13. Marks, D. (2014). *Posture and Collection.* Author's personal lecture notes. Barefootworks Seminar, Aberdeenshire, Scotland, UK.

14. Bennett, *Principles of Conformation Analysis.*

15. Marks, *Posture and Collection.* Author's personal lecture notes.

16. Karl, P. (2008). *Twisted Truths of Modern Dressage: a search for a classical alternative.* Brunsbeck, Austria: Cadmos Verlag GmbH.

17. Sandel, K. (2015). R*iding in Lightness: A whistlestop tour of the principles of Legerete.* Author's personal lecture notes, Bruton, Somerset, UK.

18. *Ibid.*

19. Weishaupt, M.A., Wiestner, T., von Peinen, K., Roepstorff, R., van Weeren, K. and Meyer, H. (2006). Effect of head and neck position on vertical ground reaction forces and innerlimb coordination in the dressage horse ridden at walk and trot on the treadmill. *Equine Veterinary Journal,* Supplement 36: Equine Exercise Physiology.

20. A.J. Equestrian. (2015). *Sculptaseat Market Research Survey Findings.* Aberdeen: Corporate publication.

21. Wanless, M. (2002). *Ride With Your Mind Essentials.* North Pomfret, Vermont: Trafalgar Square Books.

22. Summerley, H.L., Thomason, J.J. and Bignell, W.W. (1998). Effect of rider and riding style on the deformation of the front hoof wall in Warmblood horses. *Equine Veterinary Journal,* Supplement 26: The Equine Hoof.

6 Transitions

MANAGING TRANSITIONS FOR BOTH HORSE AND HUMAN

There are thousands to tell you it cannot be done,
There are thousands to prophesy failure,
There are thousands to point out to you one by one,
The dangers that wait to assail you.
But just buckle in with a bit of a grin,
Just take off your coat and go to it;
Just start in to sing as you tackle the thing
That 'cannot be done' and you'll do it.[1]

The act of reading this book suggests that the reader has already chosen to take an ethological approach to horse keeping, or otherwise is very interested in integrating an up-to-date evidence base into their current paradigm. The authors hope that this book supports a substantial and long-lasting shift in the reader's personal perspective. During the last fifteen years the authors and their colleagues in Barefootworks have had direct contact with hundreds if not thousands of people who have decided to keep their horses barefoot. Reflecting on

The author Anni Stonebridge and friends descending Mount Keen, Eastern Cairngorms.

these experiences, it is clear that the choice to transition is crucially embedded in the act of making significant changes in thought patterns, associations, beliefs and behaviours. Maintaining new behaviours over time can be hard work and requires considerable planning and commitment. The authors would like to acknowledge the significant changes that many clients have successfully achieved. The positive improvements in the health and well-being of the horses that share their lives are testament to this fact.

Redundant peripheral loading devices.

PRO COMMENT

Why include a specific chapter on change? In our daily work as hoof care professionals, being agents of change is part of the job. HCPs also work within a chronological timeframe. Barefoot hoof care is not the same as it was as little as ten years ago, and we can anticipate that there is significantly more change ahead. We regularly find ourselves helping clients towards education and resilience on behalf of their horses, and we would like to share that insight further.

shod to barefoot. Other people's experiences may be enlightening but there is no one way a horse should be expected to transition. Some horses may show no differences at all, others will need a lot of support.

Professional support

The support of an experienced HCP should be arranged at least one shoeing cycle before the shoes are removed. Most professionals

PREPARING TO DE-SHOE

Anticipating a transition process from shoeing a horse to a barefoot lifestyle has become a normal belief for people choosing barefoot horse keeping. Many years of assisting horses and humans in transition give insight into common themes and factors.

Individual experiences

Encouragingly, today more and more horses never experiencing shoeing. However, for those that have, each horse is an individual and will have a different experience of changing from

The author Jane Cumberlidge at work.

schedule their diaries at least one trimming cycle in advance and may not have space at short notice, but will be very happy to discuss and give advice on preparing for transition. The week a shod horse becomes overdue is too late to call a barefoot specialist.

Preparing the whole horse

The transition period may place additional demands on the rest of the horse's body. Preparing the horse by establishing a suitable diet and management plan well in advance can pay huge dividends in horse comfort and easy transitioning. Using a barefoot friendly vitamin and mineral source and reducing sugar and starch intake, as discussed in Chapter 4, are useful preparatory steps. Gradual internal changes can be established several months in advance, and will ensure the horse is as healthy as possible and growing strong horn before it becomes completely reliant upon it. The authors' experience in the UK suggests that many horses find transitioning less challenging during the winter months. Shorter daylight length means the grass is less active and variable in carbohydrate content. The main forage source (hay or haylage) may be providing a more consistent nutritional profile. The hormonal state of most healthy horses is also more stable during the winter months than during the breeding season.

Do barefoot horses abscess during transition?

Despite historical rumours to the contrary, in the authors' experience abscesses are not routinely part of the transition process. There is no evidence that barefoot horses are more susceptible to abscesses than shod horses. In fact, barefoot horse keepers are probably more successful at finding out and identifying the

causes of repeat abscessing than shod horse keepers.

When the shoes come off, the white line may appear recessed, or the hoof material can be crumbly, or black and smelly in the white line area. This is a common 'under shoe' situation; it isn't healthy, but it will improve as the whole of the hoof begins to receive proper stimulation. If there are pockets of white line infection, it is a good time to discuss them with the HCP. Vitamin and mineral supplementation should be part of a treatment regime for white

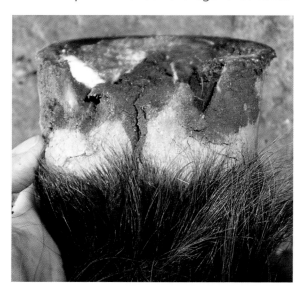

Recently de-shod foot.

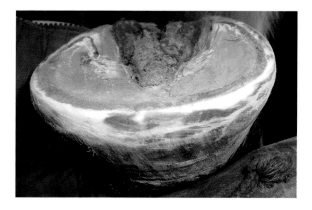

Same foot subsequent trim.

line infection, as should cleaning and 'hoof friendly' general hygiene treatment.

Trimming at de-shoeing

The day the shoes come off, the horse should receive a minimal trim, which should just address areas of the hoof wall exposed to extreme leverage. No sole horn should be removed unless it is excessively built up. Overlaid and very steep bars should be gently relieved if the HCP evaluates that they are likely to provide a pressure point. Where horses have very high heels or extremely long toes, careful balancing can be started, but the slower the better so the body has time to respond. Regular body work can assist horses facing substantial biomechanical change, so ensure that bodyworkers and HCP share their assessments, and understand each other's approach and care plans.

Age

There are some important considerations in transitioning the older horse. In the wild horses live to an average of fifteen years. Many domestic horses may have many more years beyond that age. There are some critical periods to bear in mind relating to age and transitioning. All horses, regardless of breed, skeletally mature at the same rate: 'no horse on earth, of any breed, at any time, is or has been mature before the age of six (plus or minus six months)'.[2] Before skeletal maturity, the horse has the best chance of rehabilitating successfully from shoeing as its active skeletal growth is on its side. For instance, research suggests that between six and eight years may be a critical period for cartilage development. The longer a horse has been in shoes, the more extensively its bones will have remodelled and be potentially osteoporotic. Older horses do not have enough lifetime to completely remodel bony changes, but they can be made much more comfortable and being barefoot can significantly improve joint mobility. Improvements can and do take place but at a slower rate than in a younger horse.[3]

An experienced HCP should be able to generally assess if a horse has well-developed hoof structure. The authors have recorded significant soft tissue rehabilitation in horses up to fifteen years old in their practice; beyond that age rehabilitation is limited.

WHAT TO EXPECT ONCE THE SHOES ARE OFF

When the HCP drives away, and an owner looks down at the feet of a newly barefoot horse, it can throw up a multitude of emotions. Planning and activity are essential to negotiate transition and can help the process go smoothly. With enough planning and support, transitioning is in most cases straightforward. The owner now has full responsibility for their horse's hoof care; there is no part of caring for its feet that they are legally excluded from, even to the extent of picking up tools and trimming them. As the authors have stressed, professional hoof care is a complex endeavour and should not be undertaken lightly, but there are huge advantages for owners who educate themselves about the hoof.

Turnout

In preparation for de-shoeing, establishing permanent turnout on conformable surfaces will establish daily movement patterns. Removing the shoes and then keeping a horse indoors can actually increase discomfort, even given a comfortable bed, as movement stimulates circulation. Research on stabled and turned-out horses indicates that normal grazing patterns in permanent turnout can increase the number of steps a horse takes by up to a third, which will gently stimulate transitioning feet to rehabilitate more quickly than static weight-bearing.

Exercise

Horses should be kept active when their shoes come off. Hand walking, ground work and riding will all support the progress of a transitioning horse. Removing shoes just before an important competition or a long journey is not a sensible idea. Movement is essential to help a horse become functional barefoot. Start off gradually, hand walking for up to forty minutes a day in the first week, or riding for half an hour on conformable ground, and then gradually increase duration as they become able to cope with it. Pay close attention to behavioural tension markers, and use boots and pads if they seem reluctant to travel over uneven surfaces. Horses have fantastic memories, and if they start to associate uneven surfaces with discomfort, it can take many years to replace that belief, even when they are completely functional. 'No pain, no gain' does not apply to horses during transition or at any other time; they do not benefit from being forced to 'just get on with it'.

Regular care

During the early days, cleaning up the horse's feet, checking and disinfecting them a few times a week is all the practical hoof care owners should need to do. Soaking is unnecessary and can contribute to feet that are too soft for the horse to be comfortable. In very wet weather, bringing the horse onto a clean, dry, absorbent bed (not straw or rubber mats) for a few hours can help dry them out. Keeping notes or a journal about comfort

level over the first few weeks can help identify patterns.

Troubleshooting

Some de-shod horses are initially sound on all surfaces immediately after the shoes are off, but become uncomfortable in the next few days. Sometimes other people categorize the discomfort as lameness, and owners may have to deal not only with an uncomfortable horse but with other people's criticism. It can be a difficult time, but barefoot horse keepers can deflect criticism by showing that they are being responsible by recruiting professional help, actively addressing the horse's comfort in the ways discussed, and understanding that there is a process and care plan involved.

There is no direct comparison in human health to de-shoeing, but using the analogy of permanently wearing extra tight walking boots, and the pins and needles, numbness and pain when they are removed, may be useful to explain what is going on. Any discomfort should start to reduce in a week or so; if it does not, then an HCP or vet should be consulted.

KEEPING PERSPECTIVE

Observing

Lots of changes are likely to take place in the newly de-shod foot. If the shoes have caused damage to the hoof wall, the wall may crumble around the nail holes before the new horn grows down and a new, intact wall comes in. It will take anything up to nine months to completely re-grow a hoof capsule. Exercise, nutrition and hygiene need to be managed effectively. It is a fascinating process, and barefoot horse keepers can become a little hoof-obsessed. The authors like owners who take pictures and prepare questions when they notice things that are interesting or concerning. Many trimmers enjoy a good discussion, and are more than happy to talk about the details. Keep in mind that there are no absolutes, and there may be a multitude of reasons behind some of the things observed. A supportive HCP is the first point of contact when hoof problems appear; they may also point out correlations, but identifying causality is more complex.

Record keeping

Taking pictures and video in the days before and after de-shoeing can definitely be useful, but it can take up to two years for a horse to go through all the possible changes to the feet that allow them to function well barefoot. HCPs often keep detailed notes and photo records themselves in order to keep track of changes. Barefootworks uses carbon copy sheets so that owners also have the opportunity to keep a file on their horse's hoof health.

Posting 'this is my horse's feet after the shoes came off today' pictures on the internet may well lead to a confusing array of 'advice'. Always refer to an HCP for help and ask plenty of questions. They are likely to have

seen and supported many more horses than online 'helpers'. Most busy HCPs do not have enough time to regularly offer online advice in internet fora. Without assessing the horse in person, most professionals would also agree that it is irresponsible to do so, as issues can be complex and a photo does not provide enough information on which to base robust advice. Professionals have also spent considerable resources in terms of time and money developing their knowledge and skill base, yet would be expected not to charge for online advice.

HOOF SUPPORT

Boots and pads

Even if at the time of de-shoeing the horse appears comfortable barefoot, obtain a set of well fitting boots and pads for it in case the situation changes. Findings from dissection suggest that internal hoof circulation and nerve behaviour are damaged by the peripheral loading shoes provide, leading to a substantial loss of sensation in the feet. If the blood flow inside the feet has been restricted, as it returns in the subsequent few days some horses may well need additional support. There are many choices in terms of boot sizing and design, and helpful online suppliers can advise on the best option for each horse's hoof shape. It is not a sign of failure to need to use boots and pads.

Record keeping after a trim.

Renegade Hoof Boots.

Equine Fusion Ultimate Hoof Boots.

Easycare RX Therapy Boots.

Easycare Comfort Pads – variable densities.

they are working on. Hoof boots allow the rider to give the horse a barefoot lifestyle but allow them to move in comfort and without anticipating changes in surface.

There is an extensive range of hoof boot designs to choose from, and a wide price range. In comparison to the limited performance of early boot designs, products are now available that provide firm and robust, or minimal solar support depending on the sensitivity of the horse. Modern boot designs are also substantially more user-friendly, both for the horse and for the rider. In the past many HCPs spent a lot of time adjusting and modifying boots for clients. Unfortunately, it is not cost-effective for most professionals to offer a boot-fitting service beyond measurement, but good support and fitting advice can be obtained from online boot suppliers.

With the wide variation in hoof morphology, it is unreasonable to expect any one boot design to cover all eventualities. The ideal hoof for boot fitting is paradoxically often the one that does not actually need the protection of boots, but the best fit will be possible on feet that:

• have even dorsal wall angles with no flares or bulges;
• are trimmed for good biomechanics, with balanced toe length and heel height;
• have appropriate wall length around the distal margin; and
• have a peripheral bevel at least around the toe from quarter to quarter.

As discussed in earlier chapters, the grazing environment and UK climate often stimulate changes in internal hoof function that can lead to digestive and hoof discomfort.

The authors and their colleagues in Barefootworks advise that hoof boots and pads are an essential part of barefoot horse keeping in the UK. Observation and practice of horses being ridden on different surfaces suggests that horses are very sensitive to the conformability and predictability of the surface

There are not many horses who permanently satisfy all these conditions, which presents a challenge for boot designers. Manufacturers have recognized this, so it is very useful to discuss individual needs with a hoof boot supplier stocking many different ranges. These companies often operate boot hire and trial services, and carry a second-hand stock. Horses can quickly change hoof shape and size.

An experienced HCP will be able to advise on what changes are likely to occur, will measure up for correct fitting and may carry a second-hand stock or have other clients looking to sell. In the authors' experience most horses go down sizes in their unshod state, but a percentage of shod horses have feet which have contracted beyond their optimum size. These horses may decontract and require wider boots in time.

Barefoot horse keepers report a range of problems with boot performance, as follows. (This list does not include 'coming off', as it is unreasonable to expect every boot to stay on on every occasion.)

- Problems getting a close fit on sub-optimal feet.
- Problems fitting horses with significant feathering.
- Lack of choice for extreme sizes, either extremely large or extremely small. Considering the number of owners of small ponies with laminitis, this is a substantial market niche ready to be exploited by boot designers.
- Problems keeping boots central with feet that torque.
- Application difficulties and poorly designed fittings.
- Boots needing modifications, such as peripheral bevelling or heat adjustment, in order to be properly functional. Any modification made by the purchaser or HCP is likely to contravene the product warranty.
- Rubbing problems and heel bulb compression.
- Problems keeping pads in place.
- Boots not draining in wet conditions.
- Poor boot hygiene when worn for long periods.

Occasionally the authors have encountered clients who are put off by the expense of buying boots. When comparing the cost and durability of a set of four boots with shoeing costs, they make a substantial cost saving, and are an integral tool to use for owners serious about barefoot horse keeping. A set of boots under normal use will last approximately eighteen months. Even if purchasing boots at the top of the price range, a set of four will cost somewhat less than shoeing over the same period (including eighteen months of six weekly trimming visits).

What boots need to provide

The principal design assumption behind hoof boots is sole protection, but, as with human footwear, the design of boots needs to achieve different things for different situations. As designs have evolved, the original clumpy, heavy, inflexible early models have gradually become lighter and more streamlined.

Equine Fusion Hoof Boots in action.

PRO COMMENT

I like the flexibility of performance boots with thinner soles, and the fact that they provide minimal thickness between the sole and the ground, somewhat like minimal trainers. Saying that, I don't ever rely on those boots for traction, just for a small amount of protection. I spend a lot of time training my horses to learn to balance on slopes, mud, short grass, ice, etc, so I rely on them gradually learning to predict and adjust their balance to cope with conditions. If there is a risk of slipping, I am more concerned that the horse will feel unstable and lose confidence, so I am more likely to go totally barefoot and slower so the horse can get the best proprioceptive feedback. If they are tender, then that's an internal issue I need to sort out, but boots and pads are supportive during exercise while I sort it.

I used to stock a lot of boots, but, rather like saddles, I found that you have to accept they are a tool, and understand the differences between them. It can be a process of analysis to get a working solution for some horses. For instance, twisting problems are usually not the boot – the horse is twisting the foot inside the boot whilst it is on the ground, which is probably coming from a unilateral postural difference. If it is just a little bit of twisting (a centimetre or so), that's acceptable as they still provide the solar support I want even if they aren't perfectly aligned.

I want to give the horse the consistent experience of having some protection, but not for it to get to rely on it. I do want a little conformability, which I can adjust with pads, but I also want the horse to feel the ground and learn not to fear it. This is a very specific psychological reason to use boots as much as a physiological one. Some horses anticipate substrate changes and learn to associate them with pain, which can then develop into a more substantial fear of surface variation. Repeatedly layering positive, pain-free, booted and balanced ridden experiences is a way of separating the emotions generated through anticipating pain and behaviour.

Performance boots are often used in competitive sports such as endurance riding, and are designed to be fitted to a functional, well trimmed hoof with good morphology. The soles of these boots are flexible, allowing the hoof to move, twist and expand as the horse weights and turns, and conform to the terrain but giving a degree of added support. This flexibility is essential so that the horse can feel the ground and adjust how it moves over different surfaces, thus avoiding injury.

General use boots are just that: boots for general use. They are often thicker in the sole, and are not as flexible as some of the performance models. Pads can easily be fitted to most boot styles, although this should be confirmed with the boot supplier prior to purchase if pads are required. They may also have deeper tread patterns to be durable, cope with variable terrain and mud.

Rehabilitation boots are a boon for horses with sensitive feet. They are easily applied, and can be used with pads and dressings. For some horses living with the effects of chronic laminitis, rehabilitation boots are essential for day-to-day comfort. Modern styles can also be used for exercise, making in-hand walking possible for horses with otherwise uncomfortable feet.

Pads

There are some booting systems that provide extensive pad density and 'cut out' pad options that make space for the frog with their boots. In the authors' experience, pads are very useful, and a selection of 6mm or 12mm mid-density pads is sufficient for most purposes. No observable difference has been noted in practice using more complex cut-outs, or firmer or softer density pads. Pad use is supported by research into hoof loading. Pressure measurements taken on rubber mats and concrete find that the area of the loaded foot when standing on rubber mats more than doubles in comparison to the foot standing on concrete. The pressure on the solar foot on rubber reduces to less than a quarter than when on concrete.[4] This gives support to even healthy barefoot hooves – horses choose to move on softer going given the opportunity.

HUMAN TRANSITIONS

New barefoot horse keepers are on the threshold of change and may also need support. The authors and their colleagues have all experienced clients for whom trimming appointments are 50 per cent horse support and 50 per cent human. Remember that change is a personal choice, and it is important to understand that moving towards any new belief and behaviour pattern is a dynamic process requiring commitment and practice. It needs to be – it is life-changing. The grandfather of change psychology, Griffith Edwards, explains: 'By and large building a new Jerusalem is difficult. By and large let people edge into something that they see as appropriate.'[5]

The authors' experience in research into how people make and sustain difficult personal changes informs how they support new barefoot horse keepers.

WHAT ARE THE NECESSARY FEATURES OF SUCCESSFUL CHANGE FOR THE BAREFOOT HORSE KEEPING HUMAN?

- Feeling that it can be done
- Enhancing motivation
- Defining the right goals for the horse and the human
- Choosing to identify as a barefoot horse keeper
- Maintaining commitment
- Developing effective support networks and social capital
- Marking the good feelings about change

Feeling that it can be done

People often exist on a continuum between optimism and realism. When preparing to make a change, finding good evidence by collecting facts, data and the experiences of others can help barefoot horse keepers evaluate their situation and estimate their chances of success. Self-education is an important part of barefoot horse keeping and allows people to take ownership of the journey they are on.

Enhancing motivation

It is important to ally motivation with commitment and action. For example, think of teenagers preparing for exams. Often they are motivated to study, but instead spend hours preparing revision timetables – hours that could be spending studying. Planning can help enhance personal commitment. Plans need to be individual and specific, with timeframes, deadlines and costings. Sharing a plan with other people can generate the energy and commitment needed to move from 'here' to 'there'.

The acronym SMART is useful in guiding planning. SMART stands for:

- Specific
- Measurable
- Achievable
- Realistic
- Timebound

Human activity in Dinnet Equine Herd Project.

Big plans like building and fencing can be overwhelming, but are do-able if chunked into small achievable steps. For example, walk round the field, take pictures and post them on the Facebook Paddock Paradise group and ask for ideas. These three steps are much more do-able than 'win the lottery and buy a forest'.

The steps on the plan need to be small enough to achieve relatively easily. Sharing thoughts can generate some good ideas, and help evaluate those ideas that are less useful, and the act of making regular contact with others to report on progress can seriously help with commitment.

Defining the right goals for the horse and the human

Appropriately defined and relevant goals are a big feature of successful change. Goals should be specific, but creative. Brainstorming is a useful technique, and the sharing of ideas can lead to openings into previously unknown possibilities.

Defining appropriate goals for the horse requires expert evaluation. Discussing individual needs with an HCP can often shed light on the detail of what changes in health and functionality might be expected.

Choosing to identify as a barefoot horse keeper

Regardless of what any individual's attitudes and beliefs are, somewhere in the world there will be other people who share them. If those people share the same resources and physical environment, it can lead to a 'peer preference' or 'group thinking' situation, where the choice to maintain good relationships with the group influences and can pressurize individual beliefs. Becoming fluent with change may require barefoot horse keepers to make visibly different choices from others, and can lead to unease and tension in yard environments. This is particularly evident in horse keeping social networks, which are frequently described as 'clique-y'. In these situations dealing with conflict is inevitable.

With a growth in knowledge and

REAL WORLD STORY: HOW THE DINNET EQUINE HERD PROJECT CAME ABOUT

One of the great things about having your passion as your job is that you can spend your time talking to people about things you really feel for, and these discussions can sometimes lead to something amazing. In an impassioned monologue in the pub with two good friends, I described how, despite all the things I did to make my horses happy at home, it seemed superficial. I wanted to let my horses live a life where their real needs came first, and where my convenience and need for contact were secondary. Watching my horses in my small, flat, paddock, I understood that it didn't matter how many gym balls, tracks, pea gravel areas, ad lib forage and interesting edible things I placed in the field, or how much time I spent connecting with them, it was still not really 'nourishing' in horse terms. If we had a bigger herd group the energy was better, but fewer than four and they only really responded to potential food appearing. I desperately wanted to find somewhere that defied conventional horse keeping, but my options at home were excruciatingly limited. Why did they like going out on the trail so much and get so excited? Home was boring.

'Well,' said my friend, 'there is that bit of rough land next to our paddocks. It belongs to the estate but the farm hasn't used it for a couple of years. The cattle used to escape and stampede up to our house but the area's quite big, I think they've decided re-fencing it isn't worth it.' The logistics fell into place comparatively easily. The charming manager from Dinnet Estate was enthusiastic about the project, I wrote a proposal and we came to an agreement in principle soon after we walked through the plot with him. He understood that what we wanted to do was not just three horsey girls wanting grazing for their ponies, and the Estate was keen to support local projects. What we wanted to do was to trial an ethological way of horse keeping that will hopefully have some lessons for other horse keepers in the UK, and it will lend some profile to the forward-thinking management of the Estate. We agreed a co-operative lease and this was the unassuming start of the Dinnet Equine Herd Project.

expectations of a brighter future, barefoot horse keepers can sometimes appear somewhat over-zealous. It is sensible to allow other people to make their own choices and not be critical. This is particularly reflected in the experiences with horse keepers who keep their animals in DIY livery or group self-boarding. People taking their horses barefoot can become the butt of considerable personal criticism. More people are making connections with the barefoot horse keeping community before taking their horse's shoes off, and if they are finding that their actions receive positive comments from others, this can considerably help their commitment to stay the course. For some individuals the internet may initially be

the only place to connect with like-minded individuals, but face-to-face contact will help confirm the choice to change.

Maintaining commitment

When life is difficult, sometimes it may feel easier to return to old behaviour. Fear of the unknown can promote a lot of internal 'what if x happens . . .' style night-time anxiety. Many HCPs occasionally say they wish they could just go back to a time when a hack was just a hack, and someone else looked after their horse's feet. For example, an owner begins to feel that their livery situation is negatively impacting

Typical UK livery yard.

on their horse's health. They want to find a new and more appropriate place to move the horse to, but the idea of first finding, then negotiating with and finally moving to a new yard seems like a challenge.

Over time, barefoot horse keepers can find that they no longer identify with their previous network of horse friends. This is an undeniably common occurrence, and can be emotional.

PRO COMMENT

In livery yard situations an owner may require much more support and may suffer a lot more extensive criticism because by their actions they challenge the group thinking. I have known owners decide to put their laminitic horses back out to grass, or put shoes back on them because they couldn't take the pressure any longer. Even though their convictions were towards making positive change, they were putting their heads above the parapet to do so. The dynamics in these yards are insidious and I try to get to know places where my clients can take their horses that are going to nourish their beliefs rather than judge them.

Developing effective support networks and social capital

Hoof care professionals will often link their clients with other barefoot horse keepers. Some also offer educational events, which are both occasions to learn and opportunities to meet like-minded people. Having a real-life support network can be an essential part of maintaining change.

Social media can be an excellent resource, when used sensibly. As well as virtual contact, Facebook can be a useful route to find real people locally. Most barefoot horse keepers are

Barefootworks Clinic.

more than happy to receive visitors and talk to a newbie about the changes they have made.

Social media and the internet

There is now a significantly large online barefoot community. The membership of the Barefoot Horse Owners Group UK on Facebook at the time of writing exceeded ten thousand. In the authors' opinion, entering large online groups is somewhat like visiting an exotic bazaar - it's best to keep a low profile and your money hidden away. There are many people in online communities who are there to provide genuine help and support, but there are also a few who will try to manipulate group trends to support their beliefs, and others who are using the internet to represent themselves as other than they are. Some discussion threads on topics such as feed products are used for commercial gain by unscrupulous companies who have vigilant online 'advisers'. These are paid staff who watch group activity, pick up people whose posts suggest that they are open to suggestion, and then recommend personal contact. Remember that feed companies are not independent, advisers will often be very

friendly and they will always try to supply a product. Effective and functional groups need to have very good moderation to manage online behaviour and prevent commercial companies from exploiting their members.

The bottom line in barefoot virtual communities is that most group members are amateur rather than professional, and therefore will have very limited experience. Large Facebook groups are useful, however, to monitor trends in behaviour, and for moral support when times are tough. It is important to remember that online 'friends' are not subject to the rules of real world relationships, and people do not behave in the same way as they would face to face.

Reliable online communities need strong moderation. Moderation of large groups is necessary in order to ensure that group behaviour reflects real-world behavioural standards. The Equine Cushings and Insulin Resistance Yahoo Group is often joined by people in crisis caring for a sick horse. Styled as an outreach group in 1999 by a horse owner with Cushings, at the time of writing this group had more than twelve thousand members and is an excellent place to obtain evidence-based advice in a crisis.

REAL LIFE STORY

When you can just watch them and you love it, and it feels like that is good enough to make you happy. These Zen-like experiences keep me on track. In their most crystal-clear form they have become way-markers that mark a place where I have felt most in touch with the universe. I can recall a few long moments at the end of the first long hill trip I made with barefoot friends. We were walking our horses south down a rocky mountain track. I was walking next to my horse and every so often he gently swung his nose over and touched the back of my arm. A stand of Scots pine trees away to the east made long shadows in the golden sun of the late afternoon. Every sound was amplified: the crunch of pebbles underfoot, the horses' breathing, the rhythm of our footsteps. My skin felt sunburned and dry, my hands were covered with sweat and dirt from my horse; I glanced down and my boots were covered in dust from the track. Before we began the descent our horses stood on the roof of the world. Those moments were pure, timeless miniatures in a stream of experience. I never want to hear a horse's shod feet strike rock again.

Horses enjoying the snow.

The ECIR Horse Yahoo group provides a place for everyone who has a horse with Cushing's Disease and Insulin Resistance in their care to share experiences, pass along veterinary knowledge, review the latest research, offer advice and help each other.[6]

Marking the good feelings about change

Although this point appears last in the list, it is probably the most important element of maintaining change. In the long term, the most powerful feature that sustains change is when it feels good, and when the efforts made have resulted in happy, relaxed, calm and healthy horses and when there is rarely a lameness in the herd, or a vet visits for anything other than routine care.

REFERENCES

[1] Guest, E.A. (1938). *It Couldn't be Done* (The Poetry Foundation). Retrieved 3 May 2015 from The Poetry Foundation: http://www. poetryfoundation.org/poem/173579.

[2] Bennett, D. (2008). www.equinestudies.org. Retrieved 3 May 2015 from Equine Studies: http://www.equinestudies.org/ranger_2008/ ranger_piece_2008_pdf1.pdf.

[3] Bowker, R. (2008). *Contrasting Structures of Good and Bad Feet*. Author's personal lecture notes, Barefootworks Seminar, Aberdeenshire, Scotland.

[4] Bowker, R.M. (2011). The concept of a good foot: its evolution and significance in a clinical setting. In P. Ramey, *Care and Rehabilitation of the Equine Foot*, Dexter, Missouri: Hoof Rehabilitation Publishing LLC, 2–34.

[5] Edwards, G. (2008, 23 August). *Griffith Edwards on personal change* (F.E. Drugs, Interviewer). FEAD.

[6] Equine Cushings and Insulin Resistance Horse Group. (1999, 8 December). *Equine Cushings and Insulin Resistance*. Retrieved 3 April 2015 from Equine Cushings and Insulin Resistance: https://groupd.yahoo.com/neo/groups/ EquineCushings/info.

7 Troubleshooting

COMMON PROBLEMS

Obesity

The horse evolved in an environment with significant seasonal variations in the availability of forage. As a response, the horse evolved to gain weight during seasons where forage is plentiful, and to lose weight during the winter with little risk to health.

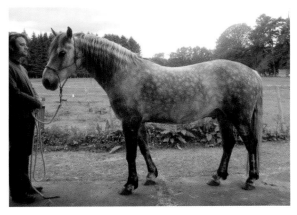

Obese gelding.

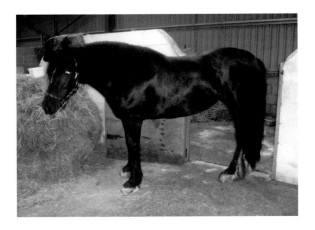

Dangerously obese cob mare.

The same gelding in good condition after losing approximately 60kg.

The causes of obesity are likely to be multifactorial, with the involvement of genetic and environmental factors, especially overfeeding in combination with minimal physical activity.[1]

As in other species, obesity in horses is linked with a range of chronic health conditions, including laminitis, insulin resistance, EMS and degenerative joint disease. Due to this evolutionary blueprint, gaining weight is much easier than losing weight, and obesity is a significant problem for domestic horses. Nutrition is discussed in greater detail in Chapter 4; here, it will suffice to say that in the authors' experience, most horse owners are much more likely to have to manage a horse's

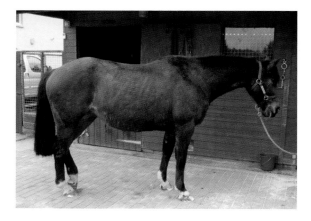

Moderately thin mare.

Thin horse. Image courtesy of eXtensionHorses (Utah_thin horse) [CC BY-SA 2.0 (http://creativecommons.org/licenses/by-sa/2.0)], via Wikimedia Commons.

weight loss than its weight gain, therefore this section includes some tried and tested weight loss and management strategies.

Body condition scoring and weight measurement

The horse's body condition measures the balance between intake and expenditure of energy. Body condition can be affected by a variety of factors such as: food availability, reproductive activities, weather, performance or work activities, parasites, dental problems, and feeding practices. The actual body condition of a horse can also affect its reproductive capability, performance ability, work function, health status, and endocrine status. Therefore, it is important to achieve and maintain proper body condition. In order to do this, one must evaluate body fat in relationship to body musculature. [2]

Body condition scoring is a system of evaluating and assigning a 'fat' score to different areas of the horse's body, and is an essential part of any weight management plan. There are a number of different well proven scoring systems, including the Henneke system, but the most commonly used in the UK is the Carroll and Huntington scoring

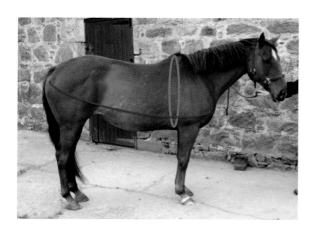

Weight tapes - where to measure.

system.[3] It is reproduced here with permission from the Blue Cross guide, Fat Horse Slim.[4]

Condition scoring should be accompanied by using a reliable weight tape and weight calculation formula. Measures should be taken monthly for maintenance and at two-weekly intervals during a weight loss programme. An

OPPOSITE: *Condition Scoring Chart. Reproduced with permission of the Blue Cross.*

Body scoring six point scale 0 to 5

0 = Emaciated		• No fatty tissue can be felt – skin tight over bones • Shape of individual bones visible • Marked ewe-neck • Very prominent backbone and pelvis • Very sunken rump • Deep cavity under tail • Large gap between thighs
1 = Very thin		• Barely any fatty tissue— skin more supple • Shape of bones visible • Narrow ewe-neck • Ribs easily visible • Prominent backbone, croup and tail head • Sunken rump, cavity under tail • Gap between thighs
2 = Very lean		• A very thin layer of fat under the skin • Narrow neck; muscles sharply defined • Backbone covered with a very thin layer of fat but still protruding • Withers, shoulders and neck accentuated • Ribs just visible, a small amount of fat building between them • Hip bones easily visible but rounded • Rump usually sloping flat from backgone to point of hips, may be rounded if horse is fit • May be a small gap between thighs
3 = Healthy weight		• A thin layer of fat under skin • Muscles on neck less defined • Shoulders and neck blend smoothly into body • Withers appear rounded over tips of bones • Back is flat or forms only a slight ridge • Ribs not visible but easily felt • A thin layer of fat building around tail head • Rump beginning to appear rounded • Hip bones just visible
4 = Fat		• Muscles hard to determine beneath fat layer • Spongy fat developing on crest • For deposits along withers, behind shoulders, and along neck • Ribs covered by spongy fat • Spongy fat around tail head • Gutter along back • Rump well rounded • From behind rump looks apple shaped • Hip bones difficult to feel
5 = Obese		• Horse takes on a bloated or blocky appearance • Muscles not visible – covered by a layer of flat • Pronounced crest with hard • Pads of fat along withers, behind shoulders, along neck and on ribs, ribs cannot be felt • Extremely obvious gutter along back and rump • Flank filled in flush • Lumps of fat around tail head • Very bulging apple shaped rump, bony points buried • Inner thighs pressing together

accurate formula for determining weight is as follows:[5]

Weight in pounds (all measurements in inches):
$$\frac{(\text{Heart girth} \times \text{heart girth}) \times \text{body length}}{330}$$

Weight in kilos (all measurements in centimetres):
$$\frac{(\text{Heart girth} \times \text{heart girth}) \times \text{body length}}{11877}$$

Several factors have a cumulative effect on weight gain in domestic horses:

- modern forages provide more energy-dense nutrition;
- horses are often sheltered and rugged in colder weather, therefore weight gained during the summer is not used to survive the winter; and
- domestic horse keeping provides ad lib winter forage without the horse having to expend any energy foraging for it.

Numerous studies examining the effect of calorie restriction on weight loss have found that there is wide individual variation in weight loss. In equines calorie restriction is likely to trigger a reduction in metabolic rate, actively reducing the rate of weight loss.[6] Research shows that it is difficult to anticipate what kind of weight an individual horse will lose on a calorie restricted diet alone.

Many different breeds were included in the above studies. Forages provided were a

Forage analysis highlights that some forages will provide considerably higher calories per mouthful than others. If forage has not been analysed, it is not possible to know what the horse is eating per mouthful.

combination of grass hay, alfalfa hay, straw and a feed balancer. The digestible energy content of the forage was analysed in some studies, but was not highlighted in others.

Consumption

Ponies have been observed to consume 40 per cent of their daily dry matter intake during three hours of pasture turnout. Another study found that they can ingest up to 1 per cent of their bodyweight in three hours of pasture turnout. Based on these findings, it could be possible for them to consume 8 per cent of their bodyweight in a 24-hour period – for a pony that weighs 300kg, that means up to 24kg in a day.

A useful strategy to manage consumption is to slow down the horse's feeding rate. Many people use small-holed haynets, and invest in slow feeding systems, which allow a trickle feeding rate. Using a slow feeder can mitigate long periods without forage, which can elevate the risk of gastric ulcers and increase stress or frustration for the horse.

Obesity and exercise

Combining calorie restriction and daily physical activity is essential for long-term weight loss and maintenance. Studies in both humans and horses have shown that a combined approach results in far greater weight loss than with calorie restriction alone.

For sedentary animals, introduce exercise at three sessions per week, including twenty to thirty minutes of hand walking, riding or lunging in walk and a little trot.

Once exercise has been introduced, increase the number, duration and intensity of the

Moderate work includes regular lungeing.

Light work – hacking.

Hard work – one of Barefootworks clients eventing at Burgie Horse Trials.

For extremely obese animals, obtain veterinary advice before starting an exercise programme. Carrying large amounts of additional weight can increase stress on the body as a whole and must be managed appropriately. The horse may need to lose a percentage of its bodyweight before beginning to exercise, and riding may be damaging.

sessions. This is important as the body quickly adjusts to activity levels. If exercise levels are not increased, they will stop being useful to weight loss. Many people find it difficult to accurately estimate how much exercise is enough. The National Research Council[7] defines workload as:

Maintenance	Grass or stable kept. Not in any work.
Light Work	Hacking and recreational riding between one and three times per week for up to an hour each time. Includes mainly walk and trot, but with a small amount of canter work.
Medium Work	Recreational riding, schooling, showing, breaking and training and low-level competition work. Ridden between three and five times per week for up to an hour at a time. Walk, trot and canter work, some low-level jumping and/or some lateral work.
Hard Work	Polo ponies, horses in race training, novice to intermediate eventing, advanced show jumping, advanced dressage and hunting. Schooling up to five to six days for an hour each day. Lateral work, jump work and fast work may all be included in the schooling sessions.
Very Hard Work	Racing (including trotting), advanced eventing, long-distance endurance riding and hunting.

OBESITY MANAGEMENT STRATEGIES

- Use *weight tapes with a formula, and body condition scoring* monthly for maintenance purposes and bi-weekly if a horse is on a weight loss plan.
- *Forage analysis and weighing hay* are accurate ways to determine and manage a horse's intake – check that your forage provides less than 10 per cent (non-structural carbohydrates) sugar and starch ESC combined.
- Hay or hay substitutes should be provided at 1.5 per cent of the *current* bodyweight of the horse.

- If minimal weight loss occurs after six weeks, the daily ration can be reduced to 1.25 per cent, and then, if still resistant after twelve weeks, to 1 per cent. With forage restriction, efforts must be made to encourage trickle feeding, with at least four deliveries of forage per day.
- Barley or oat straw can be substituted for up to 50 per cent of the forage ration to *lower the calorific value* of the forage. Ensure that the straw is clean of grains, which will increase its calorific value, and has not been chemically treated.
- Soaking hay - complete immersion in a large volume of fresh water – for 30–60

minutes will leach out some of the sugar content.

- Place a horse's forage in small-holed haynets or slow feeders to reduce their intake rate.
- Severely restrict or eliminate pasture grazing, particularly in the longer days of summer when the plant growth and sugar content will be at its highest.
- Provide a daily vitamin or mineral balancer and sea salt, as most forages are inadequate. The gold standard is a balancer custom-designed to fill in the nutritional gaps identified through forage analysis, but there are some very effective products available off the shelf. Make sure a balancer does not contain additional sugar, fillers or iron.
- Introduce a *progressive exercise regime* and be realistic about what activity levels the horse is doing.
- Grazing muzzles can be helpful with managing grass intake, but some horses find wearing a muzzle very difficult and can become aggressive or depressed. Make sure the muzzle is fitted comfortably and the horse can eat and drink when wearing it.

THRUSH

For many years thrush was attributed to fungal infection. However, research now shows that it is not fungal but an anaerobic bacterial infection. Although there are many bacteria that can cause thrush infection, fusobacterium necrophorum is commonly responsible. Fusobacterium necrophorum is a normal inhabitant of the gastrointestinal tracts of animals and humans. Since this bacteria is present in animal faeces and pretty much all soil samples, the horse's hooves will be regularly exposed to it. Fusobacterium necrophorum is anaerobic, which means it

thrives in dark, moist environments that have minimal or no exposure to oxygen.

Thrush most often infects the central sulcus of the frog, the collateral grooves and along the frog/sole junction. Although not as common, thrush has also been seen to infect the white line and sole of the hoof.

Thrush infects the collateral grooves and the frog of a pony with co-existing PPID and laminitis.

Thrush has frequently been associated with dirty or unhygienic living conditions. However, this does not explain why some horses get it and others don't when they are kept in the same living conditions (same soil, feed, management). There are some theories that suggest that a hoof with optimal structure and plenty of movement should self clean, thereby reducing the risk of thrush becoming a major problem. However, in moist, muddy and therefore anaerobic conditions, it seems that thrush infections are common.

For some horses with Cushings Syndrome, resistance to this bacterial infection appears to be limited. Even in hygienic conditions with daily treatment, thrush can be a significant challenge. If a horse has persistent infections that attack the whole of the underside of the hoof, including the defoliating sole, discussing the possibility of Cushings with the vet may be a sensible decision.

In humans with diabetes, bacterial skin and nail infections are common due to peripheral vascular disruption, and there may be a similar infection pathway linked to circulatory restriction at work here.

Signs and symptoms

Fusobacterium necrophorum causes a black, smelly, oily discharge which is often seen in and/or around the frog, central sulcus and collateral grooves. Thrush infection often causes a foul smell, which can be noticed when picking out the hooves or while trimming. A hoof that has become infected with thrush may also be very tender around the frog and collateral grooves. Also commonly seen is a disintegration of healthy frog tissue.

Thrush around the peripheral sole after shoe removal.

Left untreated, thrush can cause bleeding, pus, inflammation and lameness. In rare cases thrush infection can spread to internal tissues, sometimes requiring antibiotics to eliminate. Where this is the case, common signs are heat and inflammation in the hoof and/or leg and mild lameness; contact the vet immediately.

Prevention

The best way to prevent thrush is to minimize environmental conditions that favour bacterial development. In very wet conditions, arrange for the horse to be in a dry place for a minimum of four hours to allow its feet to dry out. Use clean and highly absorbent bedding, hose/wash off excess mud and pick out the feet. Make sure the horse receives regular five weekly trims. Some people report that preventative soaking in apple cider vinegar solution at a ratio of 1:4, or Milton at a ratio of 1:10, can be effective. Other management strategies include regular exercise, removal of droppings from paddocks and inclusion of hard standing in the horse's living enclosure.

Hoof care

Thrush does not clear up instantly and may take days or even weeks depending on the severity of the infection. The most obvious sign that it is clearing up is the disappearance of the foul smell and black, oily secretions. If the thrush bacteria or treatments have destroyed living tissue, the hoof may be tender until healthy tissue is regenerated.

A number of treatments have been found to be effective for thrush infection and vets will sometimes prescribe topical sprays. The table below details other remedies that have been found to be effective, and which may not be as costly as special treatments:

Symptom severity	Intervention	Protocol
Mild/preventative	Soaking in apple cider vinegar solution, 1:4 ratio	Preventative – weekly hoof scrubbing for one minute per hoof with Betadine or Hibiscrub Solution
	Soaking in Milton solution, 1:10 ratio	Weekly hoof soaking for ten minutes per hoof using apple cider vinegar or Milton solution
	Scrubbing with Betadine solution or Hibiscrub solution 1:10 ratio	Proprietary hoof care products such as those from Red Horse Products Ltd can be useful for prevention and management.
Moderate/severe	Daily scrubbing with Betadine solution or Hibiscrub solution, 1:10 ratio	Daily soaking or scrubbing for one week. Four times weekly in week two. Twice during week three.
In severe cases the authors recommend horse owners consult their vet	Iodine and Chlorhexidine (or other antibacterial cream) mixed into a water-based hydrating cream until it has the consistency of mustard. (Chlorhexidine is commonly available as Hibiscrub.)	Clean the hoof as above. Apply neat hydrogen peroxide to the affected areas. Leave in contact for 30 seconds and then rinse away with clean water. Dry the hoof, apply the iodine and chlorhexidine cream, packing the collateral grooves and central sulcus with cotton wool. Cover with a hoof boot to keep the hoof clean.
		For severe cases keep the treatment constantly in contact with the hoof for five to seven days, using a hoof boot or poultice boot, then apply daily for three to four hours in week two, and twice in week three.
	Equimins cream	Equimins does a similar job to the treatment above, but without the gooey mess. Wash the hoof in betadine solution, apply hydrogen peroxide to the affected areas as described above, and pack and treat the same way.
	Sugardine paste Povidone iodine and table sugar mixed into a paste.	Clean hoof with mild soap and apply paste daily or twice daily to infected areas.

In humans, *fusobacterium necrophorum* is associated with bacterial throat infections. In some cases these infections progress to become peritonsillar abscesses. There may be an as-yet-undefined relationship between this bacterial infection in the foot and hoof abscesses.

WHITE LINE DISEASE

White Line Disease (WLD), White Line Infection and Seedy Toe are all names for bacterial and fungal infection in the stratum medium horn situated next to the yellow-coloured actual white line. The white line itself is rarely infected but may be absent adjacent to the infected area. This area supports the margin of the sole as it joins the hoof wall and can be subject to considerable leverage forces.

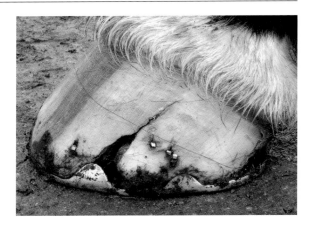

White line infection maintains a crack in a shod hoof.

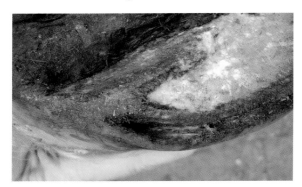

A mild case of white line infection.

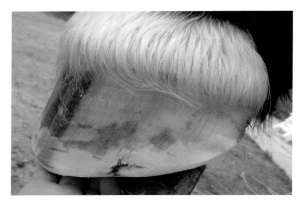

The same crack nine months later with barefoot trimming and treatment.

White line infection can travel extensively in the stratum medium.

Although it is called a disease, it is not something that you would treat with antibiotics. The problem is caused by common fungi and bacteria entering the hoof as a secondary infection, after an initial hoof problem or imbalance. Predisposing factors can include laminitis, flaring, nutritional deficiency or any hoof imbalance that has caused hoof wall separation. Anaerobic bacteria enter the hoof capsule through the weakened connection and eat the nutrient-rich inner portion – the stratum medium – of the hoof wall. Studies have identified twenty-five different strains of common environmental fungi alone that have been cultured from WLD samples.

The most obvious external sign is a black line or separation at the inner edge of the hoof wall or toe, or black, crumbly, smelly areas within cracks or fissures. An HCP may decide to open up the infected area. When examined closely, the areas affected by bacteria are the whiter areas around the top edge of the infection. The crumbly material that the bacteria leave behind then becomes infected by fungi. The fungi absorb oxygen, and serve to keep conditions anaerobic for the bacteria.

White line disease is particularly interesting in several ways: there is discussion as to whether it is actually a symptom of, or the result of, low-grade laminitis, and the symbiotic relationship between bacterial and fungal infection has only relatively recently been determined. White line disease is common to shod and unshod horses, and is equally prevalent in wet and dry environments.

White line disease is very common and is rarely a serious problem, but if it is not treated, and the mechanical issues that allowed bacteria to enter the hoof capsule in the first place are not addressed, it can result in significant disconnection of the hoof wall right up to the coronary band.

Signs and symptoms

Symptoms and severity of WLD vary but most cases are minor and do not present with accompanying lameness.

- Soft, chalky, crumbly horn in the mid-wall, which can extend from the ground-bearing surface of the hoof up to the coronary band.
- Black finger-like 'spikes' in the middle wall. Separation at the white line can appear as a small 'pocket' that, when probed, opens into a larger one or goes up into a spike.

- Severe cases may have large areas of completely separated hoof wall that may sound hollow when tapped. These large pockets may be visible on X-rays.
- The white line itself may become thickened and irregular.
- Commonly at the quarters, wall separation can occur between the hoof wall and sole.
- Pockets of infection can establish at the toe, commonly called seedy toe.

Prevention

Micro-nutrients are an essential part of preventing white line weakness, which leaves the foot open to infection. Regular hoof care to manage leverage and deal with early infection is advisable. Maintaining hoof hygiene, particularly using dry, absorbent bedding, will ensure that urea from urine and droppings will not damage the white line and hoof wall. Donkeys are particularly prone to white line infection and really need dry conditions to maintain hoof health. Infection rates vary across the year, with cases increasing in the spring and through the summer. Occasionally a cluster of very aggressive infections will occur, which appear to be linked to environmental conditions favouring micro-organism proliferation.

Hoof care

HCPs will be able to give advice on suitable management strategies. One of the most difficult things to achieve is getting sufficient anti-bacterial agents to the leading edge of the infection site. Trimming approaches for white line infection are very technical and should only be undertaken by an HCP or vet. For best results the area of hoof wall below the infection needs to have ground contact and leverage removed. The infected hoof material

Symptom severity	Intervention	Protocol
Mild/preventative	Establish good levels of micronutrients	Forage analysis. Introduce a hoof-specialized forage balancer and feed at recommended levels
	General hoof hygiene	Preventative – check hooves at least weekly
		In mild cases, soak with an anti-microbial (such as Hibiscrub) daily for one week, then four times weekly in week two and twice a week in week three
Moderate	Establish good levels of micronutrients	Forage analysis. Introduce a hoof-specialized forage balancer and feed at recommended levels, as specified by the manufacturer
	Use antimicrobial hoof treatment products	Refer to care plan
	Discuss appropriate care plan with hoof care provider	
Severe	Establish good levels of micronutrients	Forage analysis. Introduce a hoof-specialized forage balancer and feed at recommended levels, as specified by the manufacturer
	Use antimicrobial hoof treatment products	Refer to care plan
	Discuss appropriate care plan with hoof care provider	
		Cover with a hoof boot to keep the hoof clean in muddy conditions. Allow the horse to spend a minimum of four hours daily drying out
	Consult vet as it may be appropriate for the HCP to remove the adjacent wall and leverage. This could be a relatively extensive area but will not invade live tissue	

needs to be carefully cleaned out so that the infection can be exposed to light and air, and is accessible for treatment. Sometimes, if the infection is slow-growing, using a medicated packing product applied in the crack can eliminate or slow the infection. Care must be taken that the packing does not seal dirt inside the crack or provide additional leverage. Following treatment, the HCP should ensure the new horn grows down well connected, whilst carefully monitoring the affected area and treating as required.

LOW-GRADE LAMINITIS

Over the past decade, many barefoot hoof care providers have observed a number of symptoms which commonly accompany 'footiness'. This constellation of symptoms has been termed low-grade or sub-clinical laminitis (LGL). Symptoms include the following:

- the horse shows signs of 'footiness' on stony ground, and will dive for the grass verge;

- sore feet after a conservative trim, when that horse has never had a problem before with the same HCP;
- the horse is reluctant to move and turn in a small circle over hard ground;
- the horse is sluggish when led or ridden;
- the horse's facial expression seems a little tense and 'unhappy', especially in the eyes;
- the horse's body posture is tense, particularly in the shoulders and back;
- the horse has a hard 'cresty' neck and hard fat around the tail head;
- there is a bounding digital pulse;
- there is tightness and tenderness upon palpation in the back of the abdomen;
- there is elevated breathing unrelated to exercise;
- the horse is unusually resistant to holding up a foot while trimming or picking out the foot;
- the horse shifts its weight from foot to foot;
- the horse pulls its front foot away when it is placed forward on the stand for trimming;
- there are on-going problems with white line separation, pink staining visible in the walls of white feet, and event lines are present;
- there is obvious relief when the horse is moved onto a soft surface or put in boots and pads;

Low grade laminitis is characterised by frequent event lines, this horse was extremely uncomfortable on anything other than conformable surfaces.

- the orbits above the eyes are full or softly swollen;
- the horse may have a swollen sheath or udders;
- there is a reduction of solar concavity;
- the hoof wall angles become shallower;
- the hoof diameter increases and boots may suddenly not fit; and
- the horse's attitude is 'not quite right'.

If there are any concerns regarding these symptoms, or a combination of them, call the vet immediately.

ABSCESSES

A hoof abscess is a localized bacterial infection that develops in the sensitive structures of the hoof, producing pus. Pus is a combination of dead white blood cells, serum, dead tissue and bacteria, and is produced by the body as it reacts to the inflammation and infection. Pus may be encapsulated or dispersed within the local tissues, and it often accumulates between the keratinized and germinal layers of the hoof wall or above the sole and frog. As a relatively rigid container the hoof capsule cannot expand, and, as the pus develops, pressure inside the hoof increases, causing the often significant pain seen with an abscess.

The pus will gradually develop a sinus to relieve the pressure and, if left untreated, will usually work its way up the hoof wall or under the sole, breaking out through the thinner and softer tissues of the coronary band or the heel bulbs.

Conventional wisdom believes the majority of abscesses are caused by penetrative injury, but in the authors' experience this is rarely the case. A large number of abscesses have been observed in twenty-five years of practice and very few of these can be related to penetrative injury or identifiable foreign objects entering the hoof. There is little research into equine

PRO COMMENT: OUR HYPOTHESIS FOR AN ALTERNATIVE EXPLANATION FOR ABSCESS CAUSATION

Poor micronutrient provision accompanied by pressure on some part of the vasculature within the hoof capsule are common elements in many abscesses we have encountered. Pressure can be caused by a range of factors:

- hoof imbalance
- bruising
- changes in hoof wall connectivity due to laminitis
- changes in hoof wall connectivity due to other disease processes going on in the body
- overgrown bars

Prolonged pressure results in necrotic tissue, which is then eliminated from the hoof via encapsulation, sinus creation and abscess exit. The worst abscess cases we have seen have been present in horses with other concurrent serious disease processes, including gastric ulcers, Cushings, laminitis and toxaemia.

The nearest analogous human model, where an abscess occurs within a physically contained space like the hoof, would be a brain abscess. Paraphysiological research has found many different origins for brain abscesses, but they are often polymicrobial[8] and are known as sterile abscesses – i.e., formed without penetrative injury. This kind of abscess can be caused by lesions, infections or disease processes going on remotely to the site of the abscess itself. Research into human leg ulcers has found that an ulcer process can be started by a small knock to the skin of a leg with poor vascularization. Venous and arterial disease is the cause of 95 per cent of leg ulcers.[9] Constant high pressure causes the skin cells to break down and form an ulcer after a knock or scratch. Expanding the understanding of the behaviour of microbial infections within the bodies of other mammals shows potential to enhance our understanding of equine hoof abscesses.

abscesses, but observations drawn from practice have generated a working hypothesis, which more sufficiently explains the authors' observations.

Early barefoot trimming theories suggested that abscesses were a natural part of the healing process for hooves going through transition from shod to barefoot. In the authors' experience this is not the case, and abscesses are as common in shod feet as they are in bare feet. Most horses do not experience abscessing in transition, and abscesses are not caused by biomechanically correct trimming. Predisposing factors include laminitis, metabolic problems, contracted feet, soft soles, shoeing damage and overlaid bars.

Signs and symptoms

Horses can display severe lameness and reluctance to let the affected hoof bear weight. A bounding digital pulse may be present, together with leg swelling. Abscesses can happen in any part of the hoof, and may be located deep within the hoof capsule or far above the wall/sole junction. Rarely, an abscess can also extend under the majority of the wall and sole. These types of formation can occur concurrently with a serious disease process elsewhere in the body and the horse will be obviously ill. During the formation of the abscess, intermittent lameness is common. The formation and exit can be very rapid and comparatively pain-free for some horses. Owners often report no sign of lameness when an abscess exit is found during a routine hoof care visit, but for others it is an acutely painful experience. Depending on the individual infection, an abscess can take between days and weeks to emerge through the skin barrier, therefore HCPs and vets often choose if possible to try to relieve the pressure if there is clear evidence for where the abscess is located.

It is normal for the hoof wall to thicken above an abscess exit as the hoof grows down. The thickening will naturally reduce in time.

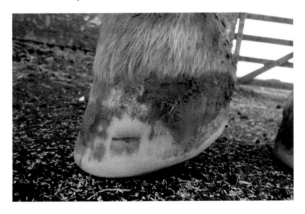

Abscesses commonly exit through the coronary band as a horizontal slit. As the hoof grows down the exit will gradually grow out.

Without that evidence, random digging can create a secondary infection ingress site.

Prevention

The horse needs to be provided with crucial micronutrients, ideally balanced to forage subsequent to analysis. In the authors' experience, recurrent abscess cases respond well to mineral supplementation at the recommended levels. Attention to hoof hygiene is essential, and horses must not be deep littered or in other ways exposed to urea around the hoof. Rubber mats and small beds are almost as much of a risk as a wet, deep litter bed.

Intervention

Consult the vet any time your horse is severely lame, or is lame for an extended period of time. A horse that is 'three-legged lame' is often just abscessing in one foot, but there is also the possibility of a fracture or joint infection, puncture wound, or other severe problem. Very deep abscesses can only be treated by a vet.

A number of things can encourage an abscess to exit, but nothing is guaranteed and it may simply take time. Appropriate pain relief is vital in these situations. Turnout is a better option, as long as there is no chance the horse is being bullied or going hungry.

Practical interventions to help an abscess break through include soaking and poulticing. Even if the abscess is still forming, twice daily soaking for fifteen minutes in an apple cider vinegar and warm water solution (ratio 1:4), or an Epsom salts/magnesium chloride and warm water solution, can provide some relief. The water needs to cover the entire hoof and ideally come up the pastern. Hoof-soaking boots are available and are very useful tools;

we use a small piece of sponge in the top to prevent the soaking solution sloshing out.

As the abscess is forming, wet poultices can help to draw it out, but poultices are most effective in the final stages where the sinus is closer to the skin barrier. Once an abscess has burst, a dry poultice can help it completely drain. Take care that the exit does not seal up before this has happened, as the opening heals from the inside out. Using an aqueous cream around the exit can prevent this occurring.

Allowing the horse to stay out with appropriate and hygienic protection, such as a poultice in a hoof boot, will allow movement according to comfort levels, which may speed the exit of the abscess. There is also less risk of anoxic laminitis in the opposing weight-bearing limb.

Following an abscess exiting through the coronet band, the exit wound will usually form a horizontal crack above the sinus itself. Above the crack the hoof will often grow a bulging area which helps to support that region of the hoof wall as the exit grows down. The sinus itself will never re-attach to the underlying laminae, and the hoof care professional must manage the resulting hollow space as it grows down. If the abscess has broken out above the heel bend, the entire wall at the heel may be disconnected. This area can break off, but commonly it will tear laterally unless the hoof care professional carefully manages the removal of loose areas. If the horn at the heel breaks, the heel will very quickly re-grow, but for a few weeks the horse is likely to be unbalanced where the wall has been lost.

COMPLEX PROBLEMS

Equine gastric ulcers

Research into the nature and prevalence of Equine Gastric Ulcer Syndrome (EGUS) indicates that gastric ulcers represent a significantly larger health challenge to domestic equines than was previously thought. The presence of ulcers in the GI tract can have a significant effect on hoof health. In cases of persistent problems with hoof wall and sole connectivity, including flaring, loss of concavity and recurrent sub-solar abscesses, the authors have seen favourable responses to ulcer treatment.

Gastric ulcers have been found in every breed and age of horse, and are not limited to performance horses. The high prevalence in racehorses suggests that the demands of racing training and performance may exacerbate their effects. Endoscopic studies have found a prevalence of 88 per cent in thoroughbred and standard bred racehorses.[10] However, even horses who are involved in typical recreational use can be susceptible to EGUS. A controlled study conducted in Iowa simulated a five-day trip to a show or training clinic environment. The study group was exposed to a trip involving two four-hour trailer journeys, individual stalling, twice daily feeding and twice daily exercise for three days between travelling. This common clinic regime of a journey and comparatively short stay away from home was sufficient to induce ulcers in 70 per cent of the horses in the study group.[11]

Research has determined a range of risk factors, many of which, unfortunately, are common horse keeping practices: stress, transportation, stabling, intermittent feeding, high starch feeding, intense exercise, performance and management changes have all been indicated as ulcergenic factors.[12]

In veterinary practice EGUS may be diagnosed based on history, clinical signs, endoscopic findings and/or response to treatment. A range of clinical, behavioural and physical signs may indicate an EGUS problem, including:

- abdominal pain, including acute and recurrent colic;

- 'picky' eating behaviour, including not finishing feeds or refusing previously acceptable foodstuffs;
- difficulty in maintaining body condition;
- distracted and restless eating behaviour;
- chronic diarrhoea;
- myofascial/neuromuscular tension patterns;
- body soreness;
- depression and withdrawal;
- behavioural and training difficulties, including persistent nervousness and anxiety, or lacking energy;
- 'grumpiness', 'bad temper' or aggression; and
- problems with hoof connectivity, horn quality, recurrent abscesses and hoof sensitivity.

The primary abdominal pain experienced by EGUS horses is thought to be caused by the effects of gastric acids attacking the stomach lining.[13] To facilitate digestion the horse's stomach continuously secretes hydrochloric acid and pepsinogen from glands located in the lower regions. The bottom two-thirds of the stomach is protected from acid damage by glandular mucosal and bicarbonate layers, but the upper third of the equine stomach is not protected by mucosal layers and is particularly susceptible to the impact of stomach acids.

If a horse is suspected of suffering from EGUS, discuss options for treatment and maintenance with the vet. Generally vets will choose endoscopic diagnosis if it is readily available. If this means a significant journey for the horse, given the findings cited above regarding travelling, discuss options for presumptive diagnosis by treatment response. Endoscopic diagnosis is currently the main diagnostic approach, but it may not be conclusive. An endoscope can only access the oesophageal tract, stomach and proximal duodenum, whereas ulcers have been found throughout the GI tract.

A Texas necropsy study in 2005 found that out of a sample of 365 horses from a variety of sources, 44 per cent exhibited colonic ulcers and 55 per cent gastric ulcers. In a second group of 180 performance horses, 63 per cent had colonic ulcers and 87 per cent had gastric ulcers.[14] A study comparing endoscopy with histology and necropsy also found that endoscopists may underestimate the number, severity or depth of ulcers present in the non-glandular stomach, and may miss glandular ulcers.[15] Other protocols for testing have been investigated. Some horses with EGUS may be mildly anaemic, but blood tests have not been found to be a reliable diagnostic tool. A urine sucrose permeability test may show promise, however, as a simple non-invasive test, as may a fecal occult blood test.[16]

Treatment

The principal aims of treatment are to manage abdominal pain, establish healing conditions in the GI tract and prevent secondary complications. There is a high rate of recurrence, and therefore the horse's lifestyle should be managed for risk factors. The vet may prescribe a combination of treatment approaches: pain relief; an acid suppressor such as Omeprazole® (sold as GastroGard® or UlcerGard®); and acid neutralizers or buffers which will limit acid production or increase the pH of the stomach, thus allowing the stomach lining to heal.

Treatment will only be effective if given at the prescribed dose for long enough to have a positive effect. Omeprazole®, for instance, has a standard of twenty-eight days at full dose and then a reduction programme; longer use may be contraindicated.[17] All EGUS treatment needs to be accompanied by lifestyle stress evaluation and reduction. What may be appropriate treatment for one horse may not be effective for another, and it may take time, in consultation with the vet, to identify what works for the horse. Generic omeprazole is an attractive and potentially cheaper alternative for treating ulcers, but if it is not a stabilized product it may not be effective in reaching the hind gut as it will be destroyed by stomach acid.

Another class of pharmaceuticals, the H2 antagonists, are antihistamine products at least one of which, Ranitidine, has been found to treat fore and hind gut ulcers, but must be administered at least twice per day to be effective.

Coating agents may also be helpful. These products contain substances that are designed to coat the site of an ulcer with a viscous compound, thus setting up an environment for the ulcer to heal, but they must be fed frequently enough for the compound to remain active and in place.

There is a large range of other products on the market that are targeted at ulcers, but very few of them have been subjected to clinical trials. They may be useful in maintenance and prevention, but there is no evidence that they are helpful in acute EGUS cases.[18] Common analgesics such as bute may be contraindicated in horses with EGUS as they have been found to exacerbate ulcer symptoms.[19]

Dietary support

Dietary management and support are a critical part of ulcer treatment and prevention, but there is limited clinical evidence for the effectiveness of supplements in terms of treatment. Some products, however, are useful as an adjunct to pharmacotherapy. Probiotics may be helpful to support the resident populations of microflora in the gut. Sea buckthorn berry has been used to treat mucosal

injury in humans and gastric ulcers in rats. In equines sea buckthorn has not been found to decrease ulcer scores, but it may prevent ulcers from getting worse. It has been suggested that calcium carbonate preparations provide an antacid effect, but they may need to be fed more than twice daily to have the desired effect. Dietary oils – flax, rice bran and corn oil – may not be effective in treating or preventing non-glandular ulcers but may be helpful in treating or preventing glandular ulcers.[20]

Maintenance and prevention

Once ulcers have occurred, it is difficult to completely eradicate them or prevent a recurrence in the future. A sensible approach is to consider the horse to be always 'at risk' and keep it on a maintenance programme, being vigilant for symptoms and promptly providing treatment. The most effective approach to prevent ulcers and maintain health manages stress and supports the horse's evolutionary ethology; this will also achieve good hoof health. Maintaining continuous access to forage stimulates saliva production, thereby maintaining greater alkalinity in the horse's GI tract. Avoiding high concentrate diets will further limit the production of corrosive stomach acids that can occur with grain feeding. Feeding alfalfa hay has been found to increase stomach alkalinity and reduce ulcer scores.[21]

Many horse owners choose to travel their horses away from home for short periods for competition or to attend training clinics, but, as the previous discussion suggests, travelling presents a considerable risk for ulcer development. Going away from home is very likely to be stressful for the horse, therefore establishing a protective gut environment by using acid suppressors is a sensible protective precaution. If frequent travelling is likely to

CASE STUDIES:

In two cases where severe EGUS was diagnosed in clients' horses by endoscopy, significant differences in dorsal wall profile, sensitivity and connection were noted after ulcer treatment with Omeprazole (Gastro Gard®). One four-year-old mare had symptoms of weight loss, body soreness, poor coat condition and behavioural problems, plus persistent quarter flares leading to white line infection. After being endoscoped and diagnosed with very severe oesophageal and gastric ulcer damage, treatment with GastroGard® was implemented. After four weeks the mare had observable improvements in all areas, and in the next few months the connectivity problem that led to her persistent lateral flaring was resolved. Subsequent endoscopic evaluation suggested that, despite the evident external physical improvements, the internal damage was too bad to allow the mare's digestion to work effectively, so sadly she was euthanized.

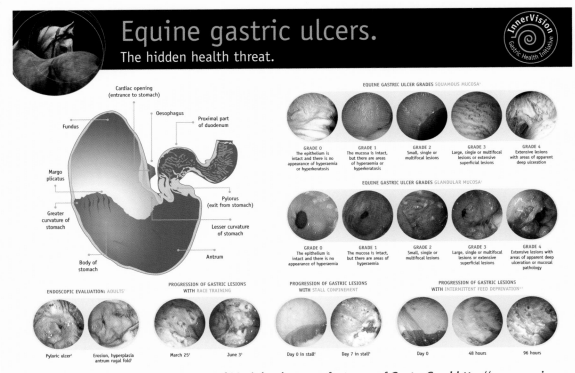

Equine Gastric Ulcers. Poster courtesy of Merial – the manufacturers of GastroGard.http://www.equin egastriculcers. co.uk/index.html

In a second case, an off-the-track thoroughbred gelding, long-term problems with low weight, wind sucking and poor condition resulted in a diagnosis of gastric ulcers after endoscopic evaluation. His overall hoof condition was poor prior to treatment, he was very body sore, and he had presented with sub-solar abscesses in all four feet on two separate occasions. After Gastro Gard® treatment his hoof condition and body score improved, although his hind gut ulcers were not resolved. His hoof condition improved in his front feet, but his hind feet became flared and sensitive again following treatment and his body soreness returned.

Both these cases had experienced significant risk factors as very young horses (racing training, and housing stress and deprivation).

be a feature of a horse's lifestyle, preparation through habituation to travelling should also be an essential part of their basic training. Establishing a predictable travelling routine is a good idea. Travelling horses in herd groups to events may also mitigate stress, as may arranging turnout with groups of herd mates rather than stabling while away.

EQUINE METABOLIC SYNDROME

Equine metabolic syndrome (EMS), previously known as developmental or peripheral Cushing's disease, characterized by J.P. Johnson in 2002, is a disorder of the horse's endocrine system that is related to insulin resistance, obesity and laminitis. It should not be thought of as a disease in the same way that something like equine strangles may be; it is rather an individual metabolic difference akin to an allergy or intolerance. The primary response to EMS diagnosis is to regulate the horse's lifestyle to manage the problem, much as one would to manage allergy triggers.

Native breeds and native crosses are particularly genetically predisposed to EMS, although most horses are susceptible given the appropriate environmental triggers. In northern climates, where many native-type horses evolved, the availability of forage varies significantly between the winter and the summer. As an adaptive response, native breeds developed the ability to safely and efficiently gain and lose a large amount of bodyweight as calorie availability varied.

Things go wrong when the system is disrupted by the horse consuming a surfeit of calorie-dense food all year round. If it is given an appropriate low-calorie, high-fibre diet, the hormones that manage appetite remain in balance. If the forage consumed is calorie-dense, the extra energy is stored as fat, and the levels of circulating hormones become seriously imbalanced. EMS cannot be 'cured',

and therefore before going into any more detail it is important to emphasize that there are only two weapons in managing EMS: diet and exercise, neither of which will be effective in isolation.

Metabolically active fat

In EMS horses unusual fat deposition on the crest, around the nuchal ligament, around the tail head, on top of the ribs and around the sheath or udders has been used to classify EMS as a clinical condition. These areas of abnormal fat deposition, which can remain in place even when the horse's body appears lean, are endocrinologically active. They release adipokines, which maintain eating behaviour even when the food eaten is calorie-dense, can trigger on-going inflammatory responses including laminitis, and make the horse increasingly insulin resistant.

Hyperinsulinemia

Insulin resistance is characterized by an elevation in the horse's circulating levels of insulin, although the glucose levels remain within the normal range. Insulin at normal levels should signal glucose take-up by the cells, but when the hormonal signalling system fails, the body responds by turning up the insulin level until the messages get through. Every cell in the body requires glucose to function, but when there is not enough circulating glucose available, the body has numerous mechanisms and conversions that can get energy to the cells that need it.[22] When insulin isn't working, fats are released, but high levels of insulin also trigger energy storage rather than usage, with the result that hyperinsulinemic horses are often weak and exercise-intolerant.

Transient insulin resistance can also occur as

a result of a co-occurring infection or injury, but may be temporary.

Laminitis

Despite the relatively recent definition of EMS, for many years owners have reported patterns in their horses' laminitic episodes that characterize the syndrome. Laminitis in these horses may be seasonal or follow an annual pattern, and may present with clinical lameness in one or multiple limbs. EMS horses may appear unusually sensitive to grass, quickly demonstrating abdominal discomfort and 'footiness', and often require complex grazing management set-ups, which may include complete removal from grass for large periods of the year.

Diagnosis and testing

Many horse owners encounter EMS for the first time when their horse is diagnosed with laminitis. The vet arrives, diagnoses laminitis, observes the body score and fat distribution of the horse and recommends they have a test for insulin resistance. In practice, the development of the syndrome is a little like a seesaw – as the horse accumulates weight through over-nutrition and under-exercise, one end is gradually weighted over the years in favour of the horse developing EMS. Eventually the seesaw tips and the horse is in crisis, but the development of the syndrome has taken some time to occur. The horse will very likely have experienced low-grade laminitis and insulin resistance previously, and event lines and dorsal wall deformations in the hoof capsules will be present, as will changes in abnormal fat deposition and tissue density. But unless the horse's history is known, and it is regularly exercised, the creeping small changes in physical comfort and attitude to exercise that occur with low-grade laminitis and developing

EMS may not have been picked up by the owner.

Management

As stated previously, EMS is not a disease and there is no 'cure' for it; the best approach for an owner with a horse which is susceptible is to plan for it. There is no UK licensed drug treatment, but pharmacological approaches tried include Metformin, a drug developed for human metabolic syndrome. Metformin testing in equines found favourable responses in the short term as a kind of metabolic 'kick-start' to improve insulin sensitivity, but the magnitude of the treatment effect diminished in the long term.[23]

As previously discussed regarding obesity and exercise, diet and fitness must be established and maintained for EMS to be effectively tackled.

CUSHING'S DISEASE (PPID – PITUITARY PARS INTERMEDIA DYSFUNCTION)

The pituitary gland is a small, pea-sized gland situated at the base of the brain. It is known as a 'master' gland, as it acts by adjusting hormonal secretions, to control a range of different body systems, including:

- thyroid gland function;
- metabolic function;
- water balance and osmotic regulation within the body;
- regulation of body temperature;
- pain relief; and
- sleep patterns.

Equine PPID has a constellation of symptoms related to problems in the regulation of the endocrine system caused by an enlargement of, or a benign tumour in, the intermediate lobe of the pituitary gland. When the pituitary gland is affected in this way, its normal hormone production becomes imbalanced. In PPID, dopamine-producing neurons in the pituitary are damaged, possibly by oxidative stress, which allows enlargement or adenoma to take place. The enlarged pituitary then produces excess amounts of a hormone called adrenocorticotrophic hormone (ACTH). The absolute cause of oxidative stress in PPID has yet to be determined. When the pituitary releases ACTH, the hypothalamus controls the release of cortisol from the adrenal glands on top of the kidneys, and thyroid hormones from the thyroid gland. In the healthy horse elevated cortisol will result in a drop in ACTH. In PPID horses cortisol does not have this effect on resting ACTH levels, which will remain elevated, and ACTH testing will reveal abnormal pituitary function.

PPID is a complex and degenerative problem to manage, and in caring for a PPID horse 'the goal posts' will often seem to move. What is effective in keeping them healthy one month will change by the next as the disease progresses. Pergolide is an effective drug therapy and can make a considerable

difference to the quality of life for a PPID horse. Cases can present with the following range of symptoms, including:

- hirsutism (failing to shed the coat);
- lethargy and depression;
- loss of top line and muscle tone;
- weight loss with fat pockets around crest, shoulders and tail head;
- swelling in the eye orbits, sheath or mammary glands;
- excessive thirst and frequent urination;
- repeated or unexplained laminitis episodes;
- laminitis episodes at unusual times of year (autumn and mid-winter);
- poor temperature control;
- excessive sweating or failure to sweat;
- changes to the thickness of the skin, scaliness;
- increased susceptibility to infections and parasites;
- heightened sensitivity to allergies and vaccinations;
- increased incidence of tendon and ligament problems;
- unusual body smell;
- increased production of smegma from the sheath;
- repeated thrush infection in the feet, despite good hygiene and treatment; and
- significant increase in hoof growth rate.

Until relatively recently, PPID was believed to be a disease of the aged horse, but the authors have experienced clients' horses testing positive for PPID at as young as six years.

A Shetland pony with diagnosed PPID. Hirsutism is a feature of the disease.

Testing

PPID is often first evidenced in small and subtle changes to the horse's level of hoof comfort, energy, their muscle condition, topline, hair shedding pattern and skin, a long time before the typical Cushing's signs become

CASE STUDY: MOSES

Moses was born in 2006 and suffered his first bout of laminitis in 2009 as a three-year-old. Despite receiving continual veterinary and farriery care, and the implementation of traditional laminitis management practices – stabling, starvation paddocks and grazing muzzles – he continued to suffer recurring bouts of laminitis and was often very footsore. He tested positive for PPID in September 2013 and commenced treatment with Prascend®. Radiographs taken in 2013 showed 4.5/8.2 degrees rotation left/right fore. Imprint shoes were applied but subsequent radiographs in 2014 showed 9.6/9.0 degrees rotation.

Moses and his friends Douglas and Jake.

In January 2015 Moses was gifted to the Scottish Animal Behaviour and Rescue Centre (SABRC) and received barefoot hoof care. Rather than stabling him, SABRC turned Moses out onto a track system and additional woodland area with two other Shetland ponies and provided hay in addition to the grass on the track. Within a couple of weeks of moving to his new home, Moses' foot soreness had reduced significantly and he was happily trotting around the track and playing with his new friends. Understanding that exercise is a vital element of overall horse health, SABRC ensure that their mini residents are taken for daily walks in hand through the woods and fields surrounding the Centre. At the time of writing, no further laminitis episodes had occurred.

apparent. At this stage blood tests may come back negative, but it is important to keep investigating any suspicions and follow up with lifestyle changes to see if the horse responds. In practice, HCPs need to highlight observed changes in hoof growth and low-grade laminitis to support early investigation.

The most commonly used test for PPID is the resting ACTH test. A single blood sample is drawn, and the ACTH results compared with normal ranges. There is evidence for seasonal variation in ACTH levels in normal horses, with elevations in autumn. If testing is conducted in the autumn, findings should be compared with a seasonally adjusted range, to avoid false positives. In PPID cases the seasonal variation may show greater elevation spikes than in normal horses.

Insulin resistance is a different syndrome that can show overlapping symptoms to PPID. It can be complex to unpick the specifics, but IR testing is recommended for horses diagnosed with PPID.

When planning testing, avoid times when the horse may be under stress or is actively laminitic. Stress has been found to increase the risk of false positives.

Treatment

The primary pharmacological treatment for PPID is pergolide (sold in the UK as Prascend®). Pergolide is a dopamine agonist – it stimulates dopamine production in the body. Each horse will have a different response to treatment and

When untreated PPID can lead to severe laminitis.

should be regularly monitored by the vet to ensure that it receives the appropriate dosage. In practice some horses show patterns of decreased appetite on pergolide, and owners become very practised at enticing their horse to take its dose each day by dividing it up and feeding it with other things that taste attractive.

In parallel with drug treatment, lifestyle management is critical for the PPID horse. It may get to a stage where it cannot tolerate grass at all, which might involve the owner in finding a solution to dry lotting the horse with soaked hay. (Dry lotting is keeping animals in grass free paddocks. In dry climates this may simply be soil with no grazing plants, or a dry lot may have a surface added, usually sand, gravel or bark.) Once pergolide has started to take effect, exercise can also help. Untreated PPID can be very painful, debilitating and depressing for the horse, and extremely hard work for the owner and HCP. Normal hormone

production regulates coat and hoof growth, but in PPID horses hoof growth can be up to four times the normal rate. Very regular hoof care is essential in such cases. Due to reduced resistance to infection, thrush may also be a significant problem for the PPID horse. Even daily treatment will not necessarily keep an infection under control. In these situations, even if there are few other PPID symptoms, PPID should be considered and treatment discussed with the vet.

Supported by equine welfare charities and the British Horse Society, 'Talk About Laminitis' is a national disease awareness initiative provided by the pharmaceutical company Boehringer Ingelheim Vetmedica which promotes ACTH testing. The initiative provides laboratory fees for blood tests for PPID, and is designed to improve awareness and understanding of the underlying endocrine causes of laminitis, as well as marketing Prascend® – pergolide mesylate, the company's licensed PPID treatment option. In 2014 the programme paid laboratory fees for blood tests for more than 8,500 horses, of which 46 per cent tested positive for elevated ACTH and PPID.

Caring for PPID horses can be very challenging, frustrating and depressing. There is an excellent source of online support, and an Equine Cushings and Insulin Resistance online community, which the authors recommend to their clients. The Equine Cushings and Insulin Resistance Group has a lot of experience in guiding owners through testing protocols and findings, feeding and management regimes, trimming approaches and the biology of the disease. For online outreach and information visit http://ecirhorse.org.

PEDAL OSTEITIS/OSTEOPOROSIS

Pedal osteitis is a term used to describe demineralization occurring at the peripheral margin of the pedal bone, which is visible on X-ray. Technically osteoporosis rather than osteitis (-itis = inflammation) is a more accurate way to describe the pathology. Vets will often point out these changes on radiographs because they are a sign of something unusual, but they may not always relate to lameness. Demineralization of the bone is a long-term process that may have little to do with a current acute performance problem.

Pedal osteitis is sometimes referred to as non-septic pedal osteitis. This can be confusing as it implies commonality between the two disease processes, which is not the case. The demineralization present in pedal osteitis/ osteoporosis clearly differentiates the disease process from septic pedal osteitis. Septic pedal osteitis is very unusual and is an infection within the bone itself, potentially caused by penetrative injury or a long-standing sub-solar abscess.

The appearance of the pedal bone in radiographs of the feet of domestic equines so commonly shows the effects of osteoporosis that many vets and HCPs may never have seen a truly healthy pedal bone. Osteoporosis is so ubiquitous in domestic equines that it was believed to be normal. It took many years before the striated, brittle, honeycomb appearance of domestic osteoporitic pedal bones was accepted to be the result of a disease process. Although it is being discussed in isolation here, it is important to be aware that in practice this is not the case. Osteoporotic changes co-occur with many other pathologies, such as laminitis, navicular syndrome and obesity. It is therefore more appropriate to think of it as simply one of a number of disease symptoms rather than a disease in itself.

Digital radiographs are more useful than film to clearly show osteoporotic changes. Radiographs should be taken at a dorso-palmar angle and a lateral view. Characteristic changes include the following:

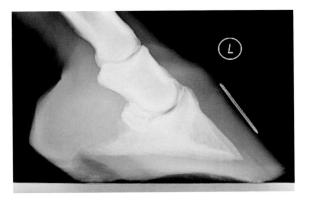

Lateral radiograph showing bone changes to the palmar processes. This horse was functionally sound, and otherwise has a good bone and hoof capsule alignment.

- the periphery of the pedal bone may appear jagged or serrated, indicating that the marginal bone has been lost, exposing the distal ends of the trabeculi;
- the bone may appear less opaque than adjacent bones, indicating that it has lost or never developed cortical density;
- the peripheral edge may be chipped or fractured, or show areas where the bone is lost completely;
- the lateral view may show changes to the tip of the bone, where the bone has been lost completely or the dermal laminae have mineralized and a 'ski tip' has developed;
- the distal margin of the bone may have a 'rocker-like' appearance; and
- the vascular channels through the bone may appear enlarged.

Radiographs are always interesting and helpful to HCPs to determine the balance of the hoof and the progression of a disease process, but it should be remembered that they are a snapshot of the horse on that day. In all but the most obvious cases of fracture, bone infection or other acute injury, unless there are radiographs available of the same animal prior to a disease process taking hold, it is often not possible to establish a causal relationship between what is seen on a radiograph and what is giving the horse the problem.

This pedal bone shows extensive remodelling in the area of the lateral cartilages, commonly known as side bone.

THE CRENA

The Crena is a small crescent shape that appears in the margin of the pedal bone at the centre of the toe. For many years it was believed that it might be the result of pressure from a toeclip on a shoe, but crena have been found in wild and feral horses and are now thought to be an evolutionary adaptation.

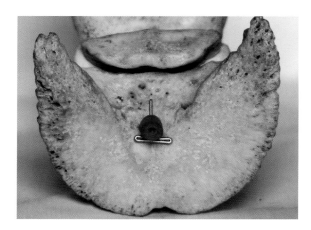

A caudal view of the pedal bone. The Crena is the crescent shaped notch in the centre of the toe.

Causes of pedal osteoporosis

HCPs are indebted to researcher and hoof function specialist Dr Robert Bowker who has shed light on many aspects of hoof development and function. In lectures, Dr Bowker regularly stresses that it is important to think outside the box and to make the distinction between what is normal and what is common. His research has explained how particularly in domestic horses long-term peripheral hoof loading and pressure leads to demineralization of P3 and the navicular bone, and eventual lameness.

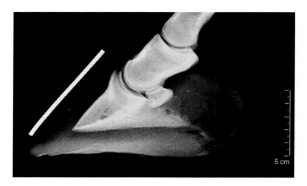

The hoof in this image is also laminitic but the pedal bone has only sunk rather than rotated.

Looking closely at the pedal bone, it is clear that there are many small surface holes or foramen. These allow blood vessels to transport nutrients and water in, and waste products out of the bone. Healthy bone requires good blood flow. Using ultrasound, Dr Bowker determined that blood perfusion of the foot is related to the conformability of the surface it is standing on. Touch is very important in stimulating blood flow, and a conformable ground surface that is in contact with the entire solar surface, such as pea gravel,

UNDERSTANDING RADIOGRAPHS

Radiographs or X-rays can be very useful aids for methodological examination of the foot, but, just like taking photographs, taking a useful radiograph is a skilled job. It can also be an expensive process, and the horse is exposed to radiation, which has its own inherent risks. There are some basic techniques and information that can help owners and HCPs get the best information from radiographs.

Radiographic terms:
Radiolucent – clear to x-rays, areas that appear black on the image;
Radio opaque – dense to x-rays, areas that appear white on the image (where fewer x-rays penetrate through to hit the film).

Preparing and marking up the foot

To produce useful images from which precise measurements can be taken, radio-opaque markers should be applied to the foot prior to x-ray. Carefully place a drawing pin in the tip of the frog and apply a wall marker (either wire, light chain or radio-opaque paste) to the centre of the dorsal wall, starting precisely at the hoof wall/hair margin. Also recommended is the use of a block with nails set at a measured distance to indicate order of magnification, and a measurement should be taken of the distance between the equipment and the block.

In a healthy foot, there are some typical features to look for on radiographs:

- the dorsal hoof wall and dorsal P3 should be parallel;
- the palmar process of P3 should be 2–5 degrees above ground parallel;
- in long-term barefoot horses, hoof walls are consistently thicker than in shod horses;
- the top of the hoof wall should be parallel with the top of the extensor process of the pedal bone. A difference in height indicates sinking due to laminitis;
- the length of P3 should be equal to the length of the caudal foot (as measured from a vertical drop from the heel bulbs to the back of the palmar processes). If P3 is longer, this indicates lengthening of the palmar processes due to calcification of the lateral cartilages;
- the sole is not uniform in thickness: there is greater depth to the sole above the collateral grooves, but solar depth below P3 should be uniform. In truly healthy domestic feet, it should measure 8–12mm in front of the tip of the frog, although the accepted norm is only 5–6mm. Assess the state of sole defoliation at the time of X-ray. Horses living on abrasive terrain such as pea gravel will not show the same sole depth as those living on soft or very hard flat surfaces due to continual solar exfoliation.

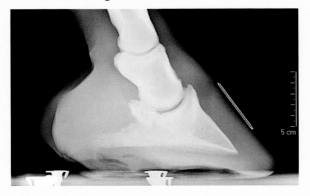

Radiograph of a functional barefoot horse.

Radiography is a very useful diagnostic tool, but there are a few cautions. Taking radiographs on an elevated block produces unusual weighting, and can result in the palmar aspect of P3 appearing lower than it actually is. Sedation can also result in changes to the individual horse's normal stance.

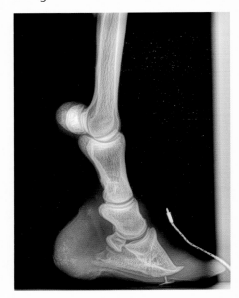

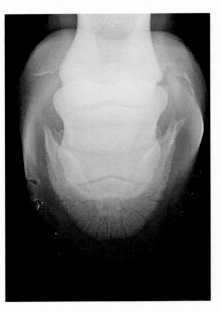

This radiograph shows a hoof where chronic laminitis has lead to rotation and sinking [see case study 'Moses']. The tip of the pedal bone has also remodelled to produce a 'ski tip', and the distal border has deformed under pressure from unregulated heel growth.

A cranial view of the pedal bone showing pedal osteoporosis at the distal margin.

encourages greater perfusion and slower blood flow through the foot, enabling maximum bone nutrition and hydration.[24] When a horse stands on a hard surface such as concrete, or has a metal shoe attached to the periphery of the hoof, blood flow through the foot is faster and there is less perfusion into the small blood vessels, therefore fewer nutrients and less hydration can reach these areas when the horse is shod or living on non-conformable surfaces. Dr Bowker established that placing even a very thin layer of material under the sole had the effect of slowing down blood flow. This suggests that the live sole has a neurosensory role in maintaining good blood flow, and may explain why even healthy horses choose to stand and move on conformable surfaces.

Treatment

Similar to EMS, pedal osteoporosis is often accompanied by other pathology. By taking measurements of pedal bone density from 200 horses of similar size and type, research has shown that P3 weight varied between 40 and just over 100 grams in the fore feet, and in hind feet between 60 and 80 grams. Bones that weighed more than 85 grams were always from more symmetrical feet. Observable pathology, including navicular, was consistently present in bones weighing between 40 and 60 grams.[25] Researchers attribute osteoporosis of the pedal bone to peripheral loading of the hoof, i.e. shoeing and trimming practices that persistently load the hoof wall and margin of the sole in preference to the sole and frog. What these findings suggest is that

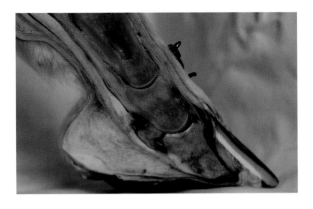

The hoof wall and pedal bone in this specimen have lost connection due to chronic laminitis.

pedal osteoporosis is something that can be mitigated against with strong, healthy development and lifestyle. Bones can and do remodel, and with appropriate stimulation and time can adapt and recover symmetry.

NAVICULAR SYNDROME AND DISEASE

Historically, lameness arising from pain in the caudal third of the foot that resolved with palmar digital nerve block, was classified either as navicular syndrome, where affected horses were radiographically normal, or as navicular disease, where bone abnormalities were detected via x-ray. However, advances in imaging modalities using magnetic resonance imaging (MRI) and computed tomography (CT) have shown that bony changes can be present that are not detected via radiographs,[26] and therefore this distinction seems somewhat arbitrary. The terms also appear to be interchangeable within the literature. Adding further to the confusion, studies have found changes to the navicular bone without any concurrent lameness. On a practical level, whether the lameness is classified as a syndrome or a disease makes little difference

to the horse and owner, therefore the term navicular syndrome will be used throughout.

Causes of navicular syndrome

Although foreleg lameness associated with changes in the region of the navicular bone has been recognized for hundreds of years, there is still disagreement as to the cause. Three main theories regarding the pathogenesis have emerged:[27]

1. Disruption of the blood supply to the navicular bone, causing ischemic necrosis when areas of bone die off due to loss of blood supply.
2. Abnormal biomechanical forces, causing chronic excess pressure on the navicular bone from the deep digital flexor tendon, resulting in bone remodelling.
3. Osteoarthritis, based on similarities in pathological changes to the navicular bone and its surface cartilage that are also seen in joints with osteoarthritis.

The authors propose that inappropriate loading of the distal limb could be the root cause of all three pathways.

In his seminal paper 'Contrasting Structural Morphology of "Good" and "Bad" Footed Horses', Bob Bowker discusses the possible involvement of the distal sesamoidean impar ligament (DSIL) and the deep digital flexor tendon (DDFT) in regulating blood supply to the navicular bone:

…During movement and stance of the horse, considerable and sudden pressure changes will most likely occur in this region and could potentially restrict or enhance blood flow to the surrounding tissues, both of which may deleteriously affect the health of the perfused tissues. The sensory detection function would ensure adequate arterial blood flow to the navicular bone… a potent vasodilatation mechanism exists under the control of neuropeptides including the tachykinin substance P (SP). SP, neurokinin A (NKA) and calcitonin gene-related peptide (CGRP) have been shown to be present in the sensory nerve fibres that course through the DSIL and the dorsal half of the DDFT and pass into the distal phalanx and the navicular bone.[28]

A comparative study looking at the stress and contact forces on the navicular bone in sound horses and horses with navicular disease found that:

...force and stress in the horses with navicular disease were approximately double control group values early in the stance phase. This was due to a higher force in the deep digital flexor tendon, which was attributed to a contraction of the deep digital flexor muscle in early stance in an attempt to unload the heels... in the navicular disease group... the horses landed toe first... and loaded the foot in a more dorsal location until about 70 per cent of stance.[29]

Osteoarthritis is a common repercussion to abnormal biomechanics.[30] Regardless of the cause, there are a number of common clinical signs:

- abnormalities in the navicular bone including the medullary cavity, trabecular and cortical bone;
- abrasion to the cartilage on the flexor surface;
- abnormalities in the navicular bursa;
- abnormalities in the deep digital flexor tendon;
- abnormalities in the collateral sesamoid ligament;
- abnormalities in the distal sesamoidean impar ligament; and
- swelling of the distal interphalangeal joint.

A review of the MRI examinations of 72 horses recently diagnosed with navicular syndrome with less than six months' lameness identified the frequency of clinical signs. The study showed that the vast majority of horses had bony and soft tissue abnormalities:

Structure	Number of Limbs Affected	Number of Horses Affected
Navicular bone	108 (75%)	62 (86%)
Collateral sesamoidean ligament	86 (60%)	54 (75%)
Distal interphalangeal joint swelling	71 (49%)	36 (50%)
Navicular bursa	58 (40%)	32 (44%)
Deep digital flexor tendon	49 (34%)	32 (44%)
Navicular fragments* (37.5%)	15/48 (31%)	9/24
Distal sesamoidean impar ligament	40 (28%)	26 (36%)

*Note: not all horses were imaged from a suitable direction to evaluate the distal border.

Within the authors' client base, horses which have been given a veterinary diagnosis of navicular syndrome fall into three distinct categories:

- horses which present with a long toe/low heel and broken back hoof pastern axis;
- horses which have an upright tubular foot with high heels, sometimes with a broken forward hoof pastern axis; and
- horses in which the hoof conformation looks relatively normal but the hoof size is small in relation to their body size/weight.

Mediolateral imbalance is also a common feature.

Regardless of which category the horses fall into, they all exhibit a clear toe-first landing. They also have poorly developed digital

Horse with a navicular diagnosis before biomechanical trimming. At this point the horse was unsound on hard surfaces.

Lateral image of a high heeled foot prone to navicular.

Over six months of four weekly trimming and rehabilitation, the angle of the dorsal hoof wall has been guided back and the horse is weighting more caudally.

Dorsal image of a high heeled foot prone to navicular.

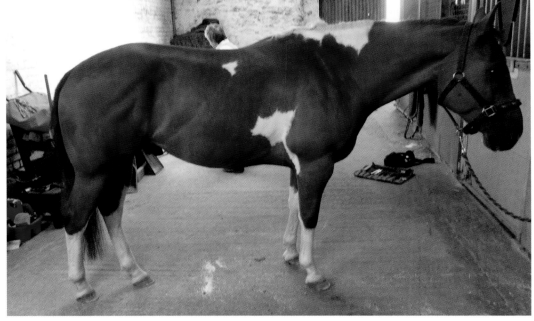

Horses with a large body size compared to their feet size are common navicular cases.

cushions in terms of both volume and density, lateral cartilages which are easily deformed by thumb pressure, and heels that have migrated forward of the rear of the frog. Commonly they also have contracted heels and caudally displaced heel bulbs. Poor hoof conformation is cited as a major risk factor by the University of Edinburgh Dick Vet School's factsheet on navicular.

Barefoot rehabilitation focuses on improving structure in the back part of the foot – the digital cushion, lateral cartilages and frog – and trimming to correct the alignment of the digit bones. Achieving these goals enables correct movement to be restored, reducing the biomechanical stress on the navicular bone and soft tissues, allowing them to become pain-free and the horse sound.

Rehabilitation strategy

The most successful navicular rehabilitation is a result of teamwork involving the owner, HCP, bodyworker and vet. Muscle tension in the body is extremely common, locking the horse into compensatory movement patterns. Myofascial release and appropriate stretching can help restore correct movement. Veterinary assistance via radiographs of the foot to precisely establish hoof balance and/or anti-inflammatory pain relief in the early stages can be very helpful. Trimming requirements vary widely between horses and in the early days may be fairly minimal, but it is important to assess the hoof frequently to maintain balance as close to ideal

Pea gravel provides a conformable surface for barefoot horses.

as possible. The owner has a vital role to play in providing movement on conformable surfaces; thrush control; turnout with companions; and a high-quality forage balancer.

Movement on conformable surfaces

A thorough evaluation by the HCP should be undertaken before a walking programme commences. A progressive programme of walking in hoof boots and pads will stimulate development or regeneration of the digital cushion, lateral cartilages and frog through repeated loading and unloading. As well as immediately improving comfort levels, hoof boots and pads serve three other key functions:

- they provide a conformable surface, stimulating neuroreceptors located in the sole and frog, and increasing perfusion of blood through the foot;
- they reduce concussion by dissipating some of the forces encountered when the foot hits the ground, reducing the amount of concussive shock transferred to the damaged soft tissues and bones;
- they provide a degree of stability to the entire foot and increase comfort. Horses with a long toe/low heel presentation often also have very weak feet. Shoes provide a very rigid structure to the foot and when they are removed, some horses find the greater flexibility in the foot uncomfortable.

Thrush control

It is very common for navicular horses with high upright heels to have a frog with a deep central sulcus and thrush problems. This alone can make the horse very sore and it will try to avoid loading the back of the foot. Treating thrush, and being vigilant with hoof hygiene to ensure it does not return, is crucial.

Turnout with companions

Transforming weak, under-developed feet requires movement. Standing in a stable for the majority of the time does nothing to help the navicular horse strengthen its feet. Gentle movement with calm herd companions is very beneficial. If the ground is particularly hard – for example, due to frost or periods of warm dry weather – using hoof boots and pads for turnout can ensure the horse remains comfortable and happy to move.

High-quality forage balancer

Where horn quality is poor, it is unable to support the weight of the horse and can crumble, split or otherwise collapse. Ensuring that the horse is supplied with the micronutrients it needs to build strong horn is vital.

LAMINITIS

Laminitis, defined as inflammation of the laminae, is a very painful condition associated with the breakdown of the lamellar connection between the hoof wall and the pedal bone. Alignment of the pedal bone with the hoof wall can be lost through rotation of the hoof capsule away from the pedal bone, or the sinking of the pedal bone within the hoof capsule, or both. It affects all breeds of horses and ponies and can strike at any age. There are currently no reliable tests that predict the severity of any laminitis event. Some horses recover complete functionality, but for others there may be irreversible damage.

Causes

A great deal of research has been undertaken to identify the causal factors for laminitis. Research is on-going, although three distinct pathways have been identified:

- endocrinopathic laminitis, in equines which have an underlying hormonal disease (equine metabolic syndrome, insulin resistance or PPID). For all of these horses hyperinsulinemia (abnormally high insulin levels) appears to be the common denominator.[32]
- systemic inflammatory response syndrome (SIRS), associated with equines which have alimentary disturbances such as hindgut acidosis or infection due to retained placenta after giving birth. Along with elevated heart rate and temperature, one of the common symptoms of SIRS is diarrhoea.
- weight-bearing or supporting limb laminitis (SLL). Famously, the racehorse Barbaro, who fractured a leg during the Preakness Stakes, was operated on and then entered a lengthy period of recuperation, only to develop laminitis in the supporting limb due to excessive weightbearing.

How common is it?

Recent research suggests that one in two hundred equines is likely to develop laminitis.[33] Earlier studies suggested a prevalence range of 1.5–34 per cent,[34] and that the majority of horses which are diagnosed with laminitis have underlying endocrine disease. One study identified that 89 per cent of cases were endocrinopathic in origin.[35] Laminitis due to excessive weightbearing is rare: a review of cases of SLL between 2005 and 2013 at Rossdales Equine Practice established that only 0.02 per cent of registered horses during that period were diagnosed with SLL.[36] Laminitis triggered by SIRS would appear to account for up to 10 per cent of cases.

During the spring and summer months many horses belonging to the authors' client base exhibit some signs associated with low-grade or sub-clinical laminitis, including shortness of stride; discomfort on hard or uneven surfaces; stronger digital pulses; event lines; ring bruising; wall staining and solar bruising. Signs of discomfort are frequently observed in response to palpation over the cecum and large intestine, and range from subtle (eyes and nostrils tight, muscle twitching and tail swishing) to the more obvious (stepping away, lifting a hind leg/kicking out, and turning to bite). Most of these horses are able to be ridden across a variety of terrain without hoof boots with no signs of discomfort during the autumn and winter when grass growth is minimal or dormant.

Image showing the epidermal laminae of a healthy and laminitic dorsal wall.

What happens to the laminae?

During a bout of laminitis, the laminae elongate and taper. The hoof wall is no longer firmly attached to the pedal bone and the laminae lose their ability to resist the biomechanical forces encountered by the foot.

Signs and symptoms

- Weight shifting from foot to foot or rocking back
- Reluctance to move
- Legs not crossing over when turned in a tight circle, but rather the feet shuffle around
- Bounding digital pulse
- Hot feet
- Swollen coronary band
- Elevated respiration
- Elevated heart rate

In SIRS cases the following may be present in addition to the above:

- Bloated abdomen
- Touch sensitive
- Oedema in sheath/mammary glands
- Loose droppings

Image showing the dermal laminae of the feet in the previous image.

Managing the laminitic horse

Establishing the horse's comfort and ability to move is the first priority. The authors have supported many hundreds of laminitic horses, and in the majority of cases the cause will be identifiable in the lifestyle of the animal. In most cases laminitis is unfortunately not a one-off event, but the culmination of a developing disease process and the start of a series of episodes. A detailed case history can be extremely helpful in identifying triggers, such as changes to turnout arrangements or recent worming treatment, but in most cases it is essential to look for the long-term underlying cause. A variety of tests can be undertaken to establish whether endocrine disease is an underlying factor. Pharmaceutical therapy, particularly for horses diagnosed with PPID, can be extremely helpful in minimizing the risk of future episodes. Anti-inflammatory pain relief is also routinely prescribed.

Dietary management

Endocrinopathic and SIRS laminitis can be improved with dietary management. If laminitis is suspected, take the horse off grass.

For horses with endocrinopathic laminitis, it is important to provide a low sugar diet and many do not tolerate grass well. Ideally, have the forage analysed to establish the non-structural carbohydrate and mineral content, and supplement accordingly. The key figure to look at is the ester soluble carbohydrate (ESC) percentage. Forage with 10 per cent or less ESC is generally regarded as safe to feed for laminitics. Soaking hay in copious amounts of fresh water for an hour, using fresh water for each batch of hay soaked, can also reduce the sugar levels and is good practice when levels are unknown. Bagged forage replacements with low ESC levels can be a good alternative where forage analysis is impractical.

PRO COMMENT

In cases of severe laminitis, the laminar connection has been disastrously affected. A common veterinary response is to use frog supports and NSAIDS, and to keep the horse stabled for up to thirty days. The reason for using frog supports is supposed to be to prevent the pedal bone from rotating and penetrating the sole, causing significant pressure, pain and ultimately bone demineralization. In the authors' experience, however, once the laminar connection has failed in severe cases, the horse needs to completely re-grow the connection, which will take a significant amount of time. Frog supports are limited in their effectiveness and have been superseded by rehabilitative hoof boots and pads, which support the entire sole.

Another common approach is to relieve pressure on the DDFT by raising or not trimming the heels in the mistaken understanding that this will help prevent rotation. A corollary of higher heels is to tip the horse's weight onto the front of the pedal bone, thus increasing pressure on the sole and making penetration more likely. Experienced HCPs understand and manage hoof balance in order to maintain a low palmar angle, which means that the risk of pressure and pain from rotation can be significantly reduced. Sinking can occur in laminitis cases with balanced feet, but the pressure is not localized to the tip of the pedal bone and rotation is often less acute.

Many horses in the past have been euthanized because it was believed that it was not possible to rehabilitate the horse from pedal bone penetration or severe rotation, but this is not the case. Many barefoot horse keepers have successfully rehabilitated laminitics using the knowledge provided by research into vascular flow and the endocrine system. Balancing the hoof to achieve a functional digital bone angle is the responsibility of an HCP with the support of good radiographs, and needs to be addressed as soon as possible with a laminitis case as it can significantly reduce internal pressure and pain. In some of the most severe cases the horse will show substantial relief by relaxing, licking, chewing and caudally weight-bearing when the HCP effectively balances pressure and reduces leverage within the hoof capsule.

For horses where SIRS as a result of hindgut acidosis is the causative factor, establishing a more alkaline environment in the hind gut is necessary, and replacement hind gut flora can be colonized using probiotics.

Provide supportive comfortable footing

A deep shavings or finer particle bed will allow the horse to dig its feet into the most comfortable position possible, and provides a yielding, conformable surface and neuro-stimulation to assist in perfusion. A similar depth of straw bedding does not provide the same cushioning and support, nor does it absorb urine well, and the horse may eat it. Straw can be high in non-structural carbohydrates and contribute to maintaining active laminitis problems.

Company

Horses in pain during laminitic episodes can easily become depressed if they are kept in isolation. Establishing a run-in shed with a deep soft bed and a grass-free yard with a conformable surface, where the horse can have a permanent suitable companion, is the easiest and most stress-free way to manage a laminitic. In serious cases isolation can contribute to the horse 'giving up'.

Movement

If laminitis is identified in the early stages and an appropriate management plan is implemented (including dietary management, biomechanically appropriate trimming, hoof boots and pads, and pain management), it is the authors' experience that controlled movement can significantly reduce recovery time. In many cases gentle hand walking in

boots and supportive pads, or on soft going, can improve circulation to the feet, reduce pain and actively nourish the damaged soft tissues with improved blood flow. Vets are sometimes reluctant to suggest movement due to the fear of rotation, but research findings support controlled movement. In laminitis cases the hoof and pedal bone connection is very weak, and will in most instances do what biomechanical forces determine in spite of external attempts to prevent this.

As far as the hoof and P3 are concerned, re-establishing perfusion with blood is the key to 'creating a healing environment' by providing needed nutrients and oxygen. While it would be everyone's dream to have a 'silver bullet' medica-tion to do this, none such medication currently exists… the first order of business in re-establish-ing perfusion in the naturally occurring disease is minimizing mechanical compression of the solar corium and stretching of the laminae within the hoof capsule.[36]

As supported by research,[37] the authors recommend a movement protocol in laminitis cases. In implementing movement it is essential that the following factors are established:

- a balanced trim that achieves a heel first or flat landing;
- well fitted hoof boots and soft pads; and
- appropriate pain relief.

Movement needs to be divided into several short sessions across the day, ideally two or three 20–30 minute gentle in hand walks rather than longer ones.[38] Walking needs to be at the horse's own pace and without the weight of a rider. Lungeing, horsewalkers and ridden work are contraindicated. As laminitic horses spend considerable amounts of time with their bodies in locked positions, massage and body work can be very supportive and pleasant experiences around walking.

Rehabilitation

Rehabilitating a horse from laminitis is time-consuming, and requires significant resources in terms of the owner's time and investment. The aim of rehabilitation should be to return the horse to full health, rather than managing the symptoms without significant improvement in pain. The authors have been part of the care team in a number of cases where serious and chronic laminitis and its associated internal health problems have significantly restricted the quality of life of the horse. If the condition is not improving and the horse is still in pain, even though pain relief is in place, decisions need to be taken regarding the horses' management protocol and progress. It should be noted that in some cases euthanasia is the final outcome, as a good quality of life does not equate to a few hours' daily standing up.

REFERENCES

1. Geor, R.J., Harris, P. and Coenen, M. (2013). *Equine Applied and Clinical Nutrition – Health, welfare and performance.* Oxford: Elsevier Health Sciences.
2. US Department of Agriculture. (1983). Condition Scoring Your Horse. E*quine Veterinary Journal*, 15:371–2.
3. Carroll, C.L. and Huntington, P.J. (1988). Body Condition Scoring and Weight Estimation of Horses. *Equine Veterinary Journal*, 20:41–5.
4. *Ibid.*
5. Ellis, J.M. and Hollands, T. (1998). Accuracy of different methods of estimating the weight of horses. *Veterinary Record*, 143(12).
6. Geor, Harris and Coenen, Equine Applied and Clinical Nutrition – *Health, welfare and performance.*
7. National Research Council. (2007). *Nutrient Requirements of Horses.* Washington DC: National Academies Press.
8. Brook, I. (2009). Microbiology and antimicrobial treatment of orbital and intracranical complications of sinusitis in children and their management. *International Journal of Pediatric Otorhinolaryngol*, 75:1183–6.
9. http://www.circulationfoundation.org.uk/help-advice/veins/leg-ulcers/ (accessed 15 April 2015).
10. Bell, R.J.W., Kingston, J.K., Mogg, T.D. *et al.* (2007). The prevalence of gastric ulceration in racehorses in New Zealand. *New Zealand Veterinary Journal*, 55(1).
11. McClure, S.R., Carithers, D.S., Gross, S.J. and Murray, M.J. (2005). Gastric ulcer development in horses in a simulated show or training environment. *Journal of the American Veterinary Medical Association*, 227(5):775–7.
12. Videla, R. and Andrews, T.M. (2009). New Perspectives in Equine Gastric Ulcer Syndrome. *Veterinary Clinics of North America*, 25(1).
13. *Ibid.*
14. Pellegrini, F.L. (2005). Results of a large-scale necroscopic study of equine colonic ulcers. *Journal of Equine Veterinary Science*, 25(3):113–17.
15. Andrews, F.M., Reinemayer, C.R., McCracken, M.D., Blackford, J.A. *et al.* (2002). Comparison of endoscopic, necropsy and histology scoring of equine gastric ulcers. *Equine Veterinary Journal*, 34(5):475–8.
16. Videla and Andrews, 'New Perspectives in Equine Gastric Ulcer Syndrome'.
17. Ridgway, K. (2012). Equine Ulcers – You really need to know more. Producer: D.K. DVM. Retrieved 14 July 2015 from Equine Therapeutic Options: http://www.drkerryridgway.com/articles/articles_ulcers.php.
18. Ridgway, 'Equine Ulcers – you really need to know more'; Videla and Andrews, 'New Perspectives in Equine Gastric Ulcer Syndrome'.
19. Tobin, T., Chay, S., Kamerling, S. *et al.* (1986). Phenylbutazone in the horse: a review. *Journal of Veterinary Pharmacological Therapy*, 9(1):1–25.
20. Videla and Andrews, 'New Perspectives in Equine Gastric Ulcer Syndrome'.

21. Nadeau, J.A., Andrews, F.M., Mathew, A.G. *et al.* (2000). Evaluation of diet as a cause of gastric ulcers in horses. *American Journal of Veterinary Research*, 61(7):784–90.

22. Finocchietto, P., Barreyro, F., Holod, S., Peralta, J. *et al.* (2008, March). Control of muscle mitochondria by insulin entails activation of Akt2-mtNOS Pathway: implications for the Metabolic Syndrome. PLoS One.

23. Durham, A.E., Rendle, D.I. and Newton, J.R. (2008). The effect of metformin on measurements of insulin sensitivity and beta cell response in 18 horses and ponies with insulin resistance. *Equine Veterinary Journal*, 40.

24. Bowker, R.M. (2008). *Contrasting Hoof Morphologies*. Author's personal lecture notes. Barefootworks Seminar, Aberdeenshire, Scotland.

25. Ibid.

26. Sampson, S.N., Schneider, R.K., Gavin, P.R., Ho, C.P., Tucker, R.L. and Charles, E.M. (2009). Magnetic Resonance Imaging finding in horses with recent onset navicular syndrome but without radiographic abnormalities, *Veterinary Radiology and Ultrasound*, 50:339–46. doi: 10.1111/j.1740-8261.2009.01547.x (accessed 23.07.2015).

27. Waguespack, R.W. and Hanson, R.R. (2010). *Navicular Syndrome in Equine Patients: Anatomy, Causes, and Diagnosis*. Vetlearn. com. Compendium: Continuing Education for Veterinarians (accessed 21.07.2015).

28. Bowker, R. (2009). Contrasting Structural Morphologies of Good and Bad Footed Horses, *AAEP*.

29. Wilson, A.M., McGuigan, M.P., Fouracre, L. and MacMahon, L. (2001). The force and contact stress on the navicular bone during trot locomotion in sound horses and horses with navicular disease, *Equine Veterinary Journal*, 33(2):159–65.

30. Roos, E.M. (2005). Joint injury causes knee osteoarthritis in young adults, Current Opinion in Rheumatology, 17(2):195–200 (accessed 23.07.2015); Andriacchi, T.P., Koo, S., Scanlan, S.F. (2009). Gait Mechanics Influence Healthy Cartilage Morphology and Osteoarthritis of the Knee, *J Bone Joint Surg Am*, 91 (Supplement 1):95–101. http://dx.doi.org/10.2106/JBJS.H.01408 (accessed 23.07.2015).

31. Sampson, S.N., Schneider, R.K., Gavin, P.R., Ho, C.P., Tucker, R.L. and Charles, E.M. (2009). Magnetic resonance imaging findings in horses with recent onset navicular syndrome but wihtyout radiographic abnormalities. *Veterinary Radiology & Ultrasound*, 50(4): 339–346.

32. McGowan, C.M. (2008). The role of insulin in endocrinopathic laminitis, *Journal of Equine Veterinary Science*, 28(10):603–7.

33. Wylie, C.E., Collins, S.N., Verheyen, K.L.P. and Newton, J.R. (2013). A cohort study of equine laminitis in Great Britain 2009–2011: Estimation of disease frequency and description of clinical signs in 577 cases. *Equine Veterinary Journal*, 45(6):681–7.

34. Wylie, C.E., Collins, S.N., Verheyen, K.L.P. and Newton, J.R. (2011). Frequency of equine laminitis: a systematic review with quality appraisal of published evidence. *The Vet Journal*, 189:248–56.

35. Karikoski, N.P., Horn, I., McGowan, T.W. and McGowan, C.M. (2011). The prevalence of endocrinopathic laminitis among horses presented for laminitis at a first-opinion/referral equine hospital, *Domest Anim Endocrinol*, 41(3):111–17.

36. Wylie, C.E, Newton, J.R, Bathe, A.P. and Payne, R.J. (2015). Prevalence of supporting limb laminitis in a UK equine practice and referral hospital setting between 2005 and 2013: implications for future epidemiological studies, *Vet Rec*, 176(3):72.

37. Taylor, D.M. (2011). Veterinary Management of the Laminitic Patient. In P. Ramey (ed.), *Care and rehabilitation of the equine foot*. Dexter, Missouri: Hoof Rehabilitation Publishing LLC.

38. *Ibid.*

39. *Ibid.*

8 Final Thoughts

Horses have hooves so that their feet can grip on frost and snow, and hair so that they can withstand the wind and cold. They eat grass and drink water, they buck and gallop, for this is the innate nature of horses. Even if they had great towers and magnificent halls, they would not be interested in them.[1]

Barefoot Horse Keeping is as much a philosophy as it is a practical approach to inform the reader about barefoot hoof care. The authors hope that this book has convinced readers of the value of taking an integrated approach to barefoot horse keeping, and they have not only found it educational, but it has stimulated thought and discussion. It is not the intention that the book be a definitive text on anatomy, biomechanics or any other topic, but rather encourages readers to make their own connections and to continue to gather knowledge to unpick puzzles and find answers themselves. In this way the field will move forward and greater numbers of domestic equines can lead healthier and more ethologically appropriate lives.

The completion of this book has been a downloading of knowledge, and has allowed the authors to introduce ideas and subjects that they frequently consider in their work, and are keen to research and develop. It is critical that barefoot horse keepers and hoof care professionals keep questioning assumed knowledge for the benefit of the horse, and evaluate the strategies they implement to establish their validity in the context of practical horse keeping.

As the authors have experienced themselves and witnessed in the choices of their clients for their horses, when attempting any kind of personal change, it is sensible to do it gradually, with care and consideration. Aiming for small incremental gains is often the most effective approach, particularly if the goal is significant. There is nothing to be lost, however, by aiming higher than it seems possible to achieve at the time.

There are many horses enjoying a healthy barefoot life who have faced difficulties and challenges along the way,but whose owners can now look back and see how far they have come.

[1] *The Book of Chuang Tzu* (fourth century BC), translated by Martin Palmer (1996), Penguin: Arkana.

Anni Stonebridge and Oro.

Jane Cumberlidge and Bucket.

READING AND RESOURCES LIST

Principles of Conformation Analysis (vols I II and III), D. Bennett
Contrasting Structural Morphology of Good and Bad Footed Horses, R. Bowker
Equine Locomotion, H. Clayton and W. Back (eds)
Physical Therapy and Massage for the Horse, J-M. Denoix and J-P. Pailloux
Horse Anatomy: A Pictorial Approach to Equine Structure, P. Goody
Twisted Truths of Modern Dressage, P. Karl
Anatomy Trains, T. Myers
Care and Rehabilitation of the Equine Foot, P. Ramey
The Lame Horse, J. Rooney
Correct Movement in Horses: Improving Straightness and Balance, K. Schoneich and G. Rachen-Schoneich
Activate Your Horse's Core: Unmounted Exercises for Dynamic Mobility, Strength and Balance, N.C. Stubbs and C. Clayton
Ride With Your Mind Essentials, M. Wanless
The Horse's Muscles in Motion, Sara Wyche

WEB RESOURCES

Equine Cushings and Insulin Resistance Horse Group: https://groups.yahoo.com/neo/groups/EquineCushings/info

Online courses in equine nutrition and PPID:
http://drkellon.com/coursedescriptions.html

Education for the prevention and treatment of laminitis in horses:
http://www.safergrass.org/

Vet Debra Taylor talks about the equine foot:
http://www.thehorse.com/videos/34609/is-the-hoof-smart-adaptability-of-the-equine-foot?utm_source=Newsletter&utm_medium=health-news&utm_campaign=09-30-2014

Licensed trainers from the School of Légèreté:
http://www.philippe-karl.com

Straightness training:
http://www.bentbranderuptrainer.com

http://academicartofriding.com

INDEX